WHY THE NATIONS RAGE

WHY THE NATIONS RAGE

Christopher Catherwood

Hodder & Stoughton

LONDON   SYDNEY   AUCKLAND

A CIP Catalogue record for this title is available
from the British Library

ISBN 0 340 69062 3

Typeset by Palimpsest Book Production Limited,
Polmont, Stirlingshire
Printed and bound in Great Britain by
Mackays of Chatham PLC, Chatham, Kent

Hodder and Stoughton Ltd
A division of Hodder Headline PLC
338 Euston Road,
London NW1 3BH

To

John S. Moore
and his daughter,
my wife,
Paulette

Contents

Acknowledgments

Religious nationalism and mass murder are gruesome subjects. Neither does much to restore faith in human nature. By pleasant contrast, few things have done so much to create faith in human nature as the wonderful help which I have received from so many kind people in the writing of this book.

Most people end their acknowledgments by thanking their long-suffering and patient spouse. I would like to break with tradition and begin with giving the profoundest possible thanks to my wife, Paulette. She has been more than encouraging. Without her belief not only in this project, but also in my return to academic life, none of this would have been possible. She has also helped to sustain me personally throughout the writing, and during this initial phase of my research.

Families are a great source of support. My own family and Paulette's have been tremendous. My father-in-law, John Moore, has for many years been active in the cause of religious liberty, and it is in recognition of that contribution that I have dedicated this book to him.

This project began with two papers on 'Nationalism, Religion and Tolerance' for the Religious Liberties Commission. I have long been interested in human rights, and

I was delighted to be able to do something concrete for them on so important a subject. I was introduced to the RLC by my old friend and great encourager, Mike Morris, whose own work on religious liberty has been lauded worldwide. To him, and to the outgoing RLC Director, Brian O'Connell, I owe profound thanks. These two have been instrumental in rescuing several religious leaders around the globe from severe persecution.

The academic community in Cambridge has proved to be the ideal haven for my research. First and foremost, I must thank the Rev. Dr Frank McHugh, Fellow of St Edmund's College, Cambridge and Director of their Von Hügel Institute. He enabled me to return to academia via a Visiting Scholarship at St Edmund's College, and was instrumental in my election as a Senior Research Associate at the Von Hügel. St Edmund's is a uniquely delightful academic community, with a wonderfully diverse and international student body. Many an important conversation originated over tea and biscuits in the Common Room.

I have also been greatly encouraged by Dr Philip Towle, Director of the Cambridge University Centre of International Studies, where I am also a Visiting Scholar. Feedback from a lecture I gave there on this topic has been helpful in the preparation for this book.

The staff of the Keston Institute have international recognition for their pioneering work on religious freedom in Eastern Europe. I am particularly grateful to their founding Director, the Rev. Michael Bordeaux and to his colleague, Dr Philip Walters, for their wise advice and help.

Christopher Cviic, of the Royal Institute of International Affairs, and Jonathan Eyal of the Royal United Services Institute, both gave me their time and insights.

The Oxford Centre for Mission Studies have been very

Acknowledgments

supportive in many ways. In particular, Canon Vinay Samuel, Dr Chris Sugden and Dr Carl Armerding have been tremendously helpful.

One of my most important helpers and advisers has been Sam Ericsson. Sam is a unique individual who has been one of the key linchpins in helping the cause of religious liberty and human rights worldwide. The organisation which he founded, Advocates International, plays a pivotal role in making sure that Article 18 of the UN Charter for Human Rights is fully implemented. The fact that both sides in many a dispute feel that they can trust and speak freely to Sam is a major tribute to his efforts. As well as being a tremendous support both to me and to Paulette personally, Sam has been a great person with whom to discuss many of the key ideas in this book.

Many academics and their work have been important in developing my own thinking. I am most grateful to that distinguished jurist, Professor A. E. Dick Howard of the University of Virginia. The writing of Professor Anthony Smith of the London School of Economics, and the lectures of Professor Lammin Sanneh of Yale University, have played a large role in shaping my own thought, as has the controversial but very important work of Professor Samuel Huntington of Harvard University. I have been honoured to be invited to many fascinating seminars, and I am particularly grateful to my old history tutor, Colin Lucas, now Master of Balliol College, Oxford, for inviting me to a Master's seminar on the subject.

Many friends have been individually very encouraging throughout the project, and the list would be far too long were I to mention them all. I would like in particular to mention Lindsay Brown, of the International Fellowship of Evangelical Students, and the members of my Wednesday home group in Cambridge. Other members of the Glebe Road community have been wonderfully supportive as well.

Financially, I am very grateful to the Religious Liberties Commission for funding the first year of the research, in preparation for their fascinating consultation on religion, nationalism and tolerance in Prague in May 1996. I am particularly indebted to Mike Morris, Brian O'Connell and Colin Saunders (of the Evangelical Alliance) who arranged the necessary finance.

The research time for this book was possible thanks to a very timely grant from the Sir Kirby Laing Foundation. I am most grateful both to Sir Kirby Laing himself and to his fellow trustee, Simon Webley, for making this possible. I am also indebted to Rev. Ken Martin, Dean of Cambridge Arts and Sciences, for giving me pupils and study supervision, which helped keep body and soul together at critical periods.

Lastly, I must give deepest thanks to my old friend and editor at Hodder and Stoughton, Judith Longman. Judith and I have chatted over potential projects for many a year, and it has been great to work on one with her at last. She has been wonderfully patient over the various delays, and a model of graciousness in getting me to rewrite passages that needed clarification. Having once been an editor myself, I know that editors are often a greatly undervalued species. This is a shame, so in paying due tribute to Judith and the tremendous hard work she puts into getting good books into print, I wish to thank both her and all her trade for the special contribution that they make.

Christopher Catherwood
Von Hügel Institute
Cambridge
January 1997

Preface

Nationalism is one of the most important forces of the twentieth century. Tens of millions have died as a result of wars since 1900. Nationalism has been blamed as the cause for many of them, right up to the recent conflict and mass murder in Bosnia. Recently, some have argued that religion has merged with nationalism, providing us with a potentially lethal mixture, just as we thought we were safe again, following upon the end of the Cold War.

This book is an attempt to look at these two forces, religion and nationalism, to examine them and to see why many of today's nations rage against one another.

How to use this book
Nationalism and religion are both highly complex subjects. In combination they are more complicated still. In writing *Why the Nations Rage*, I have done my best to simplify those two topics in order that non-specialist readers can understand the issues more clearly.

I have therefore divided the book into five sections. The section introductions are designed to explain the basic points, which the chapters then go on to elaborate in more detail. So if all this is quite new to you, it might be a good idea to read the section introductions first, so that you can get the general flavour of where the book is going.

I have tried to use non-technical language if at all possible. Sometimes it was impossible to avoid technical terms, though I trust that I have used such words sparingly. For those who want a reminder of what such expressions and other key terms mean, I have included a brief glossary as Appendix A.

Those not familiar with East European geography and history can also consult the Appendices, so that they can distinguish the ethnic groupings, countries, former Empires, and events leading to the East/West split within Christendom which are essential to the discussion.

The argument in the book is cumulative. That is to say, it begins with some basic arguments in Section One, and goes on to explain each of them in Sections Two, Three and Four. Section Five offers what I would like to think might be a solution to the whole issue of religious nationalist rage.

You might occasionally become confused with material new to you. If that is the case, you can use the Section Introductions to give you the gist of the chapters you want to skip. You can then read those chapters where the material is more familiar, without missing too much of the cumulative argument of the book. When you have done this, you can then return to the chapters you missed and, I trust, find them easier to follow second time around.

I have also used many sub-headings in each chapter in order to make the text easier to follow. They act as signposts, so that readers can understand the direction the material is taking them. They should also make it possible to go back a page or two, if you need a second glimpse, without having to read all the previous paragraphs.

Preface

A wish for the reader

Religious nationalism, the rage of nations, is a crucial issue of our time. Hundreds of thousands of innocent people have died in the past few years alone because of it. We cannot understand our own times, or the dangers that we ourselves might have to face, unless we come to grips with it.

I trust, therefore, that this book will help you in doing so. May it make complex issues clearer, your comprehension of the basics better and your world a safer place as a result.

The Parable of the
Good Bosnian Muslim

A Western journalist was travelling from Sarajevo to Mostar. He fell among fighting militiamen and was robbed. A Serb Orthodox Archimandrite passed by. 'A journalist,' he thought, and sped away. Then a Croat Catholic priest noticed him in the ditch. He shuddered, and made his exit as quickly as possible. Then a Bosnian Muslim found him. He bound his wounds, drove him to a good hospital and gave him some dinars.

Section One

Nationalism and Self-Identity

Nationalism and religion have combined in many parts of today's world to form the phenomenon of *religious nationalism*. Some have argued that this phenomenon might lead to a new Cold War. The most famous exponent of religious nationalism, Samuel Huntington of Harvard University,[1] has called it the 'clash of civilisations'. His theory has travelled well beyond the confines of academia. It has been discussed in newspapers and magazines as well as in common rooms and university seminars.

However, if we are to understand something that could be a threat to world peace, we need to ask some fundamental questions before attempting to come up with answers. Why do people perceive Islam as a potential threat? Why are people in Bosnia killing each other in the name of both God and nation?

We need to look at some key concepts before getting down to the details.

What is nationalism? How can we define it? Why do some people kill each other in the name of nationalism while others regard their own nationality as comparatively unimportant?

1

To accomplish this, we need some political and historical analysis of the nature of nationalism. But we also require some psychological insights, both individual and collective, to understand why some nations have been more gripped by murderous forms of nationalism than others.

Chapter 1, 'A Question of Identity', takes us to this important starting point, the psychology not just of ordinary people, but of nations themselves. Chapter 2, 'The New World *Dis*order', looks at why nationalism has come back on the international agenda with a vengeance, especially since the fall of the Berlin Wall in 1989 and the demise of Communism in Central and Eastern Europe. Chapter 3, 'Imaginary Kingdoms', looks at the nature of nationalism itself, historically, politically and sociologically. Nationalism is so massive a subject, that not everyone agrees upon what it is and how to define it. Is it an innate natural phenomenon, common to us all, or is it purely a human creation, an 'imaginary kingdom'?

My hope is that after reading these three foundational chapters, the reader will be properly equipped to embark on a more detailed examination of religious nationalism.

1

A Question of Identity

Who am I?

For those of us living in the West, a question such as 'Who am I?' might be one of passing interest, but not one worth dying or killing someone for. It is an issue which we would place in the realm of popular psychology, perhaps, well below matters of life and death. Taxes, health care or education are all far more important on our scale of priorities.

Religion and nationalism
The reason for this book is that there are many parts of the world where that simple question is the number one issue, transcending everything else. If such an unusual view puzzles us, my main aim in *Why the Nations Rage* is to explain how this has come to pass, and why an understanding of this very different perspective is essential for all of us.

Religion and nationalism, the two basic ingredients of the world-view under discussion, have placed themselves firmly back at the top of the late twentieth-century agenda. Let us begin the process at what I think is Square One.

3

Why the Nations Rage

Religion and nationalism seem at first glance to be theological or political issues. To many rational, late-twentieth-century Westerners, that is precisely what they are. But that is exactly the problem.

One theme we need to grasp is that other people think in radically different ways from ourselves. We will see as our book progresses that the outlook we have in the West came into being over many centuries, after a long period of historical development. Each part of the world has a history unique to itself. The histories of China or Central Africa differ sharply from each other and, in turn, from our own.

Europe itself is equally diverse. The story of Western Europe diverges considerably from that of the Eastern half. What we take for granted in Denmark or France is by no means always presumed to hold true in Romania or Russia. Their experiences, while similar in some ways, are utterly unlike those of West Europeans in other ways.

Two areas that separate West and East are nationalism and religion, the themes of this work. Where I come from and what I believe are both key ingredients of who I am as a person, or what we can call our self-identity. In the West, we have increasingly divorced these two facets of our lives, thus reducing their relative importance in the way we think.

Sixteenth- and seventeenth-century Western Europe saw many wars of religion. Hundreds of thousands died because they were Protestant or Catholic, or because they were citizens of a country in which you were only allowed to be one of these things.

By the twentieth century, religious wars had ceased in the West. Wars ignited by a nation's or ethnic group's self-identity still continued, and with a vengeance. These wars were based on nationalism. The 1900s began with the First World War from 1914 to 1918. Although the conflict began in Eastern Europe, in the Bosnian capital of Sarajevo, the war spread because of the nationalism of a country at the heart of the West, Germany. By 1939, and the start of the Second World War, German nationalism was both the cause and beginning of what was to be the worst war in human history, with over fifty-five million people killed.

Nationalism seems to have replaced religion as a cause of war. Nationalism is a 'Who am I?' question, as we shall discover. The core of nationalism is the fact that who your ancestors were and what kind of ethnic origins you have is the most important ingredient of your self-identity. So crucial is your background to who you are that it can be worth killing for, especially those who do not share it.

The puzzle of faraway countries
In today's Western Europe, with the twenty-first century upon us, to murder someone because they are of a different religion or ethnic grouping from our own seems thankfully alien to the vast majority of our fellow citizens. English Catholics or French Protestants are no longer burned at the stake. Irish Americans do not plot the death of white Anglo-Saxon Protestants. France no longer fears military invasion from Germany. We have come to regard such conflicts as somehow uncivilised, a remnant of an embarrassing, more primitive past, forgetting in the process that the Second World War ended in the lifetime of many alive today.

When we turn on our televisions and see pictures of ethnic cleansing, mass murder and concentration camps, happening both now and in Europe, we are instinctively astonished. How could this be? Even more extraordinary to us is the seeming fact that both religion and nationalism are central to the conflict in the former Yugoslavia. For us, religion is a purely private matter. Our ethnicity, our national sentiments, may be something we hold dear, but nowhere near enough to murder someone whose ancestry is not the same as our own. It all seems very puzzling, very far away.

A history lesson

In our bewilderment at nationalist violence, we are echoing the perplexity of many decent-minded people back in the 1930s. The violence of Nazi Germany, and the genocidal loathing of the Jews, parallel the similar brutality of the Serbs, with their murderous hatred of the Bosnian Muslims, in our own day.

Many Westerners in the 1930s confused the particular brand of nationalism of Nazi Germany with a new kind of political perspective. To Neville Chamberlain, a Birmingham businessman-turned-politician, dealing with Adolf Hitler was an act of political necessity. Today we sit in our armchairs and condemn Chamberlain for surrendering Czechoslovakia to Hitler at Munich in 1938. As a specialist in 1930s Balkan history who has studied the dreadful consequences of Chamberlain's mistake, I can well sympathise with Churchill and others who proclaimed that Hitler was a maniac who had to be stopped. But the sheer cruelty and deviousness of Hitler is much easier to comprehend with hindsight than it was in 1938. The intrinsically demonic nature of a Hitler was quite beyond the experience and comprehension of a decent, middle-class businessman like Neville Chamberlain for whom Germany was the land of literature, music and art. Even the worst German atrocities in World War I were insignificant in comparison to the unutterable depravity of the Holocaust that was to follow.

Czechoslovakia was a 'faraway country of which we know nothing', according to Chamberlain. The Balkans are equally mysterious for many. The central issue which

has ignited the powder keg is not simply a question of
Serb nationalism in the way that German nationalism
was the major problem in the 1930s. Religion is also
crucial to an understanding of what is happening in that
troubled area. The former Yugoslavia is a paradigm of the
issue of religious nationalism. If we want to comprehend
what many regard as one of the key movements of the
post-Cold War era, we must turn to the Balkans.

Living in a big cage

I was a regular visitor to the Balkans in the 1970s and
1980s. Yugoslavs were very proud of the fact that while
they lived in a Communist regime, theirs was not an
Iron Curtain country. The level of repression, while
sometimes an irritant, was gentler than that experienced
by my friends in Czechoslovakia. One critical freedom
which Yugoslavs possessed was that they could travel
abroad without permission. The post-war generation of
Yugoslavs enjoyed this freedom to the full. As my friend
Radovan once said, 'Here in Yugoslavia we live in a cage,
but it is a big cage.' To some of us, a cage is still a cage,
and any kind of restriction is irksome. But to a Yugoslav,
the fact that Tito had removed Yugoslavia from Stalin's
orbit in 1948 and had opted for non-aligned neutrality
instead, made the country a far better cage to live in than
those cramped, confined spaces next door.[1]

In a sense, Yugoslavia was a showcase country, something of which its inhabitants were very proud. So when
the country started to fall apart, it was not surprising that
another middle-class, civilised, Western politician said
that Yugoslavia should stay together rather than break
up.[2] Tito had kept it together and relatively harmonious,
and that was how all civilised, rational people ought
to see it. Surely rampaging nationalism in Europe had
disappeared with the fall of Nazism in 1945.

As we saw with Hitler and the 1938 Munich crisis, hindsight can be a matter of pride for the people who were eventually proved right. Churchill was correct: Hitler was a serious danger to humanity, perhaps far worse than even Churchill himself could have realised.[3]

As stories of Serb concentration camps and ethnic cleansing came out into the open, it was very tempting for those of us who opposed the continued union of Yugoslavia to say, 'We told you so.' Nationalism was not dead. Far from it; it was all too alive. Rather than dying in 1945, it had merely slept, and had now awoken with renewed energy and what seemed to be a desire to make up for lost time. For Germans, one could substitute Serbs, and for Jews, the Bosnian Muslims.[4]

So how was it that in 1938 and 1989 intelligent, civilised, rational, educated people in power could not see what was glaringly obvious to others? To understand why things happened one needs to look further, beyond dates and the meeting together of politicians.

Finding the roots: a matter of self-identity
Above all, one needs to try to understand that most elusive of concepts, human nature. Who are we, and why do we do what we do? Are we just economically-determined robots, or are there more basic, possibly even primeval, forces at work?

As a historian, not a trained psychologist, I am aware that parts of this book will take me beyond my main areas of speciality. The great escape clause of historians, when asked a question they cannot answer properly, that 'it's not my period,' applies with even greater force here. To ask a twentieth-century specialist about the fifteenth century can produce a hesitant answer. Psychology is, of course, a stage further away, in that it is a different academic discipline altogether. So with that caveat in mind, let us begin to explore the question of 'Who am I?' and, just as important, 'Who am I not?'

Most of us at some stage in life indulge in varying degrees of introspection on the subject of what makes us into who we are. One of the reasons why this is so complex an issue – and why we all too often evade it – is that when it comes to the question of identity, we actually have more than one. This is not to say that we are all suffering from varying degrees of multiple personality disorder! It is simply that just as many individual trees make up a forest, so many elements combine together to comprise the totality of who we are as individuals.

Meeting the author: an exploration of one self-identity

Let us start our discussion of identity with some self-revelation: my own sense of identity. As the myth of objectivity in history went out with the nineteenth century, this examination can also alert you to any innate prejudices that you might detect throughout this book.

As this is a book on nationalism, I should begin by saying that I am British. This seems on the face of it an easy concept to grasp. But even in something as simple as being 'British' there are complications.

Britain is made up of several historically distinct countries: England, Scotland, Wales and Northern Ireland. With the last country, many in Northern Ireland do not see themselves as British at all: they are Irish. The divide is along the lines of *religious* nationalism. In Northern Ireland, it is religion that determines what you call yourself, Protestant or Catholic. This is important to my own ethnic identity.

I am every component of British except English. My father is an Ulster Scot (someone from Northern Ireland of Scottish descent, but not Irish, and almost invariably

Protestant). My mother is Welsh. So that makes me an Ulster Scottish Welshman, a true hybrid that is all too rare in Britain.[5]

A cosmopolitan's dilemma

I am, therefore, what Michael Ignatieff,[6] himself an ethnic Russian brought up in French-speaking Canada, would call a 'cosmopolitan'. Should Wales play Scotland at rugby football, I have a dilemma – which side do I support? No one ethnic grouping has exclusive claims upon my loyalty. I could call myself a Celt, but how purely Celtic my Scottish ancestors were is open to doubt. Lowland, as opposed to Highland, Scots are ethnically far nearer to their English neighbours than many a modern-day Scottish nationalist would like to admit.

Not being English creates interesting problems when I go abroad. In the United States, I can be British, or, less euphoniously, 'a Brit'. I could just about get away with 'Ich bin ein Britischer' in Germany, though I may not be readily understood. But to say, 'Ja sam Britski' in Eastern Europe provokes nothing but incomprehension.

The races of Britain are known by their individual nationalities – Scottish, English, Welsh, etc. So 'je suis anglais' or 'sie sind Schottisch' is the norm, both at home or abroad – which is fine if you are English or Scottish, but not for someone like me, who is more than one of these.

English nationalism

Furthermore, English nationalism, hitherto quiescent, is growing again. Many have argued that until recently it was subsumed in being British.[7] Most Britons are English, and most of the wealth is English, too. But with the nationalisms of the other parts of the island coming more to the fore, specifically English nationalism is becoming increasingly evident.

English nationalism can have a strongly Protestant component.[8] The State Church is the *Anglican* Church, or the Church of *England*. Many English Anglicans link being English with the way in which they express their faith. I was once at a meeting in a beautiful old historic Anglican church, where it was argued that the building should be used for an exhibition to show God's special relationship to England. If I had called such people religious nationalists, they would probably have been both surprised and upset at the same time.

Such nationalist sentiment, especially when expressed in a church whose purely theological sentiments so closely match my own, angered me somewhat. I identified two reasons for my anger, both of which have some bearing on the future subject matter of this book.

First, I have in my own family folk-memories of English oppression. My maternal great-grandmother had many bad experiences when young. As a schoolgirl, she had to wear the 'Welsh knot' – a wooden collar around the neck similar to those worn by African slaves transported to the USA. She was disciplined in this manner if she was caught speaking her native Welsh at school. This took place in Wales itself, not England. My great-grandmother never lived to see Welsh, the national tongue of her own country, given legal recognition in the 1960s, nearly a century after she was born. Today it is the other way around: Welsh is compulsory in all schools in Wales.

But that recent memory, plus the more remote family memory of a Scottish ancestor whose army routed that of the English way back in the fourteenth century, have always made me wary of English nationalism. Whether my more cosmopolitan ethnic roots have prejudiced me against any kind of nationalism *per se* is something that you will have to read this book to discover.

However, what shocked me far more in the statement

at the church meeting was the linkage between God and a particular country. It is this linkage that is at the core of religious nationalism.

Transnational faith and religious nationalism

My own particular brand of Christianity, Protestantism, should normally be *transnational* by its inherent nature. Protestants should believe that it is your Christian faith that makes you what you are, rather than your place of birth. Indeed, it is the breaking of the link between nation and faith that is at the core of tolerant, pluralistic society, of precisely the kind that we have seen growing in the West. If people are not Christians it is something that needs a spiritual solution rather than one based on nationality.

Since my student days, I have been involved directly or indirectly with an international Christian organisation working among students, the International Fellowship of Evangelical Students (IFES). Because it is international by definition, it is deliberately federal in power, rather than being tied into leadership of one predominant nation. What unites all members, European, Asian, African, Australasian, North and South American alike, is belief in a common creed. What was so unique about the student conferences I attended in the 1970s was that we had all races and cultures together, each with their own very clear distinctive characteristics, but all united around a common spiritual focus.

My wife, Paulette, comes from a similar background, both ethnically and religiously. Like most Americans, she is a mix: in her case, every British component (English, Scottish, Irish and Welsh) along with a small sprinkling of French Huguenot and Choctaw. In America, this is something of which to be proud, a fact given away in small things such as genealogy. In England, one normally traces only one line back, usually the paternal. In the USA, the aim is to trace all your ancestors: two parents, four grandparents, eight great-grandparents, and so on. Interestingly this also reveals a plethora of religious ancestral backgrounds for most Americans: Anglican, Baptist, Methodist, Presbyterian, etc.

Paulette also has an IFES-style background, having worked for its North American affiliate. This, too, has inculcated a sense of proportion. While all of us who call ourselves Protestant would believe that certain core biblical truths were essential to an understanding of Christian faith, we would not insist that any one denominational expression was in and of itself absolutely true.[9]

These are all themes that will be looked at in much more detail throughout the book. I raise them autobiographically here as an opener, both to introduce them and to make them accessible in a personal way.

Some other forms of identity

So far I have concentrated on my religious views and upon my nationality – religious nationalism being the subject at hand. But we all have numerous other forms of identity as well.

For those of us who are married, our marital state is obviously central to our identities. As I am a husband, I am also a man, and although gender roles are seemingly up for debate in today's post-modern society, my maleness is clearly once again a key component in who I am.

I am probably what you might describe as an upper-middle-class professional. I am an Oxford-educated Cambridge academic. This means that I live in a cosmopolitan, international, intellectual milieu, with all that that implies for my world-view. My undergraduate college, Balliol College, Oxford, and my current academic affiliation, St Edmund's College, a graduate college at Cambridge, are both known in their respective universities for the exceptionally high number of students from different countries, which thereby strengthens the cosmopolitan milieu I have just described.

So I could describe myself, albeit rather cumbersomely, as a male married Ulster Scottish Welsh World Christian interdenominationally-minded Protestant upper-middle-class cosmopolitan Oxford-educated Cambridge academic.

That is clearly a large number of means of self-identification! To this I could add other things such as being a historian, a heritage devotee and much else besides. The main point is that we all have loyalties within such forms of self-identity. Our *prime* identity or identities are the focus for how we live and think about ourselves.

Finding our prime self-identity
Other than when Wales beats England in sport, I do not regard my nationality as of crucial weight in my self-identity. To me, my personal religious faith and the fact that I am Paulette's husband are of far greater importance. I thoroughly enjoy being part of the Cambridge intellectual community, but if circumstances took me to another university, it would not be the end of the world. If Paulette were to be run over by a bus, though, I would be devastated. Different forms of self-identity have differing priorities in each individual, and those same forms have differing levels of importance at particular times of our lives as well.

However, most of us manage to keep our self-identities in some kind of reasonable balance. These self-identities are not usually harmful, certainly not in psychologically healthy individuals.

But, from time to time, self-identity can become profoundly unhealthy. Sometimes this is relatively harmless both to the individual and to society, especially if the distorted self-image is not violent. Criminal psychopathology, though, is extremely dangerous in its effects. Limited to random individuals, it can, with a good police force and enough secure mental institutions, be kept in check.

Healthy and unhealthy States
What if, though, a whole society becomes unhealthy in its self-image? What if the police and the politicians, rather than locking up the criminally insane, are actually among their number, urging them on?

The daily bulletins on our TV screens at home have brought to our attention a country where the key instigator of criminally-insane behaviour is a psychiatrist-turned-politician. In Serbian Bosnia, an increasingly violent country, many in the West would say that the lunatics have truly taken control of the asylum.

One of the greatest tragedies of Bosnia, and of the whole former Yugoslavia conflict, is that the region was until recently seen as an example of a robustly healthy state. The old Yugoslavia and Britain had much in common, in that they were united countries with different nationalities who lived peaceably side by side. While I think that some of the more enthusiastic defenders of Bosnian unity overdo the extent to which harmony existed before the civil war began, it is certainly true to say that actual physical violence between the different communities was rare.

However much I may dislike English nationalism and its attempts to hijack Protestantism, I know full well that no one is going to make non-Anglican expressions of faith, whether Baptist or Catholic, illegal. Furthermore, not even the most ardent religious nationalist in England is going to kill me because my views differ from theirs. In today's high technology, post-modern (let alone modern) world, such sentiments would seem quite incomprehensible. But our complacency on such matters has been rudely shattered by war on the most brutal scale within Europe itself: the conflict in the former Yugoslavia.

This book will be looking in far more detail at that war, as it is a paradigm of what religious nationalism can lead to. Having introduced myself as one example of self-identity, let me discuss two further examples, as their very personal dilemma is at the heart of the issue. Before I give details about some of my friends in the former Yugoslavia, I need to give a brief background outline of the extraordinary ethnic mix of that country.

Yugoslavia: a case study in national self-identities

In essence, Yugoslavia, the 'Land of the South Slavs', was composed of lands from three quite distinct Empires: Austro-Hungarian, Ottoman and Venetian. The Venetian part of the country came under Austrian rule early in the nineteenth century. The parts under the Austro-Hungarian Empire had different rulers: most of Croatia, for example, was under Hungarian rule, but the Dalmatian part was Venetian until the late eighteenth century, becoming Austrian in the early 1800s. In fact, part of what is now Yugoslavia was Italian until 1945, and the Italo-Yugoslav frontier was not finally rectified until 1954. It actually gets more complex than that, but the precise details need not concern us here.

The key fact is that there was no such country as Yugoslavia prior to 1918. Earlier, when parts of Yugoslavia were under Roman rule, much of what is now Croatia and Slovenia were not under Illyria, but part of Italy itself.

The multi-ethnic nature of Empires

Empires are, by their very definition, multi-ethnic. This was true of the Austro-Hungarian, Ottoman and Venetian Empires. Ethnicity was not an important factor so far as the rulers were concerned. Indeed, it was more a source of problems than something to be encouraged. If all the ethnic groups around you were also suppressed, then there was a very real sense in which you were all in it together. There were important exceptions, the main one being if you were of the same ethnic or religious group as the ruler. The classic example of this was the ethnic Germans throughout the Austrian domains, and Muslim subjects within the Ottoman Empire. Most of the 'Sudeten Germans', Germans living in the old Czechoslavakia, were expelled after World War II. But the Muslim converts, the descendants of those Slavs, converted to Islam as far back as the fifteenth century and remain in Bosnia to this day, with the tragic consequences we will see later on.

The key thing is that whereas, in a country like England, nearly everyone whose family has been there for three or four generations is considered English, in a formerly imperial country like Yugoslavia, there is enormous ethnic diversity.

Tito's multi-ethnic, multi-religious Yugoslavia

Under Tito, Yugoslavia was divided up into several republics with a degree of self-rule: Croatia, Slovenia, Bosnia, Serbia, Macedonia and Montenegro.[10] Serbia itself was divided in three: Serbia proper and two autonomous areas, Kossovo (which had a large ethnically Albanian population) and Voivodina. Voivodina literally means 'governorship' or 'vice-royalty', while Montenegro is a geographically-based name, which means 'Black Mountain'.

Many languages were spoken in Yugoslavia, including the predominant dialect, officially called 'Serbo-Croat', but usually referred to as 'Croat' in Croatia and 'Serbian' in Serbia. To complicate matters further, the country had two alphabets: the Latin alphabet which we use and the Cyrillic, used in religiously Orthodox countries or areas such as Serbia, Bulgaria and, above all, Russia.

From a political point of view, Yugoslavia was officially non-religious while under Communist rule. But what made the country so interesting was its unique religious diversity. Most European countries have one predominant form of religious expression – for example, Protestantism in England or Norway, Catholicism in Italy or Belgium. Some, like Germany, have two. But Yugoslavia had three: Catholicism, Orthodoxy and Islam. This unique matrix, and the way in which religious expression ties in with national identity, is one of the most important themes to be considered here.

The American 'melting-pot': the diversity and unity model

It is critical to remember that ethnic boundaries often get confused, if not completely muddled, in countries which were once under imperial rule. For people in a nation like England, where most people are the same, this is difficult to understand. This holds too in the USA, with its 'melting-pot' mentality. Although ethnic diversity can be enjoyed and celebrated, the key to who you are is your 'Americanness'. Even if you are a 'hyphenated' American (i.e., Italian-American, Native-American, African-American), the American part of the component is generally present.

In addition, apart from people whose ancestors crossed the Bering Straits thousands of years ago, the USA is a nation of recent immigrants, historically speaking. The

A Question of Identity

same is true in Britain; those not ethnically British are usually also recent immigrants.

A consequence of foreign imperial rule

In a country formerly under imperial rule, however, ethnic and religious diversity has been there for centuries. As a result, one small village can have people of distinct ancestry and different religions. Catholic Croat, Orthodox Serb and Slavic Muslim families can all have lived in the same small area for hundreds of years. A village can have a mosque, a Catholic basilica and an Orthodox church all side by side.

When your ruler is many miles away in Vienna or Istanbul or Venice, this ethnic/religious difference may not be the crucial factor in self-identity. The key component could be that all of you are being taxed too highly, or that last year's harvest was bad, or any one of a whole combination of factors that have much to do with everyday survival and little to do with your ancestry or your next-door neighbour's religion.

Real lives, real dilemmas: multiple identities in a nationalist world

You can see this clearly in the unusual ethnic background of several of my friends (whose real names I have changed).

Voivodina, the ethnically very diverse part of Serbia, had numerous groupings living side by side: Hungarian, Slovak and Romanian, as well as Serbian. One person living there, Ileana, was ethnically a Romanian Yugoslav, many of whose relatives lived over the border in Romania itself.[11]

Olga's background was more complex. Most of Voivodina had originally been part of the Hungarian part of the old Austro-Hungarian Empire. Up until 1918, what is now Slovakia, a predominantly Slavic state, had also been under Hungarian rule. In fact, while most of Hungary was under Ottoman rule from 1526 until the end of the seventeenth century, the modern Slovak capital of Bratislava was actually the Hungarian capital.

Olga was an ethnic Slovak. But she was raised in a mainly Hungarian area – all within Yugoslavia. So she spoke fluent Slovak and Hungarian, as well as the national language, Serbo-Croat. After a few years, she moved to Istria. Istria is within Croatia, but was part of the old Venetian Empire and then briefly under Austrian rule for around a century or so. The Italian influence was very strong. As we saw, some parts of the Italo-Yugoslav border region were Italian as recently as 1945.[12] So Olga soon became an Italian speaker as well, also learning English and German. (She is now living in Italy, married to an Italian.) She was thus a Slovak, Hungarian, Serbo-Croat, Italian speaker by necessity and an English and German speaker for fun: six languages in all, or seven if, as is increasingly the case, Serbian and Croat can be counted as separate languages.[13]

My final illustration is Franjo and Maria. Franjo's ancestors show the ethnically diverse scope of the old Habsburg Empire. His surname (we will call it Van Rijn) was Dutch or Flemish. The Netherlands, and present-day Belgium in particular, were under Habsburg rule for centuries, albeit under the Spanish branch of the family until the early eighteenth century. So his ancestors must have gone from Flanders to Croatia, both regions being under the rule of the Habsburg family. Other than his Flemish ancestry, Franjo was predominantly Croat, but with a small smattering of Slovak thrown in.

His wife Maria was more of a mix. Her family were from Mostar, a Bosnian city famous for the destruction of its old bridge which survived for over four hundred years, including both world wars, only to be destroyed in the 1990s conflict. Before the fighting, Mostar had a healthy Croat/Muslim mix, now torn apart by the bloodshed between those two sides.

Note that I say 'Croat' and 'Muslim'. Croat is of course an *ethnic* description, Muslim a *religious* one. Once again, this is at the heart of the issue.

Maria is an ethnic Croat, with a strong dose of Italian ancestry. She now lives in Croatia itself, and the idyllic family holidays in Dalmatia that she, her husband and three children used to take have been terminated by the brutal fighting.

Solving a problem like Maria: identity and ethnicity in Bosnia

But what is Maria in essence? Is she a Bosnian by political allegiance of birth, a Croat by ethnicity, or a Croat because she lives in Croatia and is also Catholic?

What about Maria's former neighbours in Mostar? Are they Bosnians? Certainly not, so far as those of Croat ancestry are concerned.

It was Tito who made the Muslims an 'ethnic group' of their own. But until the fighting, many wore the 'Muslim' label lightly. They had many other forms of identity, several of them primary: teacher, citizen of Mostar, someone's spouse or child. In the old Yugoslavia, you could, if you wanted, identify yourself simply as 'Yugoslav', in the same way that I would describe myself as British. Today, while being a Slovene or a Serb is fairly self-explanatory,[14] being Bosnian is to be of a very confused identity. Some ethnic Serbs and ethnic Croats certainly describe themselves as Bosnians, who just happen to be of Croat or Serb ethnicity. Their political identity and their ethnic identity are separate. In that sense, they have dual self-identities.

Increasingly, those of Maria's fellow ethnic Croats left behind are having to choose. The question is not, 'Are you a Croatian Bosnian?' but 'Are you Croatian *or* Bosnian?' Bosnia is being linked either (*a*) with a disintegrating ideal, that of a genuinely multi-ethnic and multi-religious State where all groups live in harmony or (*b*) with an 'ethnically-cleansed' remnant State in which the overwhelming majority of the population are Muslims. For those who are Muslims, being specifically Muslim, as opposed to a teacher or factory worker who just happens to be Muslim, is playing an ever greater part in determining primary self-identity. The Islamicisation of the Muslim community is growing.

We thus have in Maria's old neighbours a clearly identified religious nationalism. Bosnians are Bosnians, not Yugoslavs any more. They are Bosnians, not Serbs or Croats. Furthermore, they are Muslims, not Catholics or Serbs. They are a people defined by a religion. As BBC correspondent Martin Bell has pointed out, we say Croats, Serbs and Bosnian Muslims, not Croat Catholics, Serb Orthodox and Bosnians. There is still a remnant of Catholic Bosnians and Orthodox Bosnians, many of whom fought in the Bosnian army against their co-religionists. Such people are, to me, doubly brave and their idealism is surely to be applauded. But in this post-modern age of increasing disintegration and splintering, such people are becoming a minority.

The slide into chaos: why do the nations rage?
What is the cause of the slide into chaos? Many in the West have been astonished at the fact that intelligent, rational, educated Europeans could descend into carnage. How do people whose families have lived side by side in harmony for centuries suddenly turn barbaric?

This question is not new. Many wondered precisely

the same thing between 1933 and 1945 as the nation of Goethe and Schiller, of poets, painters and composers, produced not only a country of aggression but also the Holocaust. This event ranks alongside Stalin's purges, Mao's Cultural Revolution and Pol Pot's Year Zero as one of the most appalling acts of genocide the world has ever seen. When the pictures of emaciated Muslim captives in Serb concentration camps flashed around the world's television screens, the horrific memories of old newsreel footage of Auschwitz or Dachau came back.

To make it worse, many Serbs had themselves been victims of Nazism. I once stayed in Serbia with a local friend, Draga. The family possessed no spare room, so I stayed in the same room as her father while her mother moved into her room. I spoke no Serbian, the father no English. So when Draga was not present to translate, we had to converse in bad German. I had learned German in school. Draga's father had learned it in a concentration camp, as a prisoner during the war. Even speaking German to someone from Britain, Yugoslavia's wartime ally, must have been painful.

Yet the nation of victims was now the nation that used concentration camps, as television news showed us clearly. But should we have been so amazed that such a thing could happen in Europe at the end of the twentieth century? To answer such a question, we must investigate the theme of this book – why the nations rage.

2

The New World *Disorder*

What bliss was it to be alive!

BBC television commentator David Dimbleby quoted these words on the day in 1989 when the Berlin Wall fell. Pictures of jubilant Berliners hacking down the wall were broadcast worldwide. The radiant face of hope contrasted starkly with what had gone before.

The legacy of the French Revolution
David Dimbleby's quotation on the night the Berlin Wall fell was from Wordsworth's poem on the French Revolution of 1789. Now in 1989, exactly two hundred years later, it seemed as if the Age of Ideology was finally over. This Age had been ushered in by humanistic ideals of the Enlightenment philosophers that had sparked the French Revolution.

For two centuries, the eighteenth-century French Revolution had been seen as the defining moment of 'modern' history. What had gone before was seen as monarchical, feudal or oppressive in its thinking. The Revolution's ideas of liberty, equality and fraternity were new. Political life was now at the centre of everything. The new views turned social life upside down. Religion was abolished from the heart of national consciousness. The ideology of liberty, equality and fraternity was all-pervasive and all-important.

The so-called Age of Ideology replaced the old certainties which had gone before. Hitherto kings had ruled unquestioned over obedient subjects. Everyone had paid obeisance to God. Now France had no King, and Louis XVI of France was to die, not in a bed in the royal palace of Versailles, but on the scaffold. God, too, was 'dethroned'. Robespierre, leader of the French Revolution and its wave of mass execution known as the Terror, proclaimed the first atheistic state. He established a 'cult of the Supreme Being'. Kings had ruled over their subjects in the name of God. Now the people ruled in their own name, in theory at least.

In practice, the revolution was led by people motivated by the humanistic ideals of the eighteenth-century Enlightenment. One wonders what the great Enlightenment philosophers would have made of the French Revolutionary regime, with its bloodthirsty destruction of all who disagreed with them, or who had the misfortune to be born into the wrong social class. Soon the revolutionaries were falling out among themselves and killing each other. Ideology became not a means of liberation to an oppressed peasantry, but a test of revolutionary purity, to see whether you deserved to live or die. Finally a Revolution that had overthrown a King ended up with an Emperor, Napoleon. The ideals of the philosophers had been twisted into new totalitarian regimes, first of the Terror and then of the Empire.

Civic nationalism
Some saw the concept of 'citizenship' espoused by the Revolution as the beginning of nationalism. 'To arms,

citizens!' was the revolutionary cry. Armies were citizen armies, and all those living within the boundaries of the state were the citizens. This has been called civic nationalism. It is inclusivist in tone. You can be born a Jew in Paris, and you are as much a citizen as a pure-blooded Frenchman.

As we will see, this view of nationalism is rather too simple. The French Revolution did have a kind of citizen-based nationalism, just as Communism had the Communist 'New Man' and 'People's Democracy'. Soon, however, the egalitarianism of a citizen's Republic led to the Napoleonic Empire and the French conquests of Europe. Likewise the Russian Revolution of 1917, while theoretically always purely Communist, led to a disguised form of purely Russian expansionism almost identical to that of the Tsars in preceding centuries.

Whether or not the French Revolution is the beginning of modernity depends ultimately on your own ideology. Marxists would be the first to admit that the 1789 Revolution went horribly wrong. So too did the Bolshevik October Revolution in 1917. Both revolutions overthrew oppressive regimes only to end up with governments that were considerably more totalitarian than the regimes which they replaced. Anyone who has had even a limited taste of a secret police state will understand the very sharp distinction between the philosophical ideal of such countries and the all too stark reality of everyday life in them.

However, the new ideology had left its legacy. It created the 'modern' era, or 'modernity'.[1] By such definitions, religion is 'pre-modern', with the result that it is often ignored in secular analyses of what is important.

Modernity, post-modernity and the deposition of God

At the same time as the political revolutions, an industrial revolution was also taking place. To a large extent, since this began in England, which had no political revolution in the eighteenth century, there is no direct correlation between the two. But the fruits of technological change in the industrial revolution gave tangible physical benefits to those entering the ideologically modern age.

We are now deemed by many to be living in a 'post-modern' age, one in which the ideological certainties of modernity are passing. Definitions of post-modernism, because of the very nature of its fluidity, are hard to come by. With nothing being absolute, a hard-and-fast definition of post-modernity is a contradiction in terms! Some have said that with the fall of the Berlin Wall in 1989 and the collapse of Communism in Western Europe, the post-modern age has now had its own defining moment.

The reason why people link the 1789 French Revolution and the ideology of Communism is their mutual belief in equality. Both world-views are also innately secular. Humankind can go it alone. As the philosopher said to Napoleon about God's rôle in science, 'I have no need for that hypothesis.'

Enlightenment philosophy, revolution and the acknowledgment of God

One can posit an altogether different set of revolutions as defining moments in history. Neither of these revolutions eliminates religion, yet both believe deeply in liberty. These are the Glorious Revolution of 1688 in England and its ideological successor, the American Revolution of 1776. Neither of these was marked by extensive bloodshed and both created regimes far more tolerant than those which existed before.

In particular, the American Revolution is still embodied in the Federal Republic of the United States. The USA certainly has its faults. But it is one of the freest, most optimistic and tolerant societies on earth. It remains a democracy, over two hundred years later. Its people are free, and the rule of law prevails. No Napoleon or Stalin has ever ruled America. The USA is also a country which is one of the most actively religious today, although Church and State are explicitly separated by the Constitution.

Later parts of this book will look more explicitly at the USA, and the whole issue of tolerance. Suffice it to say here, when the Iron Curtain fell in 1989, it was not surprising that many in the USA took a rosy view of the future. American optimism is one of that country's strongest features, going back to the 'can-do' mentality of the early settlers. The President in 1989, George Bush, felt that a post-Communist 'New World Order' was coming. A Japanese-American historian, Francis Fukuyama, wrote an internationally best-selling book entitled *The End of History*. Marxist ideology stated that Communism was the inevitable conclusion to the historical process. Now Communism had collapsed. So 'history', as understood in those terms, was now finished, since Communism was no more. The kind of totalitarian ideologies that had oppressed humankind since 1789 had vanished. Now there would be a new world order of peace and prosperity in which liberal capitalism would replace ideologies such as Communism. Benign, peaceful and freedom-loving American capitalism would conquer the world.

The new world of *dis*order
All too quickly, the much-vaunted New World Order became the 'New World *Dis*order'. Those of us who

believed that it was romantic Cloud Cuckoo Land were vindicated far faster than we would have liked. This was because the era of peace and prosperity that it promised soon declined into war and chaos: Bosnia, Rwanda, Chechnya, the Gulf War. Seldom has a prophecy been proved to be wrong so quickly. And let's face it, who actually wants to be proved right when what you prophesy is a return to chaos and anarchy?

Yet with Bosnia, Rwanda and Chechnya, that is precisely what took place. As we saw in the last chapter, we had murder on a mass scale such as Europe had not witnessed since World War II. Furthermore, because the Age of Ideology was supposed to be finished, so too was genocide. Genocide was part of Nazism, where people were killed because of a racial ideology that said Jews were inferior beings. Or it was part of Communism, where people were slaughtered under Stalin because they were rich peasants. Under Pol Pot in Cambodia, tens of thousands were murdered simply because they were educated and middle class. Millions of people had died in similar circumstances in Mao's China during the collective madness known as the Cultural Revolution. But was not Communism supposed to have collapsed? (This is not to deny that Communists were reappearing in new guises, but the murderous Maoist/Stalinist version was thought to have disappeared.)

In reality, however, 'history' had never gone away. 'History', the study of the past, might have been hijacked by various ideologies. Hitler used it to prove the inevitable rise of the German master race and Marx felt that it made inevitable the rise of the working class, and an egalitarian society. Such ideologies, Fascist or Communist, that proclaimed a Messianic 'New Man', a humanity fully in accord with their particular ideology, may have faded.[2] In the sense that Communism proclaimed that the 'inevitability of history'[3] was on its side, that kind of history may well have ended. (Although, as almost no one predicted the demise of Communism in 1989, it is now only unusually brave or exceedingly foolish historians who ever proclaim anything to be over forever.)

The return of nationalism

But to many of us, especially those historians who had studied the Balkans, and that region's confusing and tempestuous past, 'history' had not been finished. Rather, it had been asleep and had woken up with a foul mood and a savage temper. Communism had not been replaced by benign pro-American capitalist democracy, however much some would have liked that to happen.

Rather, it had been replaced by a beast that many thought had died back in 1945 – *nationalism*. The fantasies of well-meaning Marxist historians[4] that nationalism was on the way out have been proved devastatingly wrong.

Psychologically speaking, it is easy to see why we all wanted a new and peaceful Golden Age to be ushered in. Who would not want it after the Cold War? Unfortunately, in wanting our own way in the new post-1989 era, we were not alone. Other forces were also at work, none of which were as benign.[5]

Nationalism: the forgotten force

We have, in fact, been here before. The Edwardian period, 1901–1914, has also been regarded by many as an era of prosperity and comparative innocence, especially in the light of the horrors that came later. For those opposed to the dominant capitalist system of the day, there were millenarian or utopian hopes very similar to those expressed in Norman Cohn's study of the Middle Ages.[6] Cohn showed how, even in medieval times, there were those who felt that an earthly paradise on earth could be created, where everyone would live together in peace and harmony, and where no one group would exploit another. Either way, whether capitalist or Marxist, there were countless people at the turn of the century whose world-view was radically optimistic and for whom their form of utopia was just around the corner.

The great political philosopher, Sir Isaiah Berlin, has expressed well the mood of that time:[7]

> The nineteenth century generated a great many . . . Utopias and prognoses, liberal, socialist, technocratic and those that were filled with neo-medieval nostalgia, craving for a largely imaginary *Gemeinschaft* [society] in the past – systems for the most part justly forgotten.[8]

Unfortunately for the dreamers, there was one vital force that they forgot.

> In all this great array of elaborate, statistically-supported mass of futurology and fantasy, there is one peculiar lacuna. There was one movement which dominated much of the nineteenth century in Europe and was so pervasive, so familiar, that it is only by a conscious effort of the imagination that one can conceive a world in which it played no part: it has its partisans and its enemies, its democratic, aristocratic and monarchist wings, it inspired men of action and artists, intellectual élites and the masses: but, oddly enough, no significant thinkers . . . predicted for it a future in which it would play an even more dominant role.[9]

But as Berlin concludes,

> Yet it would, perhaps, be no overstatement to say

31

that it is one of the most powerful, in some regions the most powerful, single movement or work in the world today; and that some of those who failed to foresee this development have paid for it with their liberty, indeed, with their lives. *This movement is nationalism* (italics added).[10]

Nationalism, class and self-identity

As Berlin goes on to say, Marxists were particularly prone to ignore the sheer force of nationalism, and the massive threat that it posed. To Marxists then (and now, I would argue), nationalism was a 'form of false consciousness'. After the class-based revolution that they eagerly anticipated, which would rid the workers of their oppression, nationalism would find itself joining 'other relics of human immaturity in ethnological museums'.

As we saw earlier, we have many basic forms of self-identity, and these can play differing roles in our lives in terms of their importance. Our social class, expression of faith, or our culture can all dominate us and our reactions to external events in one way or another.

When war came to Europe in 1914, Marxists and others naturally hoped that the working classes in different countries would combine together against what they felt to be a capitalist-inspired war. This, as Berlin has written, proved to be a gigantic mistake.

The most powerful appeal of all these centres of devotion and self-identification has historically been the nation state. The revelation of its hold on its citizens in 1914, when it proved so much stronger than class solidarity of the international working-class movement, exhibited this truth in a peculiarly devastating and tragic fashion.[11]

Nationalism, self-determination and the 1919 Peace Settlement

The First World War and its causes have been discussed, argued over and debated by numerous historians in many countries. But I think that most of them would agree that nationalism was at least one of the crucial triggering factors, if not the most important. The war began in Sarajevo, the Bosnian town that has once again become synonymous in the 1990s with fighting and death.

Regrettably, the victorious powers at the end of World War I who were drawing up the Treaty of Versailles did not truly understand the nature of the nationalist genie. Nationalism was perceived as a good thing in large measure because of the way in which it was understood. Ever since the French Revolution, nationalism had been seen as a positive force, the desire of a free people to enjoy their liberty. In the context of the time, it would be difficult to disagree. Why should the Czechs or the Croats not be a free people in their own country?

Unfortunately, the doctrine of self-determination espoused by the idealist President Woodrow Wilson had an underside. In essence, his doctrine was that every State deserved its independence. Such thinking went back to the Declaration of Independence from Britain in the eighteenth century. However, by the twentieth century, things were not so simple. Independence from the ruins of the multinational Habsburg Austro-Hungarian Empire was far more complex. For all the Czechs who had become free in 1919, there were millions of ethnic Germans in countries such as Poland and Czechoslovakia and ethnic Hungarians in newly independent States such as Romania who found themselves as national minorities. Because the Austro-Hungarian Empire had been multi-ethnic, these different ethnic groupings had been living cheek by jowl for centuries. All had been imperial subjects. In the Austrian half of the Empire at least, the Habsburgs had done increasing amounts to keep all nationalities happy in order to perpetuate their rule. Jews, for example, were treated unusually well by the ruling dynasty.

With the new Peace Settlement agreed at Versailles by the victorious Allies, some people were happy with the new countries that had been created, but many were not. For every problem that was solved, a new one arose. The basis of the new States was supposed to be *ethnicity*. This concept of the primacy of ethnicity replaced that of subjection to an Empire. As Franz Joseph remarked, the key question in the old Empire had been, 'Is he a patriot for me?' the 'me' being the person of the Emperor himself. Now it was an ethnic question: are you a Czech, a Pole, a German? This was at the heart of the doctrine of 'self-determination'. However, the new States were not ethnically uniform. They were like the old Habsburg Empire that they replaced, ethnic patchworks but simply on a smaller scale.

The nationalist consequences of self-determination

So we find that the doctrine of 'self-determination makes its way from the enlightenment of the eighteenth century to the darkness of the twentieth,'[12] a darkness about which we now know all too well. As Woodrow Wilson's adviser Colonel Lansing himself recognised, self-determination unalloyed would 'create trouble in many lands . . . The phrase is simply loaded with dynamite . . . It will, I fear cost thousands of lives.'[13]

As a consequence, disgruntled nationalism provided the pretext for another, far more devastating, conflagration: World War II. It was not thousands of lives that were lost but tens of millions in the worst loss of life ever seen in human history.

The ethnic consequences of Versailles: from peace treaty to the Holocaust

At the heart of World War II, so far as the Nazis were concerned, was the issue of ethnicity: the ethnic superiority of the German master race. This is not to deny that they collaborated with other ethnic groups in their quest for Empire and domination. But the chickens of 1919 had truly come home to roost. The peaceable Woodrow Wilson, with his genuine desire to see freedom restored to many European peoples, had destroyed an Empire which had kept the different ethnic groups together in peace, and unleashed a devastating ethnic genie from its bottle. Over fifty million died in World War II, millions of whom died for no other reason than that they were born into the wrong ethnic group, whether Jew, Slav, Gypsy or other ethnic groups deemed to be somehow undesirable.

The horrors of the Holocaust are so well known as to need no elaboration here. We will look in more detail at Nazism, especially its religious or pseudo-religious elements, in another chapter. The fact that other massacres took place alongside the genocide of the Jews is sometimes forgotten. These involved fewer casualties, but were equally distressing and have had long-lasting consequences. Thousands of Yugoslavs perished in the war, murdered not by the Nazis, but by their fellow nationals.

History has become a political tool in today's Balkan conflict. Exactly how many were slaughtered, and by whom is still hotly disputed.[14] All that can safely be said is that many Croats, Serbs and Muslims were murdered, and that in countless cases, ethnicity or religion was the reason for murder.

However, in theory, all this came to an end in 1945, with the imposition of Communist regimes throughout Central and Eastern Europe. This is not to say that Communists did not exploit nationalistic sentiments. Ceaucescu, the dictator of Romania, did so to full effect, stirring up hatred against his country's Hungarian minority and even managing to make Dracula, a real historic figure called by the appropriate name of Vlad the Impaler, into a national hero.

A Hobbesian view of the Yugoslav conflict

Britain, like the former Yugoslavia, once experienced civil war. The insights gained from that seventeenth-century conflict remain useful for an understanding of the nature of this uniquely brutal kind of war. One of the contemporary writers who well understood the feelings of those unsettled times was Thomas Hobbes, a political thinker whose book, *Leviathan*, is still in print and read today, three hundred years after it was written.

He is best known for one of the key phrases in that book, namely, that life is 'nasty, brutish and short'. While England experienced civil war, Europe had just recovered from the Thirty Years War. This was a kind of civil war in the Holy Roman Empire, with the outside intervention of countries such as Sweden and France. Religion – the struggle between Catholics and Protestants – played a key role in that struggle (with Catholic France siding, for political reasons, with the German Protestants). Here, for thousands of often innocent peasants caught up in the crossfire, life was indeed very nasty, very brutish and all too tragically short.

In his television series, *Blood and Belonging*, and book of the same name, Michael Ignatieff quotes Hobbes in relation to the current Yugoslav strife. Michael Ignatieff, while best known for his television arts coverage and literary novels, has an interesting perspective on nationalism. He is a Canadian of distinguished Russian ancestry and has an impressive academic and diplomatic background.

But as his book shows, he has, like me, realised that the cosy internationalism of High Table and civilised after-dinner conversation are many miles away from the experiences of ordinary people. Ignatieff observes,

> Thomas Hobbes would have understood Yugoslavia. What Hobbes would have said, having lived through religious civil war himself, is that when people are sufficiently afraid, they will do anything.[15]

In other words, there are forces which can turn normally well-behaved, outwardly rational people into the kind of person who will do things which they might never have contemplated before.

Religious nationalism and the new world disorder

It is the contention of this book that nationalism, especially nationalism reinforced by or combined with religion, is precisely such a force. Rather than a 'new world order', we have, in effect, a 'new world disorder' in many parts of the globe. As Ignatieff has commented, the key component

> of the new world order is the disintegration of nation states into ethnic civil war . . . and the key language of our age is ethnic nationalism . . . The repressed has returned, and its name is nationalism.[16]

We will be looking in detail at different terms and concepts on the issue of nationalism as this book progresses. Much that has been written already is unfortunately in the rather impenetrable language of sociology, with terms such as 'narrative', 'discourse', 'story' and so forth. I will attempt to translate these concepts into language which is not overly complex.

Some key definitions of nationalism

For his television series Ignatieff also had to use terms

familiar to a wider audience than that of the university seminar. He was therefore able to give some very helpful and concise definitions of nationalism – though as we will see, his full definition has left out a vital component. He writes,

> As a political doctrine, nationalism is the belief that the world's peoples are divided into nations, and that each of these nations has the right of self-determination, either as self-governing units within existing nation states or as nation states of their own.[17]

We shall soon see that this is an excellent starting definition, but one that needs further resolution. For as Ignatieff and numerous others have shown, there are two very different concepts of nationhood – civil and ethnic. An inclusive or civil definition says: anyone born in this country belongs to it. This is the premise on which the classic 'civil' nation, the USA, is based. Ideally, it does not matter in America whether you are black or white, Jew or gentile, of English ancestry or Chinese. An American is an American. However, American nationalism certainly exists. At the time of writing this book, I was watching some of the Presidential election debates. Both candidates were careful to affirm the greatness of the American nation. Rather encouragingly, in the Vice-Presidential debate, both candidates indirectly, but firmly, reaffirmed the multi-ethnic character of the USA today. So whatever America's faults, ethnic nationalism is not trumpeted as an ideal in most circles.

However, many countries or nations make ethnicity central to their concept of what a nation is. This is, of course, exclusivist, not inclusivist. No Jew, even if their family had lived for centuries in Germany, was truly a German under Nazi ideology. Likewise, even though Muslims and Serbs had lived for centuries in the same village, when ethnic nationalism came to the fore, such peaceful co-habitation became something of the past. Ethnic cleansing was born.

Why should such a thing be important? Once again, Ignatieff has a helpful definition. He writes,

> As a cultural ideal, nationalism is the claim that while men and women have many identities, it is the nation which provides them with their *primary* form of belonging [italics added].[18]

Nationalism and self-identity

We saw in the last chapter how we can have many identities and that different identities have varying degrees of importance in different circumstances. Nationalism, in this cultural context, says that while you may be a husband, a schoolteacher or factory worker, a football enthusiast and many other things besides, that if you are also, say, a Serb, then the primary identity you have is not your marriage relationship, your job or your hobby, but your nationality. Your Serbianness is what counts first and above all.

Those who have healthy self-identities can afford to be inclusivist in their identity, and outwards in their relationships with others. To put it another way, positive self-images are defined by what they are for, not by who or what they are against.

However, much ethnic nationalism is the opposite: if you were a nationalistic German in the 1930s, you regarded Jews as the enemy, in the same way in which nationalistic Serbs today think of Bosnian Muslims as 'Turks', national enemies to be ethnically 'cleansed' from a pure Serb homeland.

Nationalism, identity and ethnic cleansing

The very term, 'cleansing', is highly indicative in itself. 'Cleansing' implies getting rid of something dirty and possibly harmful. The concept that people need to be cleansed from society, whether Jews or Muslims, implies that by their very identity they are in and of themselves harmful. 'Ethnic cleansing' thereby demonstrates that an entire people or ethnic group are likewise all, by definition, harmful.

It is important to add here that while those of us in the West decry ethnic cleansing, we cannot be complacent. The notion in British and American inner cities of ethnically non-white ghettoes, and the phenomenon of 'White Flight', in which middle-class whites leave a residential area when middle-class black people move in, is, while a less ostensibly violent phenomenon, nevertheless a very similar concept. Western whites may not accept the wilful murder of those of a different colour, but the mentality is there. Consequently, to take Ignatieff's final definition, 'as a moral ideal, nationalism is the ethic of heroic sacrifice, justifying the use of violence in defence of one's nation's enemies, internal or external.'

In some contexts, the concept of a national enemy can be healthy. Opposition to Nazism, for example, can surely be described as a good thing. But as the genocidal ferocity seen in Rwanda has shown, it can be profoundly unhealthy as well. When the great eighteenth-century English thinker, Samuel Johnson, once quipped that 'patriotism is the last refuge of the scoundrel', he could not have imagined the depths to which some people would take his adage.

Fear as a motive for ethnic cleansing

If we seek to understand how people can murder each other after living side by side for so long, we need to appreciate the nature not just of ethnic exclusivity, but also of fear.

Fright, terror – these emotions are incredibly powerful. You might think of yourself as a normally rational being. But if you saw someone seizing and hurting your child, what might happen to your natural, rational and possibly pacific tendencies? It would be quite understandable if they flew out of the window while you used hitherto untapped reserves of physical strength to get your child back. Rationality would normally say that one stopped there. But we can all imagine that in the heat of the moment, an angry or scared parent might hit the assailant with some nearby object, like a stick or a brick. This would not be to validate such a response. However much we may, at a gut level, understand the vigilante mentality, most of us, in sober moments and upon calmer reflection, might well opt instead for a campaign for better street lighting, school education for children on 'street danger' and for the local authority to press the police for increased neighbourhood patrols.

Most of those of you who read this book will probably come from middle-class backgrounds. But what of those who live in, say, a British 'council estate' or an American ghetto? Often survival is possible only through bargaining, especially with those who wield the most physical power. As many policemen know all too well, this is frequently the reason why decent, law-abiding citizens in such areas do not inform on those they know to have committed crimes. Intimidation is simply too great for someone to come forward and say, 'X and his gang did it.' The forces of law and order are just not powerful enough to protect those citizens who, while privately entirely on the side of the police, need the protection, directly or indirectly, of the local gangs in order to survive.

This is precisely what happens, on a national scale, when law and order collapses countrywide. This is the very phenomenon we see in the former Yugoslavia (and which arguably, but controversially, happens everywhere in totalitarian regimes where the rulers practise criminal behaviour on a massive scale).

As we saw from Hobbes, scared people in a world that is nasty and brutish will do anything to protect their own lives from being short as well.

In my trips to Yugoslavia, and as confirmed by those of Michael Ignatieff, this became very clear. As Ignatieff observes, 'there is one type of fear more devastating in its impact than any other: the systemic fear that arises when a state begins to collapse.'

The logic of violence

As my own friends used to point out, while the regime used to suppress political dissent, at least it kept law and order. It might be illegal to go to certain types of meetings but at least you were not in such danger of being mugged. But when Tito died, his State began to unravel. In Ignatieff's words,

> Ethnic hatred is a result of the terror which arises when legitimate authority disintegrates . . . In the ruins [Tito's] heirs and successors turned to the most atavistic principles of political mobilization in order to survive. If Yugoslavia no longer protected you, perhaps your fellow Croats, Serbs or Slovenes might.[19]

Indeed, as many social anthropologists have pointed out, 'nationalist violence' is often by no means as irrational as we often suppose it to be. When we watch the television, we feel that those perpetrating such acts of brutality, especially on a mass scale, must be irrational. After all,

42

we would never do such a horrible thing ourselves. Or would we?

Yet what is truly scary about such violence is that its motivation is frequently entirely rational. Terrorists often use such means to draw attention to their cause. Many of them actually want the State to come down with a heavy hand, to be provoked into what the terrorists hope will be a major over-reaction. The local populace will then be so disgusted by the newly-imposed regime of suppression that they will join together with the terrorists in creating the revolutionary environment that will overthrow the State altogether.

So it is with the ethnic violence that we have seen in the former Yugoslavia. An act of violence creates a desire for revenge. The only people who can protect you against that desire for revenge are those who instigated it in the first place.

Complicity in murder: how the innocent become guilty

Suppose that irregular Serb forces murder fifteen Muslims in your village. You are an ethnic Serb. You yourself might have opposed such violence. But do the brothers, cousins and friends of the murdered Muslims believe you? Even if they do, living near them will still create a powerfully distrustful atmosphere. If they do not, and sadly but understandably that is far more likely, then they will quite probably want to kill you in revenge. The murderers were Serbs. You too are a Serb. Suddenly the fact that for the past thirty years you were the village baker, selling bread to Serbs and Muslims alike, no longer matters. All that is left is that they are Muslims, fifteen completely innocent Muslims have been slaughtered, the murderers were Serbs, and so are you.

What then do you do if the same Serb killers come to

you and say, 'We will protect you against the Muslims in the next village who are plotting to kill you.'? It would, of course, be pleasant to think that we would throw our hands up in horror and tell the Serb gunmen that they are evil monsters with whom you wish to have no dealings. That would be the morally correct choice – anyone who kills innocent civilians is an evil person by any standards, even in today's relativistic post-modern permissive age.

However, most of us are not made of the same material as heroes or martyrs. Confronted with such a repugnant choice, it would take someone incredibly brave to refuse such an offer, even though it was the very barbaric act of those same gunmen that put you in such a position in the first place.

Ethnicity, murder and a sense of place

As we all know, the gunmen went well beyond just the first question. For the Serb gunmen, it was not simply that your 'Serbianness' was the only thing that mattered. They went a stage further by linking *ethnicity* with *place*. Everyone living in a particular place had to be Serb. So if you were not Serb, it did not matter how many centuries your ancestors may have lived there, the time had now come for you to leave. If you did not, then they killed you. Thus was that terrible phenomenon of ethnic cleansing brought to Bosnia.

This, too, naturally, made any Serbs who watched or assisted, complicit in the crimes of the gunmen. Any Muslim returning would want to avenge not merely his or her murdered relatives, but also the theft of their own home. Serbs were moved into the houses of those expelled, and this too made them complicit in the crime, because they lived in stolen property. They would need the protection of the gunmen to prevent Muslims or Croats from trying to return and from expelling them from what had now become *their* home, their new home, the one given to them when the Croats or Muslims were expelled in ethnic cleansing.

So as we can see, what appears on the surface to be an act of savage, irrational barbarity is, by its own warped internal logic, strongly rational. This is all the more true if by getting hitherto innocent people caught up as collaborators in your acts of rational barbarity, they become completely dependent upon you for protection for the consequences.

Needless to say, it is not that simple. There is another fundamental mobilising force to get people to do what you want, and to give them a rationale for what would otherwise seem savage or meaningless. This is a force that is at the core of most belief systems around the world today. But as most commentators are part of the secularised, humanistic West, they ignore it or underplay its influence. The force is, of course, religion. Section Two develops this theme.

3

Imaginary Kingdoms

Our discussion of religious nationalism now brings us to the history of nationalism itself. What is it? When did it begin? Is it new? Is it old? Is it something old in nature that reinvents the ways in which it presents itself in different generations?

To the everyday world, the concept of nationalism may seem fairly straightforward. To academics, particularly sociologists and anthropologists, it is incredibly complex.

The origins of nationalism debate
Even the most informed writers disagree on how nationalism began. Each viewpoint has its eager proponents, especially among sociologists. It is therefore difficult for me, as a mere historian, to come down on one side or another. Let me give a practical example.

In preparing this book, I had read with much enjoyment the books on the subject by someone I shall call Professor William X. I then found myself in conversation with an equally eminent sociologist, who told me that he got fed up with all his students endlessly 'quoting Bill X'. They were being so unoriginal! Alas, that clearly meant that in his eyes I was unoriginal too.

Yet to me, Professor X was original in his thought, with a synthesis that I found very appealing. But, then, I had pre-existent ideological reasons for tending towards his view. Objectivity, while always sought by writers, is in practice very hard to achieve.

How we believe what we believe

I was once having dinner with some Peruvian evangelical Marxists. (To those who find the idea of an evangelical Marxist bizarre, or even impossible, all I can say is: my friends are genuinely both Protestant evangelicals and political Marxists at the same time. Such 'constructs', as the sociologists put it, really do exist.) They asked me what the predominant ideology was in the Cambridge history faculty. Finding this very difficult to answer, I asked a friend who had been in the faculty longer than I had what his view was. He responded in one word: documents.

Documents? What my Cambridge colleague was saying in effect was that pragmatism, *inductive* research, is fundamental to how history is done. You look at the evidence and only then do you come up with a theory.

This may seem startlingly obvious to many readers. Philosophers call this pragmatic methodology an *a posteriori* approach – you decide *after* examining the evidence. This is the opposite of the *a priori* approach in which you look for evidence to back up a set theory.

If we are to look at nationalism, we need to discover and to acknowledge what we believe and why we believe it. Our belief system needs to be based on the 'documents' of history, the hard evidence. We must also take into account the nature of human existence, the uninterrupted history of human achievement and failure. Just as judgment and mercy must be meted out with sane balance in a stable society, so we must approach history with enough

47

detachment to see our own failings, not just those of our neighbour. Otherwise we can be as guilty as the nationalist extremists and others whom we are condemning for killing people because of an interpretation of history.

Objectivity and prejudice: *why* we believe what we believe

Most of us like to think of ourselves as objective: *I* have true views; *you* have prejudices. In fact, if we are honest with ourselves, we all have prejudices. A prejudice is a *pre*-judgment of something. This is often conditioned by what we call a *world-view*. All this is tied in closely with the issue of self-identity, which we discussed at the beginning. How we see ourselves often determines how we see not only other people, but other views as well.

This also predetermines how we react to opinions different from or opposite to our own. If we see a particular viewpoint as self-evident objective truth, it becomes all too easy to believe that when people disagree with us, they do so not because they are genuinely convinced of their opposing viewpoint. Rather, we convince ourselves, they do so with the secret knowledge that we are teaching the truth. Therefore they surely have a hidden, probably evil, motive for concealing the truth when they oppose us.

Both sides of the political spectrum, usually in their extreme forms, are guilty of this. A right-wing nationalist and a Marxist internationalist may have politically opposite views, but their mindsets are often very similar, as the history of Germany in the 1920s shows us all too vividly. What to one person can be a stimulating, but purely intellectual, debate can arouse in other people enormous anger and sometimes a violent response.

Three views of nationalism

So when we look at the issue of nationalism, it is vital

to bear this in mind. What to some people is history is to others life and breath itself. We have what amounts to three basic views of nationalism and nation formation:

- (a) the 'modernity' view
- (b) the 'primordial' view
- (c) the 'pragmatic' view

There are, as always, variants of each of these, but to examine all the combinations in minute detail would be too complicated here.

The modernity view

The classic exposition of the 'modernist' view is the fascinating work by American Professor Benedict Anderson, called *Imagined Communities*. Other modernist proponents are the late Ernst Gellner and the British writer Eric Hobsbawm.[1] In summary, this school of thought believes that nationalism is a product (or a 'construct', to use the correct sociological term) of the modern age ('modernity'). Again, to simplify matters for the non-specialist, this era is deemed for all intents and purposes to have begun around the time of the French Revolution in 1789.

Those who call 'modernity' by the alternative name of 'the Enlightenment Project,' after 'Enlightenment' philosophers such as Rousseau and Voltaire, should logically have an earlier starting date. The name 'Enlightenment' is, by its very nature, rather loaded as it has the connotation that life before it was unenlightened, in darkness.

Some thinkers, both Christian and post-modernist, see the modernity era as having ended in 1989, exactly two hundred years later. Writers who are opposed to the 'modernity project' see it as having failed with the collapse of Communism in Eastern Europe. For them, the destruction of the Berlin Wall is somehow equal in symbolism to the violent eighteenth-century overthrow of the French monarchy, the symbol there being the physical destruction of the hated Bastille prison. As the Berlin Wall was also a kind of prison, is it significant that the overthrow of two eras in history was marked with the demolition of objects that kept people locked up?

Of course, many sociologists are not rigid in describing the eras when things begin or end. In strict chronology, 1991 – the year the USSR dissolved – could be a better date than 1989 for the end of the 'modern age'. Likewise, Benedict Anderson himself makes a convincing case that the seeds of nationalism go back to the era of printing, to the growth of Protestantism and capitalism, three crucial factors which some have argued meshed together to create a new world-view.

Protestantism and the rise of modernity

For example, the very act of reading the Bible in your own language, whether English or German, as opposed to the universal church language of Latin, certainly created a sense of unity and identity that had not existed before. In addition, with both printing and increased literacy comes standardisation. Instead of many local dialects being spoken in different regions of the country, everyone is reading the same book, printed throughout the area, in one standard form.

Likewise, Protestantism dissolved the old medieval concept of 'Christendom'. Under Christendom, while people lived in fragmented political units, everyone in Western Europe lived under the spiritual authority of the Pope (see Chapter 8). This unity was a centripedal force, giving people of all the many and very diverse parts of Europe a common self-identity, from Scottish crofters to Florentine bankers and from English playwrights to Transylvanian barons. *Prime* loyalty was to the Christian ideal rather than to any one particular region or kingdom.

Religion and the modernity debate

One of the keenest debates with the 'modernist' school and those with differing views is that about the place of religion. Some argue that nationalism replaces the medieval notion of Christendom. People cannot believe in a vacuum.

Undoubtedly, those who state that the Reformation severely damaged the notion of Christendom have a major point. No longer did all Christians profess allegiance to the Pope. The Reformation compromise, *cuius regio eius religio* (whose Kingdom, his religion), which enabled each local ruler within the Holy Roman Empire to determine that state's religion, played a key part in particularising religious loyalties.

All this preceded the French Revolution by over two hundred years. The religious map of Europe in 1700 was very similar to the one we see today. It would be hard, therefore, to think of the French Enlightenment replacing Christendom in the eighteenth century as the original medieval notion of Christendom had long ceased to exist.

What the Enlightenment and French Revolution, with its 'cult of the Supreme Being', does show is that Chesterton's dictum, if people cease to believe in God they will not believe in nothing but in anything, is true when it comes to the post-Christian views the Enlightenment created.

The primordial view

Both to nationalists and to non-nationalist writers such as the distinguished Irish thinker Connor Cruise O'Brien, this view simply does not stand up. It seems extraordinary to them to say that national sentiment does not pre-exist the French Revolution. As O'Brien points out, in his book, *God Land: Reflections on Religion and Nationalism*, one only has to read the Old Testament to see that strong feelings of *national* identity existed in the children of Israel thousands of years ago. Therefore, to this particular school of thought, nationalism is 'primordial'.

The primordial view might seem to make common sense to many. However, as the 'modernist' school might properly point out, there is much in the primordialist view that is rather artificial. Many of today's nation-states have not existed in their present form since time immemorial. Indeed, the boundaries of many present-day States have only existed since this century. However much it can be argued that nationalism goes back to King David, if one looks at real life, the existence of present-day States is incredibly modern.

An invented past?

Further, the modernists would argue, nationalists and others actually invent countries. States are moulded by deliberate design, rather than States being things that mould us. The key phrase such sociologists use is 'imagined communities'. (This phrase is also popular with post-modernists for whom the idea of objective reality is always tenuous: nothing is true except that nothing is true.) In other words, the glorious past described by nationalists, the golden age when warriors conquered all the nation's foes – the pre-Ottoman era of Serbia's Empire under Stephan Dushan, for example – is more mythic than real.

As for religion, it does not form an essential part of nationalism, so far as modernists are concerned. Nationalism is a secular construct, in a post-Christian, post-Christendom era. Not everyone agrees with this – we will discuss this issue when looking at Fascist nationalism in Nazi Germany. If ever proof were needed that nationalism is religious in scope, either directly or as a substitute religion for those no longer believing in traditional faith, Nazi Germany is a good case.

The pragmatic view

There is, between the primordialists and the modernists, a compromise view. This is propounded above all by Professor Anthony Smith, a sociologist at the London School of Economics of the University of London.

It is not surprising that many do not agree with his compromise, and that those who do are, like him, shot at from both sides. It is by no means perfect, but to me it makes much sense. It is also important to say that what you will read in this chapter, while influenced by Smith's theories, is very much my own view, especially since I probably attach far greater weight to religion than Smith does. In this age in which secular world-views still dominate the university, sociologists, while realising the importance of religion, often underestimate the innately religious nature of humanity. That is a reflection of my own world-view, of course.

Naturally I would see my own views as being objective reality. Even if you, the reader, hold a different view of religion, it is important to understand the mentality of others in examining the outside world. Those of us who grasp modern technology may inwardly laugh at the strange 'cargo cults' of Pacific Islanders. Yet to them, their beliefs are sincere and genuine. Because we do not like something ourselves, that does not negate the feelings of others. So even if you are a militant atheist, the fact that religion and nationalism are frequently closely inter-twined can be true whether you believe in God or not.

New nationalism but old ethnicity: the compromise view

What therefore is the compromise view? It is that while

the present reality of nationalism might have started in the 'modern' post-1789 era, the core beliefs of nationalists are based on genuine pre-modern ethnic or people groups.

In other words, Country X, as a political unit, might only have begun effectively in 19XX. But the *people* of X were a genuine ethnic people group way back in the early Middle Ages. So when, in 19XX, they formed their own nation-state, their *political* nation may have been brand new and recently created – an 'imagined community', if you like. But their folk memories and symbols could be ancient, going back over a thousand years. They might, legally, be a new nation, but their feelings as a people could properly be described as primordial.

As Smith puts it in his *The Ethnic Origin of Nations*, 'Usually there has been some ethnic basis for the construction of modern nations, be it only some dim memories and elements of culture and alleged ancestry.'[2]

Someone has joked that many an 'ancient' folk custom goes back to the nineteenth century, when it was 'revived' by enthusiastic folklorists. A classic example of this is the Welsh Eisteddfod, where prize-winning bards are crowned and chaired every year. No doubt the original meetings were very different from the televised versions that we see today. But equally, the slightly artificial twentieth-century version is based on a real primeval original.

By contrast, the political version of nationalism that we see today – nationalism as *ideology* – is recent. It does, however, need something to base itself upon in order to be effective.

This applies also in African countries, most of which are completely artificial in origin, with their boundaries drawn up by nineteenth-century European colonialists. Many African states are therefore multi-ethnic, often with the dreadful consequences we have seen since independence. But their names sometimes hark back to great pro-Colonial regimes, such as Mali, or to famous African monuments such as Zimbabwe. So while these present-day African states might be precariously artificial, they too hark back to a genuine ethnic past. Furthermore, when a country comes unstuck, such as the former Yugoslavia, religious and ethnic feelings are often the only components left.

Yugoslavia as an example of the pragmatic view

Yugoslavia was a country that had never existed prior to 1918. Not even under the Roman Empire was post-1918 Yugoslavia in a single Roman province. In the nineteenth century, though, many intellectuals and nationalists had the dream of creating a Southern (or Yugo) Slav state. This movement was called Illyrianism, after the name of the old 'imagined community', since the historic, linguistic and cultural background of the groups coming together was far more diverse than the romantic founders of the idea realised. In addition, political reality soon led to strong Serbian predominance, thereby cutting out the Croats and Slovenes from effective power within ten years of the country's creation in 1918.

As a recent book has shown, Yugoslavia existed twice, from 1918 to 1941 and then from 1945 to 1991. The first period saw royalist dictatorship under the Serbian Karageorgevic dynasty. The second period was also under dictatorship, but for most of that period under the deliberately multi-ethnic Tito.

Tito, however, never created what the Czech playwright and President Vaclav Havel has called a 'civic society'. So when Tito died, the country was all too open to nationalist politicians, whether Serb, Croat or Muslim, exploiting the internal divisions for their own ends. By 1991, the 'imagined community' of Yugoslavia was dead, unravelled into its constituent parts.

The States that emerged were also ones that possessed strong religious sentiments, Catholic Croatia, Orthodox Serbia and Muslim Bosnia. Bosnia itself had been a microcosm of Yugoslavia, having all these three religious groups within its boundaries. Soon, alas, as the unravelling process began and nationalism's pull was felt, Bosnian came to mean Muslim, in essence. This is not to deny the existence of those brave ethnic Croats and Serbs who insisted on maintaining a deliberately Bosnian identity. If only there had been more of them, the carnage might not have happened, or certainly not on the scale that actually took place. But, tragically for Bosnia, the pull of ethnic/religious nationalist ties was too powerful, and Bosnia has suffered the fate of Yugoslavia itself, ethnic disintegration.

Muslim anger and the fall of Bosnia

With good reason, many Muslims in different countries, from Malaysia to the Middle East, were upset that the West did not go to the aid of the beleaguered Muslims of Bosnia. Earlier and more effective intervention would, they argue, have lessened the casualty rate and prevented the chaos caused by ethnic cleansing and the mass rape of Bosnian women.

Much Muslim anger was religious. They saw the spectre of the Crusades returning, with innocent Muslims being slaughtered by 'Christian' armies, and the 'Christian' Western Powers doing almost nothing to stop it. As an American Council of Foreign Relations book has pointed out, the weakness of the West in relation to Serb aggression is appalling.[3] But as the book also shows, it was the *Governments* that took no action. The authors feel that popular opinion would probably have approved more vigorous action earlier.

Western Governments, Yugoslavia and religion

But so far as Western leaders were concerned, religion was really no part of their decision making process. The fact that different ethnic groups had particular religious views made no difference to the Governments of Britain, Germany or France. Whatever the Serbs may say, Croatia's Catholicism did not influence Germany in its support for Croatia's desire for freedom. In fact, when the fighting came, the Catholic Croats were left equally in the lurch. Certainly this was so until the USA decided to turn a blind eye to attempts in 1995 to supply weapons to Croatia, to enable the Croats to reconquer territories lost in 1991.

So far as foreign policy goes, religion is altogether out of the reckoning among Western politicians. In this they are unlike their equivalents in the Muslim world, where the two are increasingly integrated.

The return of religion is therefore something which statesmen and women have to take into account. Many would argue that, in some cases, the return has been artificially induced for political reasons. The prime example is the former Yugoslavia, where the Serb leader, Slobodan Milosevic, used Serbian Orthodox religious sentiment to stir up nationalistic hatred.

As I write this chapter, the Serbian Orthodox Patriarch, or religious leader, has turned against Milosevic personally, but has done so as part of an anti-Milosevic coalition which contains several nationalist groupings. While political leadership in Serbia may well change during the lifetime of the print of this book, the basic principle remains: there continues to be a strong link in Eastern Orthodox countries between nationalism and religion.

We will go on to examine whether or not this is in fact the case. Regardless of the 'imagined' nature of much of present-day religious nationalism, it is impossible any longer to argue that religion has no role in the politics of the post-1989 world.

Section Two

Religion and Nationalism: The Origins of Conflict

The New Cold War: Religious Nationalism Confronts the Secular State

This is not a quotation from a sensationalist press article, but in fact the title of a serious, carefully reasoned academic study, published by the University of California Press. The idea that religion could once again be a threat to world peace might have seemed extraordinary until very recently. Yet in the post-Cold War climate, since 1989, such notions are now being taken very seriously.

One only has to look at the war in the former Yugoslavia to see that there is a very convincing case for such alarming theories. In that area, Islam, Catholicism and Orthodoxy all clash against one another. An event over six hundred years ago can still provoke hostility between Orthodox Serbs and Muslim Bosnians. The crushing defeat of Serbia, in 1389 at the Field of Blackbirds at Kossovo by the invading Ottoman armies, is remembered as if it had happened yesterday.

Why the Nations Rage

The foremost theory which states that religion and culture can have an impact on contemporary politics is Samuel P. Huntington's 'clash of civilisations' theory. He argues that what is important today is *civilisation*, a cultural concept with religion at its centre, which has far-reaching political and strategic consequences. If wars come in the future, they will come as a result of clashes between different civilisations or world-views. The core cultures of the world are Western Christian, Eastern (Orthodox) Christian, Islamic, Sinic (Chinese/Confucian), Shinto (Japanese) and Hindu, with African and Latin American also classifying as civilisations of their own.

This list is by no means perfect or exclusive. How would one regard Israel, for example? Where would Thailand fit in? Huntington admits in his new book, *The Clash of Civilizations and the Remaking of World Order*, that his thesis is essentially a paradigm, a theory among many.[1] For our purposes in this book, Israel and Thailand, along with other possible anomalies, are outside our scope. His thesis is relevant to the former Yugoslavia, since three of his 'civilisations' are present there: Western, Orthodox and Islamic.

Two of the chapters in this section examine the nature of religious conflict. 'The Field of Blackbirds' looks at conflict in the former Yugoslavia and how three religions or civilisations came to clash there. What caused the war there? How far back does the tension go? What rôle did religion play in nationalist hatreds? 'The Clash of Civilisations' looks in more detail at religious nationalism and the scope for future conflict. We look at theories other than just that of Huntington, to see what they have to tell us. We have a cursory glimpse at Islam, at the Islamic concept of Jihad, or Holy War, and at the Muslim doctrine of the two 'abodes': the Abode of Islam and the Abode of War. Does the fact that Islam sees itself as a unitary entity, based upon its own religion, create a kind of religious nationalism of its own? We look both here, and later in the book, at the results of this particular form of religious nationalism in terms of inter-religious conflict.

Lastly, in 'The Paradise of Belonging', we examine the way in which states, or nations, can develop the mentality which leads to such terrible conflict in the first place. We do so by considering the concept of 'unhealthy' States, an idea which suggests that nations, like humans, can become mentally ill. Perhaps the best example this century of a psychotic nation is that of Nazi Germany, where nationalistic fervour took on a strongly religious flavour, with Hitler portrayed as a Messianic figure. The chapter's subject matter should keep Westerners humble: genocide is not the prerogative of Serbs or Hutus, but a condition any nation can develop.

4

The Field of Blackbirds

Many have puzzled over what it is that divides people who have lived together for so long. 'Surely,' they say, 'isn't everyone in Ireland Irish, for example, or fellow Slavs in the Balkans? If they are of common nationality, there should be no reason for fighting.' Yet family feuds and civil war have been part of mythology and of historical reality throughout time.

Religion and conflict

In a place like Northern Ireland, religion is obviously part of the ongoing conflict. Likewise, a large component of the tragedy of the Middle East is the mutually Semitic ancestry of Jew and Arab. Arabs look to Abraham in much the same way as Jews do. This is because both Arabs and Jews claim Abrahamic descent. They should, therefore, see themselves as kindred members of the same family, rather than, as so often happens today, as sworn enemies. Once again, it is clearly a religious difference that separates them: Jew *versus* Muslim.

We will be looking at varying aspects of all this in forthcoming chapters. So what we have here is by way of an *hors d'oeuvre* to introduce us to this complex subject.

One of the things that many people note about the Middle East is that a Jew can be born anywhere in the world and have the right to live in Israel. This is known as the 'right of return'. But one can be born in the Middle East and not be a Jew – especially if you are a Muslim. Furthermore, as recent research on DNA has shown, many Jews who have come to Israel are not, genetically speaking, of Jewish ancestry at all.

Ethnicity and belonging

This is true of the black African Falasha Jews from Ethiopia, a group of people who are ethnically African but who are Jewish in terms of their religious faith. During the Ethiopian civil war in the 1970s, the Israeli Government was able to airlift many of them out of the danger zone into the safety of Israel. Medical and genetic research has now demonstrated that many Jews of Yemeni origin are clearly descended, not from Jews, but from Yemeni Arabs who converted to Judaism centuries ago.

The Old and New Testaments make many references to 'proselytes', people not of Jewish ancestry but who converted to Jewish faith. The Jewish authorities recognised these people as being as Jewish as those of Jewish faith whose ethnic ancestry was also Jewish.

Religion rather than ethnicity is a key element in the struggles of the Middle East. Arabs and Jews are genetically very similar, but religiously different. That much is obvious. I would argue that the same holds true elsewhere.

Ethnicity and belonging in the former Yugoslavia

What is interesting is that, if you trace back far enough, the actual *ethnic* distinctions between Serb, Croat and Bosnian are all very small.

Until the civil war began, the official language was

one called 'Serbo-Croat'. The difference between the languages spoken in, say, Zagreb, Sarajevo and Belgrade was fairly minimal, maybe even less than that between British English and American English and certainly not as great as the difference between German and Dutch.[1]

Nowadays this has changed. Newly independent regimes are emphasising the differences in language, seeing Croatian and Bosnian as distinct, separate and independent languages. It is probable that, as time passes and as political divisions continue, the distinctions between languages will increase. Unfortunately, language, like history, has become a political football, with thousands of people dying as a result. One's dialect or language indicates one's nationality. During a civil war, dialect may identify certain people as belonging to 'the enemy' and mark them out for death.

This emphasis on separate dialects or languages, alongside the issues of ethnicity and religion, has further underlined the need to identify the distinctive characteristics of those called Bosnians. This apparently straightforward ethnological question has become, through politics, immensely complex. Too much hinges on the answer for a simple and honest solution now to be found. To say that a Bosnian is someone who lives in Bosnia is no answer.

The central part of the issue is the identity of *today's* Bosnian Muslims. We have seen two things about their identity: they are Muslims by religion and, like most of their neighbours, they are Slavic by ethnicity.

Interpreting history
Once again, though, nothing is that simple. Here history comes in. History, to those of us in the West, is relatively straightforward. Furthermore, we are used to several different schools of thought flourishing simultaneously.

Historians can, and often do, disagree with each other vigorously. Debate is part and parcel of the vigour of academic life. (One hopes that it does not always get to the stage of the two historians who, disagreeing profoundly over an aspect of early modern history, each refused ever to be in the same room as his rival.)

If interpretation is free in some countries, in others it is not. Under Communism, with its absolutes and often rather inflexible Marxist interpretation of the past, those wishing to challenge the orthodox 'party line' had to do so indirectly. I recall an East European historian and dissident friend who became an expert on medieval heretics. For him, to write of the injustice of the suppression of these groups helped him to express, in a safe form, his deeply-held feelings about the Communist regime's twentieth-century repression of his own people. As the oppressive regime about which he was writing was both medieval and feudal, and thus by definition reactionary, the Government did not mind what he wrote about it so long as he never drew the obvious parallels explicitly in print.

Rediscovering and misusing the past

History in such countries – both right-wing reactionary and Communist – was seen by the State as serving a purpose. (This is not to say that history does not serve political ends in democratic countries. But in the West, dissenting history is not only permitted, but can also flourish.) With the downfall of Communism, many countries were able freely to rediscover their own past. In a country like Yugoslavia, once it broke up, history became a tool in the hands of competing nationalist groups. We will explore the way in which politicians have misused history for their own political ends later in the chapter, but let us look first at the practical effects it had on what happened on the ground.

At the battle of the Blackbirds' Field, Kossovo Polje, in 1389, the great Empire of the Serbs fell to the invading Ottoman army. The Islamic conquest of the Balkans continued, with another disaster following on with the fall of Constantinople and the final destruction of the ancient Byzantine Empire in 1453. By the sixteenth century the Ottoman armies were at the gates of Vienna itself. That siege was unsuccessful, and by the end of the seventeenth century, the Ottoman Empire was in retreat, beginning with the successful reconquest of Hungary by the Habsburg armies.

Much of the history of the pre-conquest Balkans is extremely complex, and this is not a book where we can go into enormous detail. What is true to say (and when it comes to Balkan history the word 'true' is often hard to define) is that there was religious diversity even then.

A beginner's guide to the Balkans

There are few areas as complex as the Balkans. As we have seen, this is because they cross one of the most ancient 'fault lines' in Europe: that between Orthodoxy and Catholicism. Just to make things more complicated, they also have a large Muslim minority.

Why is all this important? Events that took place centuries ago have led to thousands being killed today. However unusual or incomprehensible some of what follows may seem to a Western reader, the issues of historical interpretation are very much alive in the Balkans. Your mind might well boggle at talk of mystical medieval groups like the Bogomils, or of obscure ethnic groups such as the Vlachs. If it does indeed boggle, I would sympathise with you! This part of the book has needed several redrafts simply to attempt to make it comprehensible to non-specialist readers.

Yet the very fact that such a chapter is necessary at all shows the hideous power of religious nationalism. The way in which weird medieval sects, most of which died out centuries ago, can have such relevance to late twentieth-century politics, is proof of this. It might seem crazy that innocent people should be murdered wholesale because of historical disagreements about whom they may or may not have as ancestors. This demonstrates clearly that religion combined with nationalism can be a very deadly mixture. Having the wrong forebears can cost you your life.

Trying to unravel some complexities of the Balkan present

Perhaps the most important tool in working out who is who, or, equally significant, who *was* who, is a good map. A sense of humour might also help!

If you look at a post-1992 map of the Balkans, you can see where the fault line lies. The northern part of the former Yugoslavia has two countries, Croatia and Slovenia. Both of these are Catholic. To the south are Serbia, Montenegro and Macedonia.[2] The Serbs, Montenegrins and Macedonians are all Orthodox in their expression of Christianity. Serbia has two provinces which have very large non-Orthodox minorities: Voivodina in the north and Kossovo in the south. For the sake of keeping things simpler, we will not go into details here.

You will notice one vital omission: Bosnia. If you look at Bosnia on a map, you can observe that it is in between the two blocks. It is right on the historic fault line. In particular, it is wedged between Catholic Croatia and Orthodox Serbia.

Reading any newspaper over the years during which

the fighting took place in Bosnia also reveals something unique about Bosnia: it has three major religious groups, Catholic, Orthodox and Muslim. One might think from the press reports that 'Muslim' and 'Bosnian' are one and the same. But this is not the case. There are numerous Bosnian Croats and Bosnian Serbs. Therefore in Bosnia, Catholics, Orthodox and Muslims co-exist.

Why this matters: massacre in the name of history

How did the Bosnian Muslims get there? What relationship, if any, do they have to the shadowy Bogomils of the Middle Ages? Why might the non-Slavic Vlach ethnic group have something to do with the Bosnian Serbs?

Does all this matter? Sadly, it does. An epithet like, 'Well, if I'm a Bogomil, then you're a Vlach,' might seem more akin to a childhood playground taunt than to an adult conversation. Unfortunately, the 'children of the Balkan playground' have massive weaponry and massacre those with whom they disagree. This is no arcane historical discussion or childish name-calling. This is fully-armed religious nationalism with hundreds of thousands of dead people. If you get bogged down and not a little befuddled upon reading this chapter, do not despair. This book will get simpler after this chapter. Find some good maps and keep a cool head, and what follows should be easier to understand.

A key fact about the Southern Slavs

Before we go into some detail about the ins and outs of Balkan history, we ought to remember one crucial fact about the Yugoslavs. 'Yugoslav' means simply 'southern Slav'. The Slavic areas are widespread, and also include Russians, Ukrainians, Poles, Slovaks and Czechs, among others.

Most reputable historians agree that the southern Slavs

were all one race. I put it that way here because nationalist historians today, in seeking to rewrite the past, are now arguing to the contrary. But the general consensus is that we are talking historically of one original ethnic grouping and not several. The Serbs, Bosnians and Croats are ethnically identical. Until 1991 they spoke a common language: Serbo-Croat. There were only different dialects rather than substantial grammatical or vocabulary differences between the three regions of Serbia, Croatia and Bosnia.

What has caused the great divergence to take place has been history, and the radically different historical experiences of the three groups. It is this wide historical diversity of experience that has created the present state of affairs, and which has made the history of the region so important.

Balkan history: a beginning

Let us start with the easiest part of the area: the Catholic regions of Slovenia and Croatia. Slovenia, you will notice, does not appear much either in this book or in most books on the former Yugoslavia. The Serbian leadership and old JNA (Yugoslav National Army) realised that there was not much point in preventing Slovenia from breaking away and declaring independence. Apart from a very brief spell at the beginning, Slovenia has been mercifully free from the conflict for two reasons.

First, nearly all Slovenia is Slovene. There are virtually no ethnic minorities. Especially important is the fact that there are no Serbs to speak of. Second, the Slovenes are Catholics, and not Orthodox. There are no Orthodox minorities who wish unity with their fellow Orthodox the other side of the fault line.

Linguistically, although Slovene is a Slav language, it is not the same as Serbo-Croat. The Slovenes, while closely related to their neighbours in the old Yugoslavia, are therefore slightly different ethnically.

Historically, what is now Slovenia was never part of the kingdoms of which Croatia and Serbia, respectively, were part. The core of present-day Slovenia was known as the Duchy of Carniola (Krain in German). This was an independent Duchy until 1335, when it passed to the Austrian Habsburg family until 1918. In comparison to other nations, such as the Hungarians, the Austrians were reasonably benign to their Slavic subjects. Slovenia's experience, therefore, was as part of the Austrian, Catholic West. Scenically, Slovenia looks like Austria even today. Not surprisingly, economically it is by far the most advanced of the former Yugoslav States. Being free of inner conflict and of war, it is a prime candidate for admission to the European Union and to Western Europe as a whole.

Croatia is also Catholic. However, its history is rather different from Slovenia's and more complex.

Croatia's core area was a kingdom in the early Middle Ages. Then it was conquered by the Hungarians in 1091. It remained a province of Hungary until 1918. The coastal part of present-day Croatia is called Dalmatia. This region was under Venetian rule. Venice wanted secure trade routes, and the Venetians conquered both the Adriatic coastline and many of the Greek islands. They lost their Greek possessions, but kept their Dalmatian Empire until Napoleon's time. For a few years in the early nineteenth century, much of this region was in a Napoleonically-created Kingdom of Illyria. But when the Allies defeated Napoleon, Dalmatia was given to Austria, who ruled it until 1918. The Hungarians, Venetians and Austrians were all Catholics. So although Croatia was under rulers of different nationalities, it was always under the rule of its fellow Catholic co-religionists.

Getting more complex: some Serbian history

The history of the Orthodox branch of the southern Slavs is slightly more complex. The Serbs, Montenegrins (who are closely related to the Serbs) and the 'Macedonians' were initially part of the great Byzantine Empire. This was the survivor of the Roman Empire and lasted until 1453. Byzantium was Orthodox and, under its rule, the Slavs became Orthodox, too.

The Byzantine Empire began to break up in the Middle Ages. Some of this was the result of the folly of the Western Crusaders. Urged on by the greed of the great merchants of Venice, they attacked Constantinople, the Byzantine capital, in 1204. The original vision behind the attack on Constantinople was to help the beleaguered Crusaders in the Holy Land who had lost Jerusalem not long before. So instead of invading Muslim-held territory, they attacked their fellow Christians.

Eventually, the Byzantines won back their Empire, but at much cost. Their Empire never really recovered. The Crusaders had destroyed the major Christian bulwark against Islam. Soon, the Balkans were to pay the price.

Initially, the Slavs in the Balkans were the beneficiaries of Byzantine decline. Various Slavic Empires came and vanished. One was Bulgarian, and another Serbian. The Serb Empire was the creation of a man named Stephan Dushan. His domain spread well beyond current-day Serbia. It included some of northern Greece and parts of what are now other Slavic Balkan countries such as Macedonia and Bosnia. It was the Serb dream of 'Greater Serbia' come true.

Unfortunately for the Serbs and other Balkan peoples, the decline of Byzantium opened the way for Islamic invaders coming from Asia. The most dynamic and successful of these were the Ottomans. They were a Turkish dynasty and strongly Muslim as well. They conquered most of present-day Turkey (which had hitherto had a large partly Greek population) and then started to make their way into the Balkans.

By the time that the Ottomans invaded the Balkan peninsula, the old Serbian Empire had been reduced to several, much smaller States. The forces of the Serbs and their allies were not as strong as those of the Turks, and a Serbian-led army was defeated at the Field of Blackbirds, Kossovo Polje, in 1389. It did not take long to extinguish Serb independence. Serbians were to remain under Ottoman rule until the 1850s – over four hundred and fifty years. Some parts of present-day Serbia were under the Ottomans right up until the early years of this century.

Bosnia: a beginning
We have not yet dealt with the kingdom in the middle between Serbia and Croatia: Bosnia.

Contrary to what many Serb or Croat nationalists now maintain, Bosnia was a kingdom of its own for much of the Middle Ages. It had a native Bosnian dynasty. Whatever nominal allegiance it might have had to other rulers, such as the King of Hungary, it was in practice completely independent. Bosnia lasted for longer than Serbia against the Turks. While the Ottoman invasion began in 1386, Bosnia was not finally conquered until 1463.

Bosnia remained under Ottoman rule until 1878, when both Bosnia and the closely related province of Hercegovina (literally 'the land of the Duke') were placed under Austro-Hungarian rule. The Habsburg Empire formally annexed Bosnia in 1908. The crisis which that seizure created is one of the many complex causes of the origins of the First World War. World War I began in Sarajevo, the Bosnian capital, when a Bosnian Serb, Gavrilo Princip, assassinated Archduke Franz Ferdinand, the heir to the

Austro-Hungarian throne. The Archduke's murder was the small spark that led to the conflagration of the 'Great War'. The Serb nationalism of his assassin clashed with the German nationalism of Austria-Hungary's chief ally, the German Empire.

The origins of Islamic Bosnia

This is where the history of Bosnia, and of the Balkan peninsula generally, becomes very complex. My wife is a specialist in the fifteenth century, with an Oxford doctorate, but even she found my initial attempts to explain what follows more than a bit confusing. I trust that what I have now written is comprehensible.

We have seen that national identity and religious identity have become very confused and intermingled in the former Yugoslavia. Catholicism and Croat nationalism, Orthodoxy and Serb nationalism: both have been increasingly enmeshed.

Within Bosnia itself, though, the largest religious minority is neither Orthodox nor Catholic, but Muslim. In the minds of most people, 'Bosnian' and 'Muslim' go together. Yet there are many patriotic Bosnians who are Catholic or Orthodox, not Muslim at all. What is also confusing is that 'Muslim' is a religious designation, whereas 'Serb' or 'Croat' are territorial/ethnic designations. The former leader of the Serbian grouping in Bosnia, Radovan Karadzic, is called a 'Bosnian Serb' not a 'Bosnian Orthodox'. Likewise, one refers to the 'Bosnian Croats' not the 'Bosnian Catholics'. The Muslims, therefore, are categorised primarily by their religion, the Orthodox and Catholics by their ethnic links to neighbouring countries, Serbia and Croatia.

Why the Muslims were massacred

As a result of these distinctions, Bosnia is in danger of

disintegration. The 'Croat' parts, which are desired by Croatia, call themselves Herceg-Bosnia. The 'Serbian' part, eyed by Serbia, calls itself Republika Srbska ('Serb Republic'). Indeed, one of the main motives for mass murder and ethnic cleansing by the Serbs was to ensure that those parts of Bosnia which could be absorbed into the 'Serb Republic' and thence Serbia, would contain only Serbs and Muslims.

Historically, Serb, Croat and Muslim had lived side by side within Bosnia for centuries. Sometimes one village would be Muslim and its neighbour Serb. In towns, the mixture was often far more patchwork, with all three groupings living fully intermingled. Intermarriage became increasingly common as the twentieth century progressed. Churches and mosques would stand close together.

Under the Yugoslav dictator Tito, Muslims became an official 'nationality'. Many Muslims, in those days, took another option. They called themselves simply 'Yugoslav', rejecting all other labels. After the events of 1991 and 1992 this naturally ceased to be possible. Many Muslims, Croats and Catholics then tried to call themselves 'Bosnian' and nothing else. In theory, this is still possible. Many brave Croats and Serb Bosnians still do this, rejecting the violent nationalism of their fellow Serbians or Croats who deny the possibility of a peaceful, multi-religious, multi-ethnic Bosnia.

There is a real sense in which even these ethnic descriptions – Bosnian Serb and Bosnian Croat – are meaningless. Unquestionably, many in these categories are genuinely of Serb or Croat ethnic ancestry. Many more, however, may have a very different ancestry.

To proclaim this in the former Yugoslavia is tremendously controversial. We have seen that such statements can cause death or exile. Ethnic claims made by Serbs,

Bosnians or Croats should be taken not so much with the proverbial pinch of salt, but with barrels, or even warehouses full.

This is the reason why an understanding of Bosnian history is so vital. I should add here that I am not a specialist in medieval history. However, much useful historical research has been done recently, both in Britain and in the USA. What you are about to read is my own interpretation and distillation of their findings. As I mentioned at the beginning of this chapter, objectivity of any kind is notoriously hard to come by. Balkan history in particular is very hard to discern, since many historians tend to use it as a political football in current ideological/nationalist disputes. Nevertheless, with that in mind, I trust that the rest of my account of the byways and highways of Bosnian history will make sense. The causes of present-day religious nationalism, mass slaughter and ethnic cleansing, go back a very long way. It is to the fifteenth century and those boggling Bogomils that we must now turn.

Who the Bogomils were and why they matter

Who then were the Bogomils? Why are they now so important? How can a fifteenth-century sect have such major repercussions on twentieth-century life?

What the Bogomils actually believed is, in retrospect, the least important thing about them. At the time, however, it mattered a lot. They were what is called Gnostic, or dualist. Gnostic beliefs began to develop as early as the first century. Influenced by the Persian mystics, the Gnostics believed that only the Spirit was good. All matter, including the human body, was evil. Like the Shakers in America, the Gnostics did not believe in sexual relationships even in marriage. By the Middle Ages, such teaching, known as Manichaean, had reached

Europe. The most famous group were the Albigensians in Southern France, who were wiped out in a particularly vicious Crusade. (Crusades were not just anti-Islamic, but were against anyone or any group which opposed the Church's teaching.)

The best-known Manichaean sect in the Balkans were the Bogomils. Originating in Bulgaria, they spread by the eleventh and twelfth centuries to Bosnia. Here, because the Church was comparatively weak, they became very influential.

The Church regarded all their views as completely heretical. Suppression of the Bogomils was not so easy. Central control was not always possible. However, the fact that the Bosnian Government was Catholic, and thus Christian, did not endear the Bogomils to Christianity or to Catholic rule.

Another slightly shadowy group was the 'Bosnian Church'. Again, at many centuries' remove, it is hard to be precise about them. Many areas of Bosnia were remote, and it was difficult for the Catholic hierarchy to impose correct doctrine in all areas.

We therefore have three groups in Bosnia at this stage: Catholics, Bogomils and 'Bosnian Christians'.

What happened next was the eventual successful capture by the Ottomans of the independent Bosnian kingdom in the fifteenth century. We can now begin to fathom why strange dualistic sects five hundred years ago result in twentieth-century rape, massacre and ethnic cleansing.

Remember: one of the key questions in religious nationalism is that of both *ethnic* and *religious* identity. The issue of the Bogomils and who their descendants are is very relevant to the religious nationalism of the 1990s.

The first theory is that the Bogomils converted *en masse* to Islam. They were fed up with decades of persecution by Christians, and so they decided to adopt the religion of their Turkish conquerors. Presumably this meant that sex in marriage became acceptable. This is crucial as the theory says that today's Bosnian Muslims are the descendants of the Bogomils who converted to Islam five hundred years ago.

What is certain is that the Bogomils effectively ceased to exist not long after the Turkish conquest. Small, isolated Manichaean groups like the Paulists somehow managed to survive until recent times. The mystery is: what happened to the Bogomils? Did they all become Muslims?

Is the simplest theory always correct?

Such a view does at least have the merit of being simple. Old Bogomils become new Muslims. As with all Balkan theories, however, it has strong, often unpleasant, political/ethnic connotations. The Turks were the enemies of Slavic freedom. They were conquerors who extinguished once proud, independent Slavic kingdoms. They were not just foreign, like the Austrian overlords of the Slovenes, or the Hungarian and Venetian overlords of the Croats. They were Muslim.[3]

Being a Christian was financially costly. Christians had to pay additional taxes which Muslims did not. Furthermore, the Ottoman State was run, as we will see later, on firmly religious lines. Only Muslims could achieve high office. Because religion mattered, rather than ethnic origin, this meant that anyone in the Empire could achieve greatness. You did not have to be Turkish, though that helped. But you did have to be Muslim.

Many Bosnian Muslims thus achieved very influential positions within the Ottoman Empire. They also became the effective ruling class within Bosnia itself. So strong was their grip by the nineteenth century, that they acted as a brake on reform within the Empire. Some Turks by then wanted the Ottoman Empire to become more efficient and cease to be what Western diplomats called 'the Sick Man of Europe'. It was Bosnian Muslim local rulers and landlords who made such long overdue reforms harder to implement. Reform meant centralisation, and this meant less power for the local Bosnian Muslim nobility.

Consequently, the local Serbs regarded the Bosnian Muslims as enemies and traitors. They were people whose ancestors were heretics, and who had compounded their departure from Christian faith by going over to the religion of the oppressor. They had then collaborated with the Turks against their fellow Slavs.

If, therefore, the present-day Bosnian Muslims are descended from the Bogomils, then they are traitors descended from heretics. They are ethnic traitors and religious heretics all in one. In an era of religious nationalism, that is a double strike.

Does complexity provide the truer answer?

It is, in fact, more complex than that. As we saw at the beginning of this chapter, nationalist-biased history is beguilingly simple. It is, in reality, *too* simple. Truth often has many strands which it suits nationalists to ignore.

First of all, we need to look at whether it can be proved that *all* the Bogomils converted to Islam. At this remove from the fifteenth century, many argue that such a proposition is simply impossible to prove. Historical research has not been helped by the destruction of the Bosnian national archives in Sarajevo by Serbian shelling. Undoubtedly, some Bogomils did convert to Islam. But many may equally well have done something else, or just faded away.

The other issue is that of the so-called 'Bosnian Church'. The adherents of the Church were in an ambiguous position theologically: neither fully in the Catholic

Church nor fully outside. Many of them lived in mountain regions too remote for them to know whether they were in or out. The official Catholic hierarchy did not have enough priests for the areas in question, so whole parts of Bosnia had no proper Catholic representation by default.

It is quite possible, therefore, that after the Ottoman conquest, many members of the Bosnian Church went over to Islam as well. It is important to remember one thing: the Bosnian Church and the Bogomils were quite distinct, whatever nationalists might now claim. However shaky its faith, the Bosnian Church was at least Christian.

The great unmentionable possibility is that both Catholic and Orthodox Christians also converted to Islam. They would, after all, have had good economic and political reasons for doing so. Conversion would have maintained both their economic prosperity and their political power, especially if they were from wealthy or influential families.

Such a view, if true, would extremely inconvenient. One could then no longer accuse today's Bosnian Muslims of being descended from heretics and oddballs.

Were there conversions in other directions?
The other great unmentioned, and politically incorrect question is whether there were conversions in the other direction. This has strong ethnic connotations today. We have seen that religion and ethnicity are powerfully linked in the religious nationalist equation. However, if there were conversions in different directions, then the straight ethnic/religious link may be far more complex than the rather oversimplified nationalistic version of history might suggest.

In particular, there would be several implications, all of great discomfort to present-day nationalists. For if there were conversions in the other directions, the Bosnian Serbs and Bosnian Croats might not actually be Serb and Croat, respectively, at all. They might be *Bosnians* whose ancestors converted in the fifteenth century either to Orthodoxy or to Catholicism. Worse still, they might even be descendants of Bogomils, but Bogomils who converted to Christianity, rather than to Islam. Worst of all, they might not even be Slavs, let alone Bosnian, Serb or Croat.

This is no mere historical curio. For if, say, the Bosnian Muslims are ancestrally Croats, then their place is in Croatia, as citizens of a greater Croatian State. This did in fact happen during World War II. The Fascist leaders of wartime Croatia, the Ustase, annexed what is now Bosnia, making it part of the Kingdom of Croatia. Many Croats today still regard Bosnia as rightfully theirs. So do the Serbs: if the medieval Bosnians were *Serbs* who converted to Islam, then Bosnia is rightfully part of Serbia, of a revived, modern-day equivalent of Stephan Dushan's old Empire.

Who are the Vlachs?

The Vlachs are an ethnic group closely related to the Romanians. They meandered over much of the Balkans during the Middle Ages, some reaching as far south as present-day Greece. Vlachs, like Romanians, are not Slavs. This is critical. Romanians and Vlachs consider themselves to be descended from Roman legionnaires who conquered much of the Danube border country in the early centuries AD. The province they created was called Dacia, which overlaps with today's Romania.

This may all seem rather remote from the issues that we are discussing, and in reality, it probably is. However, *perceived* reality and actual truth are frequently two very different things in the Balkans, and in the whole issue of religious nationalism.

With religious nationalism, if you can prove that someone is a different ethnic group from the one that they claim to be, then their ethnic rationale for holding on to a particular piece of territory ceases to exist. For example, nationalists in Serbia and Croatia have often claimed that there is no such thing as a Bosnian. Bosnians are simply Serbs or Croats whose ancestors converted to Islam in the fifteenth century. That means that Bosnia 'really' belongs to Serbia or to Croatia, because its inhabitants are 'really' Serbs or Croats.

It is the same with the Vlachs. Back in the Middle Ages, many Vlachs converted to the Serb Orthodox faith. They settled in what is now Bosnia. Over the centuries, a large number became absorbed into Serbian culture, religion and language. Consequently, according to some Croats, the present-day Bosnian Serbs are not Serbs at all. Ethnically speaking, they are 'really' Vlachs. This means that Serbia has no claim on any part of Bosnian soil, since the so-called 'Bosnian Serbs' are really non-Slavic Vlachs, ethnically unrelated to the Slavic Serbs. These are often the same Croats who argue that the Bosnian Muslims are 'really' Croats.

Bosnia, having no 'real' Serbs, ought therefore to cease to exist and be part of Croatia.

Religion and self-identity in the Balkans
As always, all claims of an ethnic religious nature should be taken with barrels, or warehouses full, of salt. But such claims do have considerable bearing on the issue of religion in deciding ethnic self-identity. At this great remove of five centuries and more, exactly who converted to what is going to be very difficult, if not impossible to discern.

Some have argued, and they may well be right, that some of the Bogomils and some of the Bosnian

Church converted to Catholicism, while others converted to Orthodoxy. Both Catholicism and Orthodoxy were faiths in opposition to the Ottoman invaders. Catholicism linked you to the unconquered Holy Roman Empire, and to Hungary, whose Habsburg rulers after 1526 were also Kings of Croatia and Holy Roman Emperors. Orthodoxy linked you to Serbia, and ultimately to Byzantium, both symbols of lost Christian rule in the Balkans.

This thesis would lead one to conclude that some of today's Bosnian Catholic Croats and Bosnian Orthodox Serbs are of Bosnian ancestry, not Croat or Serb. The reason they think that they are Croat or Serb is not their ancestral ethnicity, but their Catholic or Orthodox faith. Over the course of time, in taking on someone's religion, you take on their ethnicity as well. Since to be Serb was to be Orthodox, for converts to Orthodoxy, to be Orthodox was to become 'Serb'.

Pure race revisited
Therefore, it is quite possible that many of today's Bosnian Serbs do have Vlach ancestry. But it is equally possible that they descend from Serbs who emigrated from Serbia into Bosnia, and are therefore 'really' Serbs after all. We know that hundreds of thousands of Serbs emigrated to Croatia, to the Krajina or frontier region of Croatia, in order to live under Christian rule. They considered it better to be Catholic-ruled than Muslim-ruled. Furthermore, the Habsburgs gave generous financial incentives to Serbs to live in the militarily strategic border regions. Over time, many Serbs could simply have stopped off *en route* in Bosnia, then stayed there instead of completing the journey.

Arguments about purity of race have unpleasant connotations in the twentieth century. They remind us all too vividly of Hitler and Nazi Germany's racial purity laws. Such notions are also genetically absurd, in that they presume no intermarriage took place for more than five hundred years. Enough intermarriage took place in Tito's Yugoslavia over forty years to make it likely that it also happened over the preceding five centuries. Even if interfaith marriages did not happen (Catholic/Orthodox, Orthodox/Islam), marriage between co-religionists did: Orthodox naturally married Orthodox.

After a century or more, people had probably forgotten whether their ancestors were Serbs who had been Orthodox for centuries, Vlachs who had converted to Orthodoxy, or Bogomils or Bosnians who had done the same. Consequently, even if some of today's Bosnian Serbs have *some* Vlach ancestry, they may well have Bogomil or 'pure' Serb ancestry, too. They are almost certainly mixed in their ancestry, the mix being all the greater the longer their ancestors lived in the region.

The main thing about them is that they are Orthodox. Their religion is what has made them what they are today. To be Serb is to be Orthodox, and to be Orthodox is to be Serb, or certainly pro-Serb.

Yet more extreme claims are made. One of these is that the Bosnian Muslims are a mixed race, with Turkish and possibly even Arab blood.

I am not sure how these claims tie in with the idea, also put forward by nationalists, that the Bosnian Muslims are 'really' ethnic Serbs, whose ancestors converted to Islam. Nonetheless, the supposed 'Turkish' view of today's Bosnian Muslims has had horrific consequences and played a major role in their murder and ethnic cleansing.

Cutting 'Turkish' throats: religious nationalism revisited

Much of this issue is connected to the linkage of a particular form of faith with a particular territory. We will be devoting an entire chapter to that theme.

The key thing here, in the discussion of nationalism and its nature, is the day to day effect it has had. Take this account of a young Serb soldier on his way from murdering some of his fellow Bosnians: 'I have cut the throats of three Turks so far, and I don't even have nightmares.' To which the American Senator who heard this could only comment, 'Barbarism has returned . . .'

The use of the word 'Turks' for the Bosnian Muslims says it all.[4] Such allegations only go to show how warped supposed academic research can become, as was also the case in Nazi Germany and in Stalin's Russia.

However, the Islamic conquerors of the Balkans were indisputably Turkish. The Ottoman Turks were the enemy, the vanquisher of Serbia and its Empire, the evil oppressor in the eyes of centuries of Serbian patriots. These Turks were Muslims. The Bosnian Muslims are, of course, Muslims too, believers in the religion of the enemy.

Orthodoxy and the resistance to Ottoman rule

Not only was the Serbian Empire Orthodox, so too, as any Greek will tell you, was the great Byzantine Empire. We will look at the psychological/religious pathology that this created. But here, in our historical overview of nationalism, it is sufficient to say that Orthodoxy, and the Orthodox Church in particular, played a pivotal role in the success of Balkan resistance to Ottoman rule. In a real sense, Orthodoxy was the one institution that not even the Ottomans could sweep away, the remnant and reminder of the good old days of glory and independence before the Islamic invader came.

The Serbs have a form of self-identity that warps this even further. As my Croat friends never tire of reminding me, even though the Serbs were at the heart of the power structure in Communist Yugoslavia (especially the army), and benefited economically from the wealth created in

Croatia and Slovenia, they still felt like a beleaguered minority. They always thought of themselves as the underdogs, however powerful they might be.

Byzantium and Serbian self-identity

Not only that, but at the core of 'Serbianness' is the memory of 1389, the lost battle of Kossovo Polje, the Field of Blackbirds. It seems extraordinary to us that at the centre of national life and identity is the celebration of a *defeat*. Can one imagine the French making a huge fanfare, every year, of Waterloo? For that matter, does Britain have a Bunker Hill or a Yorktown station in London? The United States certainly mourns over the losses in Vietnam, and some Southerners over Lee's surrender at Appomattox, but not in the way that the Serbs do over Kossovo Polje.

It was the use made by Serb leader Slobodan Milosevic of the six hundredth anniversary of Kossovo Polje in 1989 that helped to propel him to power. He was able to use it to inflame Serbian nationalist sentiment, to arouse old feelings of hurt and resentment, with all the horrible consequences that we see today. (That is not to ascribe *sole* responsibility to Milosevic for the subsequent war. But I would strongly agree with those who say that he deliberately triggered off a nationalist-inspired chain of events that made conflict more than likely.)

What was interesting too, watching it at the time, was the very high profile of Orthodox clergy at the event. Yugoslavia still existed in 1989, and it was still a Communist State. Milosevic himself was still a Communist apparatchik. Tito had forced Orthodox and Catholic hierarchies into a low profile, remembering all too well the link between nationalism and religion. (By contrast, my Protestant friends, being neither Orthodox nor Catholic, had an unusual degree of religious freedom, greater

Why the Nations Rage

than that in other Communist countries.) Yet here was Milosevic, the Communist, standing on a platform cheek by jowl with leaders of the Orthodox Church. How could this happen?

Some historians and political scientists now go so far as to say that religion is at the heart of future world conflict, maybe even of a new Cold War. Orthodoxy is one of the candidates for such an ideology. This is a controversial view, but one, I would argue which has considerable relevance to religious nationalism, and to wars like those in the former Yugoslavia. We turn now to examine this comparatively recent theory called the 'clash of civilisations'.

5

The Clash of Civilisations

The Cold War is dead;
long live the Cold War.

The old Cold War, with capitalist West pitted against Communist East, is thankfully over. There are many, though, who warn us that there is no cause for complacency in our post-1989 world. The most eminent of these warnings is a new theory, entitled 'the clash of civilisations'. At the heart of this theory is the belief that future wars may well have a major religious component. This theory has been propounded since 1993 by Samuel P. Huntington.[1] Some have gone even further – religious nationalism, a combination of religious faith and nationalistic ideology, might create a new Cold War.

This line of thinking is highly controversial, creating considerable and sometimes heated debate. It is relevant to the issue of religious nationalism, so it cannot be avoided. Before going on to discuss it in specific detail, it would be helpful to look at the kinds of religion involved in what one might describe as 'civilisational clash'. In particular, some religions are stronger than others, with more potent beliefs and symbols to keep them alive and active.

Let us look first, therefore, at the nature of such religions in order to understand what gave them their strength.

Religions, symbols and staying power
Religion is often the repository of ancient symbolism, symbols that give life meaning as well as explanation. The Jewish star of David, the Christian cross, the Islamic crescent, the Hindu spinning wheel, all have powerful symbolism. The Nazi swastika was originally a common oriental symbol. Hitler inverted the one usually found in the East. It comes from the ancient Sanskrit word *svastika*, meaning 'conducive to well-being'. In India the Jains, Hindus and Buddhists all used this symbol. Hindus used two variants, the left-handed variant being that of Kali, the goddess connected to death and destruction. I well remember being startled by seeing one in northern China.

Many ancient religions have become extinct. Those that have not are either a mix of religions, such as Jainism or Hinduism, which have strong ethnic links, or missionary or 'salvation' religions, such as Christianity and Islam. Judaism is not really a missionary religion, but it could be described as a 'salvation religion'.

Salvation religions
For those nations or ethnic people groups adopting a salvation religion, that religion's symbols were to develop potent symbolic force, especially when flag and conquest of others combined with missionary zeal.

As one sociologist has written, 'Only the dynamic salvation religions proved their staying power as repositories of ethnic symbolism and mythology, and bulwarks of ethnic sentiments, values and memories.'[2]

Furthermore, as we saw in the last chapter, such memories, by keeping the ethnic flame alive, can lead eventually in modern times to a Nation State. As a result, the ancient and medieval history of surviving *ethnie* [ethnic groups] and nations today is *invariably religious history* [italics added], because a salvation religion has furnished the inspiration and forms of their communal experience, as well as the modes of their self-understanding and self-renewal.[3]

This ties in also with the discussion of self-identity that we saw at the beginning. The experience of being an Orthodox Christian Serb under Muslim Ottoman rule has clearly played a major, if not pivotal, role in the self-identity and self-understanding of present-day Serbs. For example, Greeks can look back to the heyday of the Byzantine Empire, which was both a political and a spiritual unit. Muslims can remember the great Abbasid Empire and the glorious days of the early Ottoman Empire when Islam was very much in the ascendant. Catholic Croats can remember when their country was on the defensive frontier of Christianity against the Islamic invader. Religious history and symbolism becomes part of the warp and woof of the ethnic/national fabric.

Ethnic destiny
Some religions go further, having what has been described as a strongly 'totalitarian' mentality, one that still exists, for example, in Saudi Arabia. First, with such faiths, you may only marry within the faith (that is, endogamously). In time, this frequently comes to mean within your own ethnic grouping. Second, such religions do not permit free exit. In several Islamic countries today, it is not legally permissible to abandon Islam if you were born a Muslim. Apostates – those who abandon faith or who change to another – have, even in the 1990s, been executed or forced secretly to flee their home countries to the safety of another. The threat to Salman Rushdie's life made

this a notorious issue, but cases of apostasy with the threat of death in Pakistan and Kuwait have also gained considerable prominence.

Obviously, some of these religions have regional variants – the Shiite version of Islam in Iran does not find favour in Sunni Islamic Saudi Arabia. But in general, the imposition of restricted exit means, as one writer has put it, that 'salvation becomes increasingly equated with a version of ethnic destiny.'[4]

Islam and nationalism

Some would argue that Islam is, in itself, a form of religious nationalism. This is because, to a very real extent, Islam sees itself as a nation, based entirely on religion.

In Islam, there are two basic religious/political entities. These are the Abode (or House) of Islam and the Abode of War. You are in either one or the other. There is no neutrality option. Membership of either Abode is determined solely by religion. You are either a Muslim, and a member of the House of Islam, or you are not. If you are not, then you are in the Abode of War.

The militaristic nature of Islam in relation to other faiths can be seen in the concept of Jihad, or Holy War. Present-day Muslims have rightly condemned medieval Christians for the Crusades. No self-respecting Christian would want to justify the barbarism of the tenth-century warriors against innocent Muslims.

Militaristic and imperialistic religion: faith out of control

However, current polemic forgets three vital things:

(1) Christians in the past were just as barbaric to each other as to those of other faiths. The history of vicious religious war, both civilised and international, in Europe

90

during the sixteenth and seventeenth centuries shows all too vividly how Christians used brute force to win conversions not just against Muslim infidels but against Christians whose form of Christianity was different from their own. Protestant and Catholic Christians have much Christian blood on their hands. Violence took place against Muslims, but not *just* against them.

(2) By the eighteenth century, such religious warfare had effectively ceased. Europeans continued to be as imperialistic and aggressive as ever. Most of Africa and much of Asia can testify to that. The concept of the 'White Man's Burden', while well-intentioned at the time, was in retrospect entirely racist in tone. The massive scale of the barbarities of the two world wars has surely proved conclusively that the moral superiority of the White Man is mythical and untrue.

Imperialism and Christian missions were, unfortunately for Christianity, linked in the nineteenth century in many areas. Christianity had by now seen clearly, for reasons we will discuss in detail later on, that conversion was and had to be entirely voluntary. Missionary endeavour therefore used persuasion, not force. No one was any longer murdered for being Muslim, Hindu or Buddhist. Forcible conversions at the point of the sword were over. In India, the ruling body for the first half of the century, the East India Company, actually hindered Christian missionary activity, lest it stir up local antagonism to British rule.

For Islam to blame Christians for using force in the past is historically justified and reasonable. To blame present-day Christian countries for the Crusades, which took place 900 years ago, is stretching the argument too far. This is, ironically, to be like the Serbs, to live in the past, to misuse history in the cause of nationalism.

(3) Historically speaking, religious war was begun by

Muslims, against Christians. This was Holy War, and it was the main way in which Islam was spread in its early years. What is now Muslim North Africa was once Christian. St Augustine of Hippo, the Church Father, was from North Africa. Spain and Portugal were also conquered by the Muslims. It took nearly seven hundred years for Christian Europeans to reclaim Spain and Portugal from Islamic rule, until 1492 when the Reconquest was finally completed.

The Middle East was also conquered. For nearly eight centuries this had been part of first the Roman and then the Byzantine Empires. Many Arabs were Christians, as they are today. When the Crusaders invaded Palestine, the Holy Land had been under Christian rule for longer than under Muslim rule. This is not in any way to pardon the Crusaders, since two wrongs never make a right. But we can understand the Crusades in terms not of a straight conquest by brutal Christians, but of an attempted *re*claiming of hitherto Christian land, by brutal Christians.

Islam continued the tradition of conquest against the West for centuries after the Crusaders had been expelled from the East. The dynamism of Islam passed from Muslims of Arab ethnicity to those of Turkish ethnicity and in particular, to the Ottoman Turks. Their Empire lasted for hundreds of years, right up until 1918, and at its peak was one of the largest in the history of the world.

Imperialism in the service of religion

Imperialism, we have argued, is undesirable. Western imperialism was often based on racist notions of white superiority and right to rule. We forget, though, that because Western imperialism had the initiative and predominance in the nineteenth and twentieth centuries, it was not always the West which had the edge. For much of history, Islam had the upper hand in the struggle with Christianity, with the legacy in Eastern Europe that we will examine in Section Three of this book.

Islamic imperialism was not racist, for which it deserves due credit. But it was religious. Military conquest and the propagation of Islam went together.

By the end of the fourteenth century, a large part of the Balkans had fallen to the Ottomans. By 1453 the great city of Byzantium itself fell, and a thousand years of Byzantine rule came to an end. By 1526 Hungary was defeated, and it was fortunate for the West that the Habsburg rulers of Austria were able to reclaim some of Hungary and preserve Western Europe from Ottoman conquest. Vienna twice came close to being conquered by the Turks, the second time as late as 1683.

All this was nearly four hundred years ago, after the Crusaders had been expelled from their last Palestinian stronghold, Acre, in 1291. It is hard to say that to besiege Vienna in 1683 was all right because Christians seized Jerusalem in 1099. Once again, two wrongs do not make a right. If Christian Holy War was wrong, so too was Muslim. Of the two kinds of Jihad, the Muslims came first, invading Christian North Africa four hundred years before the Crusaders attempted to recapture Jerusalem.

Present-day Islam

As I mentioned earlier, a full-length discussion of Islam is beyond the limited scope of a book like this, fascinating though the whole subject may be. Other writers have looked at the renaissance of Islam in recent years. One can sympathise with the way in which many Muslims feel ill-treated by the West. The seizure and treatment of countries like Egypt and Syria by European powers in the nineteenth century and after 1919 in the Treaty of Versailles cannot be excused.

Why the Nations Rage

We turn now to examine some distinctive features of present-day Islam. The divide between Sunni and Shia forms of Islam, like that between Catholic, Protestant and Orthodox Christianity, prevents Islam from being completely monolithic. But the way in which Islam strongly integrates religious faith with national life does open it to the possibility of *Islamic* nationalism (as opposed, say, to *Arab* nationalism) arising, with all the consequences which follow.

The increasing Islamicisation of many Muslim countries is bound to have political consequences. Saudi Arabia, for example, has seen acts of Islamic terrorism against American troops stationed there, even though US forces have been there since the Gulf War to defend Saudi Arabia against external aggression.

Interestingly the aggressor, Iraq, is essentially a secular State. Saddam Hussein unquestionably uses Islam in his propaganda against the West. But Iraqi Christians have greater freedom than in several neighbouring Arab countries, and one of Saddam's key ministers, Tariq Aziz, is from a Chaldean Christian background, one of the most ancient surviving groups of Christians in the world.

Fundamentalism and 'anti-modernism'

Increasingly, those Muslims who integrate faith and politics see friendship with the West as incompatible with true Islam. Often such people are described as 'fundamentalists'. This is a rather unfortunate description, and some writers prefer the phrase 'anti-modern'. Fundamentalists, whether in Iran, or Christian fundamentalism in the USA, are portrayed as wild-eyed violent extremists. While this may well be true of some, it is by no means universally true. 'Fundamentalist' has also become an unhelpful term of abuse for those who take a position different from your own. Sadly this has happened in the USA, where it has

94

become part of the internal warfare between different Christian groups within denominations. For these reasons, I am not using the term in this book, although many other authors do so.

The 'clash of civilisations' concept

The use of the phrase 'clash of civilisations' began with an influential article by Princeton University Professor Bernard Lewis in *Atlantic Monthly*.[5] In discussing Islam and the reaction of Muslims to the West, he writes,

> We are facing a mood and movement for transcending the level of issues and policies and the Governments that prove them. This is no less than a clash of civilisations – the perhaps irrational but surely historic reaction of an ancient rival against our Judaeo-Christian heritage, our secular present, and the worldwide expansion of both.[6]

He concludes with an important plea for mutual understanding, something as difficult, in my view, for the secular West as for the religious Islamic world.

A good flavour of the mutual incomprehensibility between the two sides is well-observed in Professor Benjamin Barber's book, *Jihad versus McWorld*.[7] It presents a slightly gloomy picture, a set of alternative scenarios, neither of which appeals – the bland, uniform, homogenised 'McWorld' or the strongly nationalistic, religious reaction to it of 'Jihad'. The author also seeks a way out, but to me, as to some other commentators, in seeking an essentially secular third way, he undermines the strongest case against both McWorld and Jihad. We will examine this in more detail when we discuss the issue of tolerance and religion.

McWorld can be seen as the essence of twentieth-century culture, a takeover bid by the secular West.

Why the Nations Rage

In both Western Europe and the USA, society sees itself in secular terms, even if there are large minorities who are actively religious. Politicians may bow to organised religion at election time, and may also have strong personal spiritual convictions. But they do not usually defend their policies publicly as being explicitly Christian. Even in countries with parties called names like 'Christian Democratic', it is realised by all that there are Christians in other political parties, with views that can legitimately be described as Christian-inspired. Either way, John Major or Helmut Kohl do not say that their policies are specifically Christian and that to disagree with them is to be anti-Christian. Western Europe and the USA are all, in that sense, therefore, secular democracies.

In Islamic countries, by contrast, the West is still seen as 'Christian'. The decadent behaviour in personal morality, of both Europeans and Americans, is seen according to Islamic standards as a reflection of the degeneracy of Christian values, rather than as a comment on secularist or post-modern morality, where paradoxically the old Christian moral codes have long ceased to be operative.

Old faith, new technology
This is not to say that the proponents of the Jihad world-view do not use modern technology. Imams and other Islamic clergy use the telephone, television and even the latest technological tools, such as the Internet. It is therefore not the twentieth century as such that they are against. Rather it is the mentality that goes behind it. Let me give a practical example of this.

I was once in an Islamic state, with a Muslim family. They had a television, and had been able to pick up the soap opera, *Dallas*. Arabs in that part of the world were as involved in the oil business as the imaginary Ewing family. But until now, the value systems had been rather different. It is the invasion of McWorld values that is so unacceptable to Jihad.

This kind of point has also now been made by Samuel Huntington. Writing three years after his original article, he reflected that in the West, we make the fatal mistake of confusing Western artefacts with Western views.[8] Drinking Coca-Cola does not mean imbibing a Western/modern world-view. It is a symptom of Western arrogance that we make this mistake, thereby exacerbating the tension needlessly. Subsequent chapters will look at this theme more closely. Suffice it to say here, when Huntington states that 'the West' is 'Magna Carta not McDonald's' he is showing the vital, innate difference between values and by-products which we all too easily forget.

The new Cold War?

Another American author has painted the possibly alarming consequences of this in his book, *The New Cold War? Religious Nationalism Confronts the Secular State*.[9] In it, Mark Jürgensmeyer writes,

> The new world order that is replacing the bipolar powers [i.e., the USA and USSR] of the old Cold War is characterised not only by the rise of new economic forces, a crumbling of old empires, and the discrediting of communism, but also by the resurgence of parochial identities *based on ethnic and religious allegiances* [italics added].[10]

This is a theme we have touched upon already: the primacy of different forms of self-identity. What has changed is that the old nuclear superpower confrontation of the Cold War is over. The Soviet Empire has collapsed, leaving a large and often bewildering number of successor States, both in the old 'satellite' countries and in the former USSR itself. Some of these, like the Czech Republic and the three Baltic republics, look very firmly to the West and the Western model. But others, especially in the Caucasus and Central Asia, are Islamic. War has already taken place between Armenia and Azerbaijan, Christian and Muslim respectively. Rebel Chechnya is Muslim. In Central Asia, there is rivalry for influence between officially secular Turkey and officially theocratic Iran. Some of the fears as to what will happen are no doubt exaggerated. But just as it was foolish to predict the continuation of Communism, so too is it unwise to write off the triumph of secular values. McWorld might prevail. So too could Microsoft-using, Internet-wired Muslim Grand Ayatollahs.

As a writer sponsored by the United States Institute of Peace has commented, 'Proponents of the new nationalisms hold the potential of making common cause against the secular West, in what might evolve into a new Cold War.'[11]

If this sounds alarmist, who would have predicted in the euphoria of 1989 that only two years later, conflict would begin in Yugoslavia, with over three hundred thousand killed and two million displaced through ethnic cleansing?

To be forewarned, according to the old proverb, is to be forearmed. If, as Bernard Lewis suggests, we understand better the world-view behind Jihad, we can perhaps stave off the conflict that some seem to fear.

Such anxiety seems in vogue, with books in the USA also predicting possible conflict over economic/trading causes with Japan. While this is an interesting debate, this book is perhaps not the place to enter the foray.

The religious rejection of secular nationalism
Some have asked why the 'religious rejection of *secular* nationalism' has 'been so violent'.[12] The violence can

perhaps be explained in the way in which Third World leaders see us in the West. Political leaders in Europe and America often worry, on all sides of the political divide, about the decline in 'family values'. Much of the 1996 Presidential election campaign in the USA was on how the two major contenders could outdo each other in showing their concern for this issue. The situation is similar in Britain. But to many Islamic leaders, the rot in the West goes further. Westerners are seen as showing a clear 'absence of a sense of moral community',[13] and of being innately corrupt.

Such Islamic leaders are therefore not only united in their contempt of so-called Western values, but also, according to one commentator, by 'a common hope for the revival of religion in the public sphere'.[14] According to this reckoning, Islamic principles ought to be extended to all countries. This 'religious revolt against the ideology that often accompanies modern society' has great inherent dangers. When seen as a 'doctrine of destiny', which quite often gives 'moral sanction to martyrdom and violence', the threat of Jihad becomes all the more apparent.[15]

Other forms of religious nationalism

Some Western commentators regard all this as rather alarmist. Some Muslims are far more moderate than others. While keen to protect their own Islamic values at home, they do not want to wage Holy War against the West.

Similarly, not all anti-Western religious movements want to expand beyond their own boundaries. A classic example of this is the revival in Hindu nationalism in India. Within India itself, the political manifestation of Hindu nationalism, the BJP, or Hindu nationalist party is a major threat to the religious pluralism and tolerance established by Nehru and the founding fathers of Indian independence. To be a true Indian is to be Hindu, and woe betide Muslims and Christians who preach otherwise. Yet however unfortunate for those within India the rise of the BJP might be, it is not likely to produce a campaign of Hindu conquest abroad. The same could probably be said for Buddhist militancy where it has arisen.

Hindu militancy, such as the violent destruction of the Ayodyha Mosque in 1992, does give the lie also to those who would make Islam uniquely guilty. In India, Muslims are the victims of religious nationalism, rather than the cause. The same applies in Bosnia, where the Muslim leadership initially responded by trying to create a genuinely pluralistic and tolerant State.

However, there has been a definite switch in emphasis in many Third World countries towards a more religious pattern, whether in the gentler form seen in a country like Malaysia or in the more aggressively Islamic reaction we see in Iran. The strongly secularist post-independence outlook of a Nehru, where leaders were also strongly Westernised in both world-view and education, is now fading.

The Huntington thesis

This idea of cultural/religious nationalism was made famous in Huntington's article, 'The Clash of Civilizations?' This article has caused considerable controversy, so anyone discussing it has to tread carefully, as I discovered when mentioning it in a talk to the Cambridge MPhil. programme at their Centre of International Studies. My audience was international, and even though I mentioned Huntington's thesis as tentatively as possible, those from Muslim and Sikh backgrounds made sure that the discussion was as lively as possible. He begins,

It is my hypothesis that the fundamental source of

conflict in this new world will not be primarily ideological or primarily economic. The great divisions among humankind and the dominating source of conflict will be cultural.[16]

He describes these differences as 'civilizations' – hence the title of the article, which also echoes the phrase of Bernard Lewis that we saw earlier. Huntington defines a civilisation as 'the highest cultural grouping of people and the broadest level of cultural identity people have short of that which distinguishes humans from other species'.[17] To him, this would go back to the discussion of prime self-identity. By these definitions, I would be a white Christian European in civilisational terms, or perhaps simply a Christian Western male. All this ties in with the issue of self-identity which we discussed in Chapter 1. In terms of that discussion, Huntington would be arguing that 'civilisation' is one's prime self-identity, and that future clashes would be based around that form of self-identification.

Religion and civilisation
Significantly, in terms of the remit of this book, religion is at the centre of civilisational self-identity. Huntington writes,

> differences among civilizations are not only real; *they are basic* [italics added]. Civilizations are differentiated from each other by history, language, culture, tradition, *and, most important, religion* [italics added].[18]

Religion, therefore, is at the core of civilisational distinction. The reason for this is clear, for as Huntington shows us,

> Even more than ethnicity, religion discriminates

sharply and exclusively among people. A person can be half-French and half-Arab and simultaneously even a citizen of two countries. It is more difficult to be half-Catholic and half-Muslim.[19]

I would go still further and say that in today's climate it would be well-nigh impossible. Religion can be absolute in its claims, especially if the individual adherent takes it seriously. Many Japanese might manage to be both Shinto and Buddhist at the same time. These two religions can be described as syncretistic, allowing for such a possibility. However, salvation religions are by their very nature exclusivist. Therefore, to be both a practising Catholic and a practising Muslim all at once is beyond the realm of possibility.

Is Huntington right? Much may depend on the *a priori* views of the participants in the debate, and in particular on whether they regard religion as important. The same criteria may well apply to civilisational clash as found in the Marxist interpretation of nationalism, where we saw that an innately *internationalist* Marxist author like Hobsbawm wrote off nationalism just before it began its reappearance with a vengeance on the world scene.

Culture and self-identity

There is a sense in which Huntington's view is not entirely new. A professor at the Massachusetts Institute of Technology, Harold Isaacs, wrote as long ago as 1975 that 'we are experiencing on a massively universal scale a convulsive ingathering of people in their numberless groupings of kinds – tribal, racial, linguistic, religious, national.'[20] Isaacs also commented that group identity, a person's 'sense of belongingness and the quality of his self-esteem' are all connected.[21] Furthermore, identity 'is a process "located" in the core of the individual and yet also in the core of his communal culture, a process which establishes, in fact, the identity of these two identities.'[22]

So our self-identity and the sense of belonging to a particular culture or religion go hand in hand. Who we are is influenced by where we come from and what we believe. As the US Senator, Daniel Patrick Moynihan, has observed, there is within us an innate 'disposition to ethnocentrism'.[23] Our nation, in other words, is a vital part of who we are. Since culture plays a critical role in what our nation is like, culture and nationality combine at the heart of nationhood.

Ethnicity in the twentieth century

Indeed, as Moynihan has also said, 'whatever Marxism may have meant to intellectuals, it is ethnic identity that has stirred the masses of the twentieth century.'[24]

Ethnicity has been the key throughout much of the twentieth century, in fact. Professor Smith, the British expert on nationalism, has accurately observed that of 'all the visions and faiths that compete for men's loyalties in the modern world, the most widespread and persistent is the national ideal.'[25]

Lastly, as the *Economist* accurately, but gloomily, predicted in its 21 December 1991 issue,

> Yugoslavia's may well be the war of the future: one waged between different tribes, harbouring centuries old grudges about language, religion and territory, and provoking bitterness for generations to come.[26]

Many may disagree about how ancient are the animosities between Serb, Croat and Muslim, especially since they managed to live in at least a kind of harmony under Tito. But the point made by Moynihan and by the

Economist surely agrees with some of the basic tenets of the Huntington hypothesis.

This is especially true since the fall of Communism in Central and Eastern Europe. How China remains Communist is something increasingly open to debate. Is 'Communism with Chinese characteristics' Marxism in the classic mode? The legendary George Kennan has aptly said,

> nationalism has developed into the greatest emotional-political force of the age . . It has triumphed most decisively, in particular, over the radical Marxism that loomed so large as an emotional-political force for a time in the early decades of this century.[27]

In fact, some, like Sir Isaiah Berlin, reflecting on the sheer power of nationalism in the past few years, have said that 'in our modern age, nationalism is not resurgent; it never died. Neither did racism. They are the most powerful movements in the world today, cutting across many social systems.'[28] As one writer has put it,

> The increasing prominence of ethnic loyalties is a development for which neither statesmen nor social scientists were adequately prepared . . . The study of ethnic conflict has often been a grudging concession to something distasteful, largely because, especially in the West, ethnic affiliations have been in disrepute.[29]

Unfortunately, however unpalatable something may be, we cannot make it go away merely through our disgust. The rise of ethnic conflict, and of cultural/religious civilisational clash, is exactly such an example.

Looking for new enemies?
Of course, the proposition that Huntington is right in

many respects does not mean that his theory is accurate at all times and in all places. It is, in effect, a working model that recent developments have shown to be true in some areas of the world, but which have still to be proved in others.

In addition, there is an element in it of looking for a new enemy, now that the old foe of Marxism has departed. This is the reaction to Huntington of many in the Third World. Some Muslims, especially those of a more moderate persuasion, strongly resent the growing demonisation of Islam in the West. There is also a danger that in so demonising Islamic countries, we create a self-fulfilling prophecy. Muslim leaders, angry at the way in which Western Governments treat them, turn to more radical Islamic views in protest, thereby fulfilling the caricature of radical Islam propounded by commentators in the West.

The need for understanding

Obviously, no one wants a new Cold War to begin. Having survived the threat of nuclear holocaust in the age of superpower rivalry, we do not want to find ourselves under the cloud of war again.

But if we want to avoid a civilisational clash, we must begin to understand the way in which other people think. There is a danger that, in seeing people using the artefacts of 'McWorld', such as Coca-Cola or the Internet, we pressure such people into becoming Westernised like us. To do so is to be insular. A taste for chicken burgers or for using CD-Rom technology does not always indicate a shift in the user's world-view as well. One may buy the product, but not the entire cultural package that comes with it.

Culturally and religiously, in fact, such people might be the same as they ever were. For those of us in the West, this means understanding that for some the secularisation of the twentieth century is unacceptable; use a computer, but still pray to Allah. The *Economist* in reviewing the Huntington and Barber theses in its 9 November 1996 issue appears to take a rosy view, to the effect that modern technology and globalisation can be benign. One can only trust and pray that they are right. But to use a modern tool does not of necessity mean that one has a modern *view*. It is perfectly possible to enjoy the benefits of modern medicine, yet to despise Western values and morality. In other words, *modernity* and *secularisation*, while the same in the West, are by no means necessarily the same in other parts of the world.

The dangers of failing to understand others

If we fail, we could see the radicalisation of many angry people. The fact that Iran helped the Bosnian Muslims should be a warning and lesson to us all. A few years ago, many of these Bosnians saw themselves as Europeans, living a Western lifestyle, with late twentieth-century secular aspirations. Being a Muslim was only a part, and maybe a small part, of who they were. Now such people are emphatically and proudly Muslim. Armed by Iran, sometimes trained by groups sent from Iran itself, they wear headbands which depict verses from the Koran written in Arabic. The 'Christian' West betrayed them.

As an embittered Bosnian Muslim, Mustafa Mahic, told a visiting British journalist,

> We are a kind people. I was a Partisan in the war [a soldier under Tito, fighting for the Western Allies] and fought all over Eastern Bosnia for the liberation of my country from the Germans . . . Then in 1992, I was rewarded by being thrown from my home and more than forty members of my family were

slaughtered like animals by the Serbs . . . It is a strange thing – we are made in the image of God and yet we so much want to destroy each other.[30]

Nearby the town from which Mahic had come, three thousand Muslims had been massacred by the Serbs, according to the local judge, Adil Dragonovic. No less than ten thousand Muslims were wiped out not far away at Prijedor. Such figures are huge and difficult to fathom. Somehow the forty murdered in one man's family is a tragedy easier to take in.

They died in the kind of war referred to as a 'religious clash'. Not only do some young Serbs cheerfully cut Bosnian Muslim throats. As the *Economist* reported in August 1992,[31] 'snipers kill refugee babies and at their funeral mortar bombs rain upon the mourners.'

What is most sickening is that so much murder is committed in the name of civilisation, in the name of defending 'Christian' values against the threat of Islamic invasion. When Arkan, one of the most notorious Serb militia leaders, was asked under whose ultimate authority he fought, he mentioned not a politician but a Serb Orthodox Metropolitan. That particular clergyman might have been horrified to hear a Serb irregular army leader say such a thing, but the fact that a man like Arkan could feel comfortable with being both Serbian Orthodox and carrying out the alleged raids many believe him to have committed is more than a little alarming.

How to make peace, not war
As Senator Moynihan has noticed about ethnic conflict after the demise of the Soviet system, there are

> attachments by no means necessarily liberal, never so irreligious as when pressed in the name of religion, restless and mutating all the time. This surely is

where we must anticipate the violent clash of communities and states in the years ahead.[32]

I am sure that we all trust that this civilisation clash will not happen, or, if it has begun in the bloody conflicts of the Balkans, that it will not spread on a global scale. Our sense of self-preservation should make us eager to see Huntington disproved, and the kind of peaceful world we dreamed of back in 1989 come to pass.

But if we do, we must be aware of reality, of the very genuine feelings of religious nationalism and anti-secular sentiment prevalent in many parts of the world today. Only by understanding can we keep the peace.

6

The Paradise of Belonging

Fog in Channel, continent cut off.

There is something wonderfully English in the sheer eccentricity of a statement such as that. The idea that it is the entire Eurasian landmass which is cut off by fog in the English Channel, as opposed to the relatively tiny and insignificant British Isles, says a lot about how the English see themselves.

It is also a blatantly nationalistic statement, revealing volumes about how the English, part of a country that has for decades been in comparative decline, view their own importance.

England as 'demi-paradise'
A more majestic statement of Englishness and of national pride is seen in the John of Gaunt speech in Shakespeare's play, *Richard II*:[1]

This royal throne of kings, this scepter'd isle,
This earth of majesty, this seat of Mars,
This other Eden, demi-paradise,
This fortress built by Nature for herself

Why the Nations Rage

Against infection and the hand of war,
This happy breed of men, this little world,
This precious stone set in the silver sea,
Which serves it in the office of a wall,
Or as a moat defensive to a house,
Against the envy of less happier lands,
This blessed plot, this earth, this realm, this England,
This nurse, this teeming womb of royal kings,
Fear'd by their breed and famous by their birth,
Renowned for their deeds as far from home,
For Christian service and true chivalry,
As is the sepulchre in stubborn Jewry
Of the world's ransom, blessed Mary's Son;
This land of such dear souls, this dear, dear land,
Dear for her reputation through the world,
Is now leas'd out, I die pronouncing it,
Like to a tenement or pelting farm:
England, bound in with the triumphant sea,
Whose rocky shore beats back the envious siege
Of watery Neptune, is now bound in with shame,
With inky blots, and rotten parchment bonds:
That England, that was wont to conquer others,
Hath made a shameful conquest of itself.

This famous declamation is known to generations of
school children around the world, not just in England, but
in the many countries of the British Commonwealth where
Shakespeare is still studied. It reflects a rather romantic
view of England. First, the English at this stage ruled
just England itself. England was still, economically and
internationally, a relatively new power, both in John of
Gaunt's time and in the reign of Elizabeth I. Not until
James I (and VI of Scotland) came to the throne in 1603,
did Great Britain exist. Even then, Scotland retained its
own Parliament up to 1707.

The Paradise of Belonging

Many nations have similarly romantic views of their own past or place in history. In fact, nationalism has aptly been described as the 'religion of belonging'.[2] Such a world-view has been given a similar name by the German psychoanalyst Erich Fromm, the 'paradise of belonging'. Regardless of our religious faith, we all yearn in some way or another for the Garden of Eden, a place where everything was perfect and harmonious. Fromm described the sense of *ennui* or restlessness that many individuals have today. Our fragmented society has made this far worse, with rootlessness being a common problem even in otherwise well-integrated and outwardly stable human beings. All of us, in that 1960s phrase, want 'to connect'.

Healthy and unhealthy nation-states

In Chapter 1, we saw that States as well as individuals can have unhealthy forms of self-identity. The same applies to the romantic longing for the past, for roots that connect present-day people to the past.

If we have a strong, integrated sense of who we are, we do not need a myth to sustain us in the present. We can relate to others without feeling threatened, either as an individual or as a nation. We can also tolerate dissent, because our own sense of toleration, individually or as a people, is high. We do not have to suppress groups or theories that might show up an alternative view, one which challenges the myth that sustains us.

Neurotic people also often have a warped sense of responsibility. On an individual basis, there are those who so surrender their sense of self, so absorb themselves into their new focus of identity, that they do anything that they are told. By focussing so strongly on their *group* identity, they absolve themselves completely of any sense of guilt or moral responsibility for their actions.

111

One of the most important of Christ's parables was that of the speck and the beam. We all too often fail to notice the beam in our own eye when pointing out the specks in the eyes of others.

Nationalism provides just such an instance. Subsequent chapters in this section will look in some detail at the continuing degree of religious/political intolerance alive today in Orthodox countries. Many commentators, from the *Economist* through to Harvard professors make a sharp distinction between Catholic and Protestant Western Europe on one hand, and Orthodox Eastern Europe on the other. As we shall see, this is a divide which contains considerable merit. In making this distinction, it is vital not to ignore Western Europe's own mistakes in this area. For that very reason I began this chapter with an example from my own country, of British nationalism. None of us is innocent. This chapter will therefore look at unhealthy *Western* States in the recent past.

Nazi Germany as the classic unhealthy State
A classical example of such a deeply unhealthy State is Nazi Germany. It has been described as a 'palingenetic'[3] State, one in which nationalism uses myths from the past to create a powerful tool for taking power in the present.

A controversial book by a Harvard historian claims that far more Germans were *actually* involved in the Holocaust than had hitherto been supposed.[4] By no means do all historians agree with the book's conclusions, and some have argued that its conclusions are not in fact as new as has been claimed. But I think that one argument in the book is correct, regardless of how many Germans physically took part or abstained from involvement in atrocities against the Jews. This is the view that anti-Semitic murder was within the realm of the possible. Many countries have had anti-Semitism, Britain and the USA included. But most countries have not countenanced mass murder of the Jews within their own borders. Both Tsarist Russia with its pogroms (made famous in the musical, *Fiddler on the Roof*) and late nineteenth-century France, with the Dreyfus affair, saw major outbursts of anti-Semitism, but no genocide, however unpleasant the manifestations.

The Germany of the Second Empire (or Second Reich) certainly had anti-Semitism as well, though, ironically, nothing as bad in outcome as France or Russia. But the effect of defeat in 1918 upon the collective German psyche was devastating.

Identifying God and nation

Nations and individuals suffering from such psychoses seek an external rather than healthy (or integrative) sense of self-identification or belonging. They will, for example, identify God with nation, in a way that is harmful. Whereas Britons or Americans may well confuse love of God and love of country, few, one trusts, will do so to such an extent as to justify mass murder on the Nazi scale.

This is in no way to excuse those Americans or British who drape God in the flag. The British Israelites, a group still extant, with a church in London, go so far as seriously to believe that the British descend from the lost tribes of Israel. In the opening chapter, I mentioned the example of the church where it was seriously suggested that there be an exhibition showing the special place of England in the scheme of God. It was intended for an audience of tourists, many of whom come from Muslim countries with vivid memories of the Crusades, or from predominantly Christian countries with no less sense of God's activity in their own history.

Drawing upon my own background, I found this exhibition scheme rather unpalatable, thereby inciting my own nationalistic prejudices. As a fully Celtic descendant of a Scottish warrior who soundly beat the English invaders back in the Middle Ages, I found the concept of God showing England special favour both chauvinistic and contrary to history. Furthermore, as the descendant of a Welsh preacher whose ministry was a major contributing factor to the Welsh Revival of 1904, I cannot understand the need to say that God has acted more favourably towards one country than another.

Neither those Americans nor those British who would identify God with a particular national flag would ever suggest killing in the name of God, let alone genocide. But the German experience in the twentieth century was to be all too different.

Folk memories from the forest: nationalism and Germany's pagan past

Germany has been a traditionally Christian country for hundreds of years, albeit slightly later in some areas than in other parts of Western Europe. Nevertheless, as recent research has shown, the memories of the pre-Christian era, when German tribes roamed the primeval forest, successfully resisting the Roman Empire, remained strong in Germanic folk memory. At a harmless level, the Christmas tree, introduced to England by Victoria's German consort Prince Albert, is a reminder of this.

But at a time of great stress, many of the pre-Christian sentiments of the German past arguably came to the fore. This was, as Yale Professor Simon Schama showed, something particularly prevalent among the Nazis.[5] If it had stopped at Hermann Goering's fantasies of recreating the old hunting forests, it might have been comparatively harmless.[6] Many of the Nazis were keen ecologists. However, it was to go far further than that.

The Paradise of Belonging

As early as the nineteenth century, the German Jewish poet Heinrich Heine was to write,

> No, memories of the old German religion have not been extinguished. They say there are greybeards in Westphalia who still know where the old images of the gods lie hidden; on their deathbeds they tell their youngest grandchild, who carries the secret . . . Not everything that lies buried is dead.[7]

The 'blond beast' and German national psychology
Publications in the 1990s on the psychoanalyst Carl Jung have made him an even more controversial figure now than he was in his lifetime. In particular, it is possible that he had strongly totalitarian tendencies.

But if that is indeed the case, it only serves to grant him greater insight into the Nazi mentality. By no means do all psychoanalysts today agree with his theses, especially that of the collective subconscious, yet his writings are valuable in their critique of the way in which symbolism was used by the Nazis and other German nationalists of the period to stir up ancient, atavistic German feelings. Jung wrote at the time,

> As the Christian view of the world loses its authority, the more menacingly will the 'blond beast' be heard prowling about in its underground prison, ready at any moment to burst out with devastating consequences.[8]

With tragic accuracy for the Jews and other groups deemed undesirable by Nazi ideology, Jung's prognosis was fulfilled. As he wrote three years after Hitler came to power,

> We would find Wotan [the old German god, after whom Wednesday is named] quite suitable as a

causal hypothesis. In fact I venture the heretical suggestion that the unfathomable depths of Wotan's character explain more of National Socialism [Nazism] than all three reasonable factors put together.[9]

As we now know, many Nazis were fascinated by the old pre-Christian 'Nordic' religions in Germany, including the SS leader, Heinrich Himmler. Some historians have gone so far as to comment that

National Socialism sought more than an Italian-style accommodation with organised religion, or even a Spanish-style alliance. It sought nothing less than to supplant organised religion and become, in effect, the official state religion of the 'new order' Germany aspired to impose.[10]

Nazism and Christianity

It is certainly true that Hitler went way beyond the other two Fascist dictators, Franco in Spain and Mussolini in Italy. Both Franco and Mussolini sought alliances with the Catholic Church, through official Concordats. Nazism, while also making a similar concordat with the Vatican, was nothing like as friendly to the Church, Catholic or Protestant. Research in the 1990s has shown the heroic resistance to Nazism by many active Catholics and Protestants.[11] There was, as some have commented, an almost demonic and hypnotic appeal in Nazism.[12]

Despite the occultic elements of Nazism and despite the brave opposition of many Catholics and Protestants, Nazism deceived many professing German Christians. Germany in the 1930s became an example of something predicted by a first-century Jewish exile on the Greek island of Patmos. St John the Evangelist foretold that there would be those who deceived Christians themselves.

Dietrich Bonhoeffer and his kind were in a minority: most German Christians either did not oppose Hitler or simply kept their doubts to themselves.

Christianity in any case posed a unique dilemma for a nationalistic movement as overtly anti-Semitic as Nazism. Not all Fascist movements were anti-Semitic; Mussolini, for example, left the Jews fairly well alone, with persecution coming effectively when the Germans occupied much of Italy after 1943. But for Nazis, the fact that Jesus was a Jew meant that much of the Bible had, in practice, to be ignored or reinterpreted. Hitler was keen to get the whole of German life under his control, and there was soon a tame German National Church owing allegiance to *Führer* as well as to God.

One can see this in the statements of two German theologians of that time:

It was their [the German Church's] mission, entrusted to them by God, to interpret to the German *Volk* [= race or people] that prevenient action of God and at the same time to help shape it in unconditional solidarity with the *Volk*.[13]

The people who decided what was in the people's, or *Volk*'s, best interests, were, naturally, the Nazi leadership. As we observe, the Church had to align itself in 'unconditional' terms with those national aspirations. Second as another churchman wrote:

If the Protestant Church in genuine inner solidarity with the German *Volk* . . . wishes really to proclaim the gospel, then it has to take as its natural standpoint the circle of destiny of the National Socialist movement.[14]

Here we see clearly the subordination of Church to national ideology. It is, in a sense, the ultimate religious nationalism, the merging of a faith with the ideology of nationalism.

Obviously, though, the kind of Christianity represented in the German National Church bore little resemblance to the New Testament model, where loving God and loving your neighbour as yourself were the two cardinal rules. Mass murder does not sit comfortably alongside 'thou shalt not kill'! The Jewishness of the Church was, naturally, completely absent.

Hitler as replacement Messiah

German propaganda even turned Hitler himself into a replacement Messiah figure. A propaganda piece, written as early as 1934, for school children shows this. When, back in the 1920s, Hitler had attempted to seize power forcibly, he had been arrested – it was in prison that he had written *Mein Kampf* (My Struggle). Relating to this period in Hitler's life eleven years previously, the children's text reads:

> As Jesus set men free from sin and hell, so Hitler rescued the German people from destruction. Both Jesus and Hitler were persecuted; but while Jesus was crucified, Hitler was exalted to Chancellor [in 1933]. While the disciples of Jesus betrayed their master and left him in his distress, the sixteen friends of Hitler stood by him. The Apostles completed the work of their Lord. We hope that Hitler may lead his work to completion. Jesus built for Heaven; Hitler for the German earth.[15]

Phraseology like this is the apotheosis of religious nationalism, with the national leader compared to God himself. Religion and nationalism are intertwined at the very deepest levels of belief.

From this it is not too difficult to see why many

concerned Christians today are more worried by Fascism than by overtly godless Communism. Marxism dismisses religion as the opiate of the people. Fascism, by contrast, seeps its way into the Church, thereby manipulating it for its own ends, sometimes even portraying itself as the Christian bulwark against atheistic Communism. This ruse has often been one of Fascism's greatest selling points, and it has been the pretext of many a corrupt right-wing dictator down to the present day. But thus are God's people deceived and the Church is suborned into supporting forces strongly totalitarian and inimical to the true spirit of Christian faith.

Franco, Catholicism and nationalism

By no means have all Fascists been as blatant as Hitler. Perhaps a more subtle example was someone like Franco, who ruled Spain for forty years, right up until the 1970s.

Franco used the Catholic Church to bolster his regime. Spanish Protestants, of whom I knew many at the time, felt the chill wind of his intolerance. For under Franco, to be truly Spanish was to be Catholic. Patriotic Spaniards were those loyal to Franco, the Caudillo. To be properly patriotic and loyal one had to be a Catholic as well.

By these criteria, Protestant Spaniards were not deemed to be truly Spanish, and were thus *politically* as well as spiritually disloyal. One of the biggest Protestant churches in Spain had to pretend to be a furniture repository. In a sense it was – it had plenty of chairs upon which the congregation could sit on Sundays!

The major problem arose for those young Protestant Spanish men who had to undergo their national conscription service in the military, which was, as in many European countries, compulsory. They had a major dilemma. Part of their regular Sunday drill was to venerate the Virgin Mary. This is an item on which Catholics and

Protestants have major doctrinal differences, and many of the Protestant recruits felt that they could not do what was required of them. But as this was the military, they could be punished, not for failing to be Catholics, but for disobedience of a military order.

I remember thinking how ironic it was that these Spanish Protestants were in some respects worse off than friends of mine having to do their military service in Yugoslavia. There, naturally, recruits had no religious duties to perform. Protestants, because they had no link with potentially nationalistic Churches (Catholic in Croatia, Orthodox in Serbia) were sometimes even treated more leniently than others of religious affiliation. Yet so far as sympathy was concerned, most Western Christians were far more supportive of Christians in the Communist 'East' than they were to their fellow Protestants in resolutely anti-Communist Spain. Indeed, if anything, ignorance among Christians of the suffering under Fascist rule made things worse for the Spanish Protestants, because people failed to look out for them and support them. Once again, Christians were being deceived by a regime which manipulated Christianity for its own nationalistic ends.

Section Three

The Historic Legacy
of Orthodoxy

*In Islam God is Caesar, in China and
Japan Caesar is God; in Orthodoxy God is
Caesar's junior partner.*

Samuel Huntington

The work of Samuel Huntington is a godsend to his
fellow authors, as he is able to write in a way which
is wonderfully quotable, whether or not one agrees with
his thesis.

As we saw in Chapter 5 on the clash of civilisations
theory, anybody who propounds the idea that religion is
politically important at the end of the twentieth century
is bound to court controversy. It is probably even more
dangerous to argue that religion is actually becoming
more important to the way in which countries and cultures
work, rather than fading away.

One of the best places to see this phenomenon at work
is in Eastern Europe, the former Soviet bloc plus the old

Yugoslavia. It is what sociologists call a *paradigm*, a classic example of fact proving theory to be true.

One reason that I have selected Eastern Europe is that it is the area which I have studied most in my academic life. It is also an area which I have visited, where I have many local friends, and for which I have great affection.

Others might wish that I had chosen a country such as Iran, or a country caught between two cultures, such as Egypt (Islamic/Christian Coptic) or Turkey (Islamic/secularist). I have not done so for the following reasons: first Islam has been discussed in many books, by Huntington himself, and by countless specialists, all of whom have far greater expertise than I do, and there is no space in a book of this nature to encompass Islam fully. To do it justice would require not only many years of research, but also a work many times the length of this book.

Second, the lands of Orthodoxy, which include Russia, Serbia, Greece, Bulgaria and Romania, are a wonderful paradigm in and of themselves. In particular, all of these countries have experienced Islamic rule, a trauma from which some would argue they have never fully recovered. Serbia, Russia and Romania have also had considerable interaction with Catholic countries, with the Croats, Poles and Hungarians, respectively, as neighbours.

Finally, Bosnia is a unique mix of all three faiths: Orthodox, Catholic and Muslim. As a result, the area is an especially interesting one to study. Whereas in Iran the Mongol conquerors adopted the Islamic religion of their victims, in Bosnia, several transfers took place to create the mix we see today. Some Bosnians became Muslims. Some, it is now argued, became Catholic, while others converted from Catholicism to Orthodoxy.

While Iran is a good example of a country where religion has come to dominate the State, Eastern Europe provides an example with greater variety. It is an area in which three historic faiths have interacted for centuries, whether peacefully or violently. If we are fully to comprehend the issue of religious nationalism, to learn why the nations rage, it is an excellent place to study.

The lands of Orthodoxy never had the Renaissance or the Reformation (and thus the Counter-Reformation), and the ongoing effects seen today. The reason for this was largely political, resulting in powerful cultural ramifications. The background for this political/cultural/religious isolation goes back centuries. However, this section begins with a snapshot of how it makes a difference in today's world.

In Chapter 7, 'Blasphemers of Our Country's Faith', we look at how nationalism and religious intolerance mingle together in Romania. Orthodoxy is under threat from outside competition in a new way, one that it finds disturbing. In the West, we have had such competition since the sixteenth century, ever since Protestantism arose to challenge Catholic supremacy. In the Romanian heartland, Orthodoxy has been the sole representative of Christianity ever since that faith first came to the area over a thousand years ago. The shock of invasion has produced a harsh response, one very much in keeping with that region's historic traditions.

To understand present-day Orthodoxy, it is essential to examine the area's historic roots. Chapters 8 and 9 'The Byzantine Inheritance' and 'The Ottoman Inheritance', do this. We discover that dictatorship and centuries of alien rule have created the contemporary climate of intolerance.

Byzantine imperialism, followed by Ottoman Islamic imperial rule, created a world radically different from the more pluralistic one that we inhabit in the West. To excuse is not to pardon, but the fact that the lands of Orthodoxy have suffered centuries of oppression, so unlike our legacy of freedom in the West, does explain how our East European brothers and sisters can be like us yet so unlike us all at the same time.

Historians should not speculate too wildly. But if certain key battles in the sixteenth and seventeenth centuries had gone the other way, Vienna, Paris and London could also have ended up as cities of the Ottoman Empire. How then would we have coped? Would our own pluralists have arisen? Or would the savagery of the seventeenth-century European wars of religion have remained alive and created the kind of intolerance in Western Europe that we see in the East? We cannot be sure, but such speculation does go a long way to proving that West Europeans have nothing about which to be complacent.

7

Blasphemers of Our Country's Faith

Starting with the days after the Revolution, at the end of 1989, at the same time as the 'freedoms' of the transitional period, we have been assaulted with radio programmes, using a language which only approximates to Romanian, one filled with great hatred. We tell you that we do not understand how these blasphemers of our country's inherited faith *[emphasis added], who call themselves the ['Organisation X'] have succeeded thus far in their deceptions.*

Their words corrupt the pure souls of the Bucovinians [a Romanian province] like the boots of the Russians once did. These Bucovinians which live near such bastions of Orthodoxy as Voronet, Putna, Sucevita . . . listen to everything that is broadcast to them by the above mentioned charlatans.

Our pain is great because, here in the north of the country, faith is pure and unadulterated. Our parishioners now tell us that even faith is for sale for dollars.

We ask you to stop them or at least to limit them, because they are completely shameless and

are indiscriminately proselytizing [= evangelising]
right in our back yard.

In order to avoid any unpleasantness (we have in
mind the possible destruction of their headquarters
by Orthodox parishioners), we ask you to con-
sider our requests because we know you are a true
Romanian.

(Letter from an Orthodox Archbishop in Romania
to the President of the broadcasting organisation, sent
in 1996.)[1]

Nowadays, thankfully, persecution by Catholics or Protestants is rare. Even where, in Latin America, Protestants
have legal disabilities in the constitution, the situation
is not as bad as it was some years ago. (That is not
to ignore incidents of real harassment, such as happen
in countries where local leaders turn against Protestants.
But State persecution, sanctioned by the Government, is
fading away.)

Likewise, persecution by Protestants of Catholics is
also fading, even in areas like Northern Ireland, where
discrimination was rampant until not so long ago.

Where persecution still exists: Orthodox religious nationalism

But there is one form of Christianity where persecution
is still a reality for those who disagree with it. This is the
Orthodox Church. Every day I receive Internet messages
with new details of various forms of harassment or
intolerance shown by Orthodox leaders to Christians of
a different persuasion.[2] Catholics and Protestants alike are
still under pressure in countries such as Russia, Romania
or Bulgaria, because of the respresentations made to the
regime by leaders of the local Orthodox Church.

The reason for this is religious nationalism, a force still

very much at work in countries where Orthodoxy prevails. This intolerance is manifested very clearly in the letter by the Romanian Archbishop to the broadcasting President, with which we opened this chapter. This letter is worth analysing in detail, because it gives a vivid example not only of Orthodox intolerance but also of the religious nationalism that caused it. I would like to argue that it is precisely the phenomenon of religious nationalism that causes such intolerance, rather than the other way round. As we shall see in forthcoming chapters, both Catholicism and Protestantism have been equally guilty of such intolerance in the past. But, for the most part, they were able to make a crucial break, one that allowed tolerance to flourish where it had not done before.

Unhealthy exclusivist religious nationalism
Therefore, in looking at such passages as the Archbishop's letter, we are not so much looking at Orthodox spirituality, or at Romanian Orthodox theology in a vacuum. Rather, we are examining it as a manifestation of religious nationalism, the enmeshing of intolerant, exclusivist nationalism with the forces of religious faith.

When we considered self-identity we realised that healthy people can accept others because a healthy individual is at peace with himself or herself. Unhealthy people, though, are *exclusivist*. As Senator Moynihan has wryly observed, nowadays different ethnic groups make 'demands in which people define whom they love by whom they hate'.[3]

So the reference to foreign, non-Romanian, non-Orthodox Christians broadcasting into Romania by radio as 'the enemy' is greatly indicative. They are not seen as fellow Christians. Nor is their different theology merely disagreed with. No, they are the 'enemy'. The desire of foreign broadcasters to spread their version of Christianity is interpreted as a 'great hatred'. This is somewhat ironic, since, if anyone is to be characterised by hatred, it is surely to be seen in the response of the Orthodox, rather than in the programme-makers themselves.

Although the broadcasters had evidently taken trouble to make radio programmes in the local language, the text of the broadcasts is seen as not being genuine Romanian. Whether or not this is true in a strict linguistic sense (many comedians, for example, make fun of those who speak well-intentioned but skewed versions of other languages), it is the attitude behind the remark that is again important. Not merely are these broadcasters foreign, they do not even speak proper Romanian!

Paranoid interpretations of what others believe

We saw earlier to what extent devotees of a particular world-view can become paranoid. So convinced are they of the rightness of their own set of beliefs, that they come to think that everyone else must know that they are true too. Therefore, if someone still propounds a different view, they must be doing so on the basis that the belief they are propagating is false.

This extreme interpretation – the other guy must know he is wrong – can be seen in the Archbishop's letter. The foreign broadcasters are seen as 'deceivers'. They cannot be people who sincerely and honestly hold genuine beliefs that are different from those of the Archbishop. No, they are seen as people who are deliberately deceiving the hapless Romanian people of the Bukovina region into believing something that they themselves know to be false.

They must, therefore, be evil people. That is why the poor Bucovinians are being corrupted. Once again, the use of words such as 'corrupt' is highly emotive. Notice, too, that the people of Bukovina are 'pure souls', untainted

– until now – by the evil influences coming in from outside.

'Pure souls'

This concept of the purity of the Romanian soul is all the more remarkable when one considers what propaganda had been poured into them for the past forty or more years. From the Second World War until the violent overthrow of Ceaucescu in 1989 – the only ruler that year to be ousted by force – Romania was subjected to the most ruthless dictatorship in the Soviet bloc. It was Communism with a vengeance, coupled with a leadership cult in Ceaucescu's time that fully equalled that of Stalin himself in Russia. While many Romanian Orthodox leaders collaborated for the sake of survival, many did not and Christians of all persuasions were rigorously persecuted.

Yet the Bucovinians are 'pure souls' who must be protected from the broadcasts of outside Christians. In the light of what had taken place during the previous forty or more years, this is hard to comprehend.

The other reason why the 'pure soul' remark is important is that it shows the real nature of the relationship between the Church leadership, the hierarchy, and their people or congregations. For the remark is, if one ponders it, distinctly totalitarian. The Bucovinian people are demonstrably seen as unable to make up as their own minds. Things must be decided for them.

The right to listen and to choose

This therefore ignores the fact that those with access to the broadcasts have a series of options. First, in a truly free society, they have the absolute right not to listen to the radio programmes, to ignore them altogether. It is only in totalitarian societies that people are forced to

sit and listen to (or watch on television) the ramblings of
the leadership.

Second, they can listen to them and reject the view
that the foreigners are putting forward. Some of us may
well have been taught by professors whose views are
different from ours. I am not a Marxist, for instance,
but my tutor for European twentieth-century history,
Tim Mason, was one of Britain's more eminent socialist
historians. Likewise, the Master of my college, Balliol,
was the internationally distinguished Marxist historian,
Christopher Hill. Neither of these men turned me into
a Marxist, nor did any of my fellow students, many of
whom were Marxists, Trotskyists and '-ists' of numerous
other persuasions.

To *hear* another viewpoint can in fact reinforce your
own. It is quite possible for the radio listeners of the
Bukovina to have their distinctly Orthodox brand of
Christianity strengthened by listening to an alternative.
But this option, like the first one, was rejected by the
Orthodox leaders.

Aliens and charlatans

Even worse, the Christian broadcasters are linked to
another hated foreigner, the Soviet Russians: non-
Orthodox Christians, Communists – they are all the
same. This is quite extraordinary, as there is the
world of difference between Communism and Protestant Christianity, quite apart from the fact that the
politics of the broadcasters is more likely to be right-
wing than Marxist of any kind. Not only that, but
Ceaucescu was the one Warsaw Pact leader in the Soviet
era who was able to exclude Russian troops from his
territory. (He was, regrettably, fêted in the West as a
result, despite his appalling human rights record.) The
Communism that crushed the Romanian people was

home-grown, although it is true to say that Soviet troops introduced it during and after World War II.

But again, the important point is the exclusivist principle – these people are alien, foreign, not like us, the enemy, 'charlatans'. They must therefore be stopped. Such broadcasting is not to be allowed. Even if it cannot be prevented altogether, it must be so limited as to make it ineffective.

This too is thoroughly totalitarian in scope. As what is being broadcast is alien to Romania, it must be banned. People can listen only to what the leaders say they may. This is ironic again, because this is precisely what Communist leaders used to do. Broadcasts – radio or television – were normally jammed, to stop people behind the Iron Curtain from listening to them. As methods of censorship go, it was often haphazard or ineffective, especially for those living near a border with the West. (East Germans, Czechs and Hungarians were all able to watch Western TV easily, as a result.) Romania being much further in geographically, meant that picking up overseas broadcasts was more problematic, and the penalties for being caught were very severe. The Romanians no longer had a Stalinist regime in power. But once again, the freedom of ordinary Romanians is being restricted, and this time by the Church, by an organisation that itself suffered under Ceaucescu.

However, the request is very symbolic of the way in which Orthodox Churches do not hesitate to use State power to achieve their own ends. Traditionally in Orthodoxy there has been a close, symbiotic link between Church and State, one that goes far beyond that of the Church of England, for example. This will be a major theme of this book, and we will explore it closely when we consider the key issue of the link between faith and 'territoriality' in another chapter. Suffice it to say that with this example we see clearly the core of religious nationalism, the belief that a particular people and a particular mode of religious belief not merely go hand in hand, but are also *compulsory*. To be Romanian is to be Orthodox; if you are Orthodox then you are a true Romanian.

Violence: the threat of religious coercion

The compulsory nature of belief in a religious nationalist State is seen in the clear threat of physical violence that begins the closing paragraph of the letter. It has a wonderful euphemism: 'to avoid any unpleasantness'. One is reminded of street gangs who threaten to burn down a shop unless the shopkeeper pays up. He would not want anything unpleasant to happen to his shop window, would he?

In this instance, who would order the destruction of the broadcasting headquarters? Would it be a purely spontaneous protest, an explosion of righteous anger by furious Bucovinians, upset at the corruption so indiscriminately spread by the 'charlatans'? How did the Orthodox authorities know that such a thing was possible? What measures were they taking to stop it? One certainly trusts that the Archbishop himself would be against such destruction. But if, as one would hope, this is indeed the case, his method of avoiding violence is an unfortunate one. Rather than getting adequate protection for the building, his solution is to close down or curtail the broadcasts altogether. Could he not preach the Christian virtues of peace and neighbourly love? Sadly, it seems he has opted for a political solution rather than a spiritual one.

The religious nationalist nature of Romanian Orthodoxy

Lastly, and very significantly, he calls the recipient of his

132

letter a 'true Romanian'. Being authentically Romanian, he will understand fully the thinking and world-view behind the letter. Presumably too he will act appropriately, and close down or curtail the corrupt messages that so upset the Bucovinian people.

This is again a highly charged and overtly nationalistic statement. True Romanians, especially those in responsible positions, will want to keep the country free from outside defilement. Patriots will defend the 'Romanianness' of Romania, and, as we see from the letter, a major component of Romanian national self-identity is Romanian Orthodoxy.

This religious nationalist component of Romanian Orthodoxy goes back a long way, to before the Second World War. It is in fact linked to the Fascist movement which existed between World Wars I and II. The Romanians had their own native variant of Fascism, one that had particular ideological variants.

Orthodoxy and Fascism: the Legion of the Archangel Michael

The writings of two of its leaders demonstrate the way in which Christianity was distorted and integrated into the uniquely Romanian flavour of inter-war Fascism. The commonly-known name for the Romanian Fascists was the Iron Guard. But this was the mass movement, founded by Corneliu Codreanu in 1930. The core was an organisation that he had founded three years previously, in 1927. This was named after a supposed vision; Codreanu called it 'The Legion of the Archangel Michael', which in turn was based on a slightly older grouping called Brothers of the Cross.

Both the Legion and the Brotherhood have visibly Christian names. A certain kind of mystic Christianity was central to Romanian Fascism. This can be seen from Codreanu's own writing. He wrote of the 'time when all the peoples of the earth will fight their way through to . . . final resurrection'.[4] Like the Nazis he was rabidly anti-Semitic, and it was probably just as well that he died in prison in 1938, in all likelihood at the hands of the secret police of King Carol of Romania, the country's royal dictator. Carol had not forgotten that Codreanu had come close to power via the ballot box, and one of the reasons that Carol seized power in 1938 was precisely to deny Codreanu the chance of becoming the Government.

One of Codreanu's chief henchmen was Ion Mota, who died in Spain in 1937, fighting on Franco's side in the Spanish Civil War. Mota was involved with anti-Semitic groups and helped to translate into Romanian the notoriously anti-Jewish forgery, *The Protocols of the Elders of Zion*, a work that was widely used as an excuse for persecuting Jews all over Europe.

A classic of religious nationalism
Mota's letter, on the eve of his departure to Spain, was published in their journal, *Libertate*: it is a piece of prose which not only captures the spirit of interwar Fascism, but is also a classic of the genre of religious nationalism. He writes,

We whom God has accepted to defend him at the cost of our blood and our lives may have a strong hope in the salvation of our soul, despite all the sins that we have committed up till now. No force, no love exists which is higher than that of the race (and can only be realised in the race) except for the force of Christ and the love of Him.

Thus we fight, we die here for the defence of our ancestral law, for the happiness of our Romanian people, for its rebirth through the struggle of the Legion, through the reconstruction of the country which the Captain [i. e., Codreanu, the Legion leader] is carrying out.[5]

In this letter we see the theme of what has been called *palingenetic*, a *myth*-based form of *populist ultra-nationalism*.

The Oxford-based academic who invented the term does not himself hold to the view that Fascism is religious.[6] This is because, as he correctly points out, Fascism has *this-worldly* solutions to problems, rather than concentrating upon the eternal, or upon a relationship with God.

But the phraseology used by the Legion of the Archangel Michael is, to me, both Fascist *and* religious at the same time. Fascism, or 'populist ultra-nationalism' always has myth or legend at its core. We can see this most vividly in Nazi Germany, with the legend or myth of the master race. But it can also be a grossly exaggerated version of historical reality.

Religious nationalism and the power of myth

We do not, at this vast distance in time, know exactly what percentage of Romanians are of purely 'Dacian' blood – that is, descendants of the Roman legionnaires who settled in Dacia. However, with the legionnaires themselves being ethnically very mixed by the time that the Western part of the Empire fell, the concept of a *Roman* Dacian race, and a pure one at that, is probably rather unlikely. It is also very probable that over the centuries there was considerable intermarriage between the descendants of the legionnaires and the numerous different races who passed through Dacia, or maybe stayed there and became absorbed into the population, unknown and undiscovered by later historians and anthropologists. By the twentieth century, the purity of the original Dacians, if it ever truly existed, was without question severely diluted.

Yet the core of reality, that Roman legions came to the area to defend the imperial borders against outside enemies, is true. It is also factual that they left descendants and that many if not most present-day Romanians have them as ancestors, however heavily-diluted that inheritance might be.

In addition, the Romanians saw themselves as the representatives of Latin civilisation amidst a sea of Slavs. This feeling therefore heightened their concept of themselves as being intrinsically different from their neighbours.

Orthodoxy, as we shall see shortly, also has an imperial feeling to it – the vast majority of Romanians are connected in some way or another to the Romanian Orthodox Church. The Byzantine Empire, surviving until 1453, saw itself as the 'second Rome'. Later on the Russians, who became Orthodox Christians, increasingly regarded Moscow as the Third Rome, the protector of true Christian – and Orthodox – civilisation.

Salvation language in religious nationalism

Many Fascist movements use what one might describe as 'salvation'[7] or 'regenerative' language. We noted earlier that it has been the salvation religions[8] which have proved the most enduring, surviving where many others in the Ancient World did not. (Not even today's neo-pagans worship Zeus, for example.) Salvation, rebirth, being born again are all religious terms.

Here they are being used twice. The Legion is explicitly Christian, though as Mota observes, he has to hope for salvation 'despite all the sins that we have committed up till now'. Rabid anti-Semitism and political terrorism are not tenets of the New Testament! But there is no question that his theology allowed him to be an active member and ideologue of the Legion. To him, his *political* beliefs and his *religious* faith were part and parcel of the same inner core of belief. He sincerely believed that what the Legion was doing was Christian, and that to go to support Franco and kill Spanish Communists was part of God's will.

Likewise, too, as *spiritual* rebirth is at the heart of Christian faith, so too *political* rebirth is at the centre of the Legion's Fascist programme. In the same way that Christianity teaches that human beings are by nature sinful and must repent of their sins and turn to Christ for salvation, so too did many Fascists believe that the nation had become innately degenerate and needed a strong man, a leader (= *Führer* or *Duce*) or captain, as a human saviour to turn to for national salvation.

The multi-racial Christian concept of salvation

Within the Church, Christians see themselves as the people of God on earth. (Both Jews and Muslims have similar concepts.) However, as the Apostle Paul pointed out in many of his letters to the early Church, Christianity is a genuinely multi-racial, international community. All Christians are God's people, and Christians come from *all* races.

Religious nationalism warps this process by introducing a powerfully racist component – it is a *race* that is chosen, whether Dacian/Romanian or Aryan/German. Codreanu was stridently anti-Semitic equating it, as many Fascists did then and still do, with Communism.

Jewish existence and activities, Codreanu wrote, constituted 'mortal dangers' to the Romanian people. They were 'undermining us racially . . . destroying the racial Romano-Dacian structure of our people, and call[ing] into being a type of human being that is nothing but a racial wreck.'⁹ The Jews were only a tiny minority of Romanians, but they were seen as bent on conquest!

We see clearly in this the profoundly unhealthy type of self-identity that we discussed earlier. Romanians were not only being defined by who they were, but by whom they hated. All this was done not only in the name of nationalism, but also in the name of God.

So although Codreanu and others propounded this-worldly solutions, their motivation was spiritual as well as practical. You murder Jews in God's name. It is therefore difficult to see how religion is not an intrinsic part of this kind of nationalism, as the linkage between the two is incredibly explicit.

Xenophobia and Orthodoxy
As the opening part of this chapter demonstrates, this xenophobia among many Romanian Orthodox still exists. It may no longer be the explicit anti-Semitism of the Legion of the Archangel Michael, but another clear example of xenophobia is the deep antipathy towards and hatred of Romania's small Hungarian minority. The expression of such feelings is not discouraged by the present regime – xenophobia is still present. In addition, Hungarians are Catholics, not Orthodox. The Protestant and ethnically Hungarian pastor, Laszlo Tokes, was one of the instruments in getting rid of Communism in 1989, but that does not seem to have done much good to the Hungarian minority. So all in all, the prognosis is not so good. Religious nationalism is still a force in present-day Romania, even as it was back in the pre-Communist 1930s.

Tragically for Romania, it was not always this bad. Present-day Romania was historically part of two Empires. Most of the country was under the rule of the Ottoman Empire until the 1850s and 1860s. Transylvania, however, was part of the Austro-Hungarian Empire right up until

1918. (Part of Romania reverted to Hungary in 1940–45, and Romania's province of Bessarabia was handed over to the Soviet Union in 1945.)

Under imperial rule, all majority nationalities were subjects of foreign rulers, native Romanians and those of Jewish ancestry alike. In 1947 a Romanian Jew, Solomon Bloom, wrote of the pre-1918 past. He was raised in the town of Harlau, but now lived in the USA. In his home town, Jews, Turks, Romanians, Slovaks, ethnic Germans (of which Romania had many until 1989) and Russians all lived in what seemed to be complete harmony, different ethnic groupings often specialising in different specialities and trades.

Then independence came to Romania. After 1918 nationalism, as we saw from the discussion of the Versailles Treaty, became even more important. Someone was no longer a cobbler or a tailor, but a *Romanian* cobbler or a *Jewish* tailor. Bloom laments,

> This autobiographical footnote to history brightly illuminates the process by which the principle of national self-determination, after World War I, tore apart the fabric of harmonious living among the varied peoples of the old Austrian and Turkish Empires and left them the embattled racists of today.[10]

Nearly fifty years on, racism, nationalism, xenophobia, ethnic cleansing and other monstrosities are as alive today as they have ever been.

How did Orthodoxy become like this?
What is it, though, about Orthodoxy that has permitted such intolerance to persist? Many Europeans have considerable cultural and theological problems about American methods of evangelism. Not everyone has the tact or sensitivity of a Billy Graham. But one does

not find the Archbishop of Canterbury or the Catholic Archbishop of Paris asking for broadcasts to be banned, with the added hint of violence that we saw in the letter. No mobs are likely to form outside the offices of the very Protestant Trans World Radio in Catholic Monte Carlo.

In addition, there has been a growing interest in Orthodox spirituality in the West. The writings and life of Metropolitan Anthony, an Orthodox leader based in Britain, command wide international respect.

It is clearly not something connected to Orthodox *spirituality* that has brought about this sad state of affairs reflected in the letter. It must therefore be another factor. This key difference, rooted in history, between Catholic/Protestant experience on the one hand and Orthodox experience on the other will form the kernel of the next chapter. It is a difference vital to an understanding of both religious nationalism and of that phenomenon's links with the issues of pluralism and tolerance.

8

The Byzantine Inheritance

The Byzantine Empire lasted for one thousand years. Surviving the fall of Rome, it continued right up until 1453. In theory it was the Roman Empire all along. Constantinople, its capital, was, as the name implies, founded by the great Roman Emperor Constantine, the man who made Christianity the official religion of the Roman Empire. Besides being a Christian Empire, it was in effect a Greek Empire, using the Greek language, culture and values. This became all the more obvious after the fall of the Western part of the Empire in the fifth century.

Byzantium and Orthodoxy

After the split between Catholicism and Orthodoxy in 1054, it was also officially an Orthodox Empire, with its own Patriarch in Constantinople, someone who did not owe allegiance to the Pope in Rome. Constantinople, as Istanbul, was to remain an imperial capital for much longer, being the capital of the successor Ottoman Empire right up until the defeat of the Turks by the Allies in World War I. The seat of the Orthodox Patriarch has remained in Constantinople (later renamed Istanbul) from 1054 until the present day.

One inevitable consequence, historically, is that the *political* and *spiritual* authorities, Emperor and Patriarch, remained side by side. The Orthodox faith was *the* faith of the Empire. When that Empire fell to the Muslims, the Patriarch was still there, guardian of the spiritual well-being of the Empire's Orthodox subjects and a reminder of happier days. This linkage, as this chapter will aim to show, was to have profound and long-lasting *political* as well as *spiritual* consequences.

This is why we need to study the past, in order better to understand the present. If we see how the interaction between the Byzantine State and Orthodox Christianity developed over several centuries, then became ossified under Ottoman Turkish rule for over five hundred years, we can comprehend why Orthodox Christianity is as it is today.

We also need to understand how Orthodoxy became different from Protestantism and Catholicism, over the course of many centuries. Let us therefore examine these crucial differences and how they arose.

Protestantism, Catholicism and individualism

Protestantism is *initially* and, properly understood, a religion of *individualism*. It is a faith based upon an act of choice. To use the biblical phrase made popular again the 1970s, it is 'born again' religion – you enter it by an act of choice.[1]

Consequently, in *political* terms, no stigma attaches *legally* on a national scale to a Swede, Briton or American who abandons the Protestant faith of his or her parents. Historically this was not always the case. Non-Anglicans in Britain had legal penalties in terms of restricted access to power up until the early nineteenth century. One reason that my own ancestors chose University College at London University rather than Oxford or Cambridge was that non-Anglicans were unable to study at the older universities until the 1870s. But even in eighteenth-century Britain, *being* Catholic or non-Anglican Protestant was perfectly feasible. Converts, likewise, had no penalties. Britain's first, and so far only, ethnically Jewish Prime Minister, Benjamin Disraeli, entered politics having converted from Judaism to Anglicanism in the early 1800s. Practising Jews were also able to enter politics not long thereafter.

Religious Jews were also increasingly prominent in Catholic Austria and Catholic France. In France, Protestants, having long been suppressed or exiled, were able to return to public life in the nineteenth century.

Religious tolerance in the West

Nowadays, countries like Britain and France are innately secular in mindset, with no compulsion to follow a particular spiritual point of view. Being Jewish or an adherent of any other faith is no longer an obstacle to high achievement in business or politics, as the large numbers of Muslim or Hindu millionaires testify. No Frenchman is persecuted if he abjures Catholicism, while in England those converting to Catholicism can even be seen as quite chic.

Even in Ireland and Poland, two bastions of loyal Catholicism, the old barriers are breaking down. Irish President Mary Robinson has done much to create a climate of pluralism and tolerance. In Poland, despite the efforts of the Catholic hierarchy, legislation has been passed in the new politically pluralist era that goes against the Church's teaching. Under the Communists, Protestants often had an easier time, because the authorities linked Catholicism with anti-Communist Polish nationalism.

Secularisation, therefore, while regretted by many Christians of all shades, has created a climate in which different varieties of Christianity have been allowed to flourish. English Catholics and Baptists and Irish Protestants generally live in a more equable climate than before.

One of the key factors in creating a spiritually tolerant atmosphere has, historically speaking, been political. This is the issue of *ultimate* spiritual allegiance.

Protestantism and political allegiance

Protestantism has never had the State as the *ultimate* source of loyalty, even where there was a State Church (as in Scandinavia) or an established Church (as in England). This is because, even though Church and State have been linked, Protestantism has no Pope. There is no one person within or without the State to whom complete spiritual loyalty must be given. No Archbishop of Canterbury could ever claim infallibility. Protestant doctrine simply does not allow it. Debate and dissent even within a legally-established, State-endorsed hierarchy is therefore permissible. Furthermore, as we have seen, legal disadvantages against those not adhering to the official faith have long since vanished.

The very name for Protestants not within the Anglican Church, 'nonconformists', says everything about their ultimate spiritual allegiance. The fact that they do not, by definition, conform to the Articles of the Church of England, shows that there is no link between faith and the established political order. Another name for such groups is 'free' churches, which proclaims the same message. Christianity is a spiritual act, not a political one. Many nonconformists have been very active politically. The British Labour Party is always said to be more Methodist than Marxist. But political involvement is, once again, a matter of choice for the individual.

Catholicism: dual political and spiritual allegiance

Catholics have always had a *dual* allegiance: politically to the local ruler and *spiritually* to the Pope. Theologically speaking, the Pope is an autocrat, not a democrat, although in practice this has often been modified. But the Pope's authority is spiritual, not political. So far as a Catholic ruler's Catholic subjects are concerned, since they both share a common Catholicism, ruler and ruled alike are both equally under the spiritual jurisdiction of the Pope. An Emperor must be as obedient to the Pope as a peasant.

This means that a Catholic ruler has subjects who, in a vital arena of life, owe allegiance to someone other than himself – to the Pope and not to the local ruler. In many countries, such as in pre-1789 France, the Catholic kings would insist as far as possible on getting appointments to Archbishoprics in their hands, not those of the Pope. But the loyalty ultimately owed by all good Catholics to Rome remained the same. The Holy Roman Emperor might exercise considerable political power. But in matters spiritual, it was the Pope who was supreme, as the great Holy Roman Emperor, Henry IV, discovered when he had to appear before the Pope as a humble penitent at Canossa.

In addition, the Emperor did not appoint the Pope. This meant that although the Christian rulers in the West might seek to influence elections, they did not have the final say.

The political diversity of Catholic Europe

Also important was the fact that politically, the realm over which the Pope had spiritual jurisdiction was broken up into several States. The Holy Roman Empire and Catholic Christendom were not one and the same area. The Kings of France and of Spain, both spiritually loyal to the

Papacy, guarded their political independence jealously. Italy itself was a patchwork of States, some small. The Pope did not control more than the central region, limited by States like the Venetian Republic in the north and the Kingdom of Naples in the south. Germany, while nominally under the Emperor, had powerful local Catholic rulers, spiritually loyal to the Pope but in reality, like the rulers of Bavaria, politically loyal to themselves.

When the Reformation came, the old Christendom concept was irreparably damaged. There were areas that were Christian but owed no allegiance to either Pope or Emperor. The dreadful warfare of the sixteenth and seventeenth centuries showed that neither side could crush the other. In the worst fighting, the Thirty Years War of 1618–1648, the Catholic French even sided with the Protestant Princes of Germany against the Catholic Emperor. France's reasons were purely political and dynastic. In addition, the Bourbon Kings Henry IV and Louis XIII gave full freedom of worship to their Protestant subjects under the Edict of Nantes. Henry, the first Bourbon king, was a convert from Protestantism, again for mainly political reasons, saying 'Paris is worth a mass'.

In other words, by the seventeenth century, any political/spiritual unity that Western Christendom may have had was dissolved. There had also been long periods of discontinuity, from the fall of Rome to Charlemagne's restoration of the Holy Roman Empire at the start of the ninth century. These were the so-called 'Dark Ages' when Christianity itself was under severe threat from outside pagan invaders whose conversion to Christianity took many centuries.

Caesaro-Papism and the Byzantine Empire
With the Byzantine Empire it was quite different. First, there was continuity with nearly one thousand years of

uninterrupted existence. The one gap, in the thirteenth century, was a result of the foolish Fourth Crusade, when the Crusaders, greedier for wealth than for the Christian cause, attacked Christian Constantinople rather than the Muslim Middle East, with results we shall soon see. This meant that the link between one unitary political State and the one spiritual realm was never broken. Emperor and Patriarch co-existed right up until 1453.

The Emperors saw themselves in direct succession to the Roman Empire, which, in the East, they were in a way that the Holy Roman Emperors in the West were not. The realm of Byzantium and the realm of Orthodoxy were the same with one important exception. When lands were lost to Islamic invaders, those Orthodox Christians retained their spiritual allegiance to Constantinople. They still looked to a city where the spiritual and political heads *both* dwelt.

By the fifteenth century, the Byzantine Empire collapsed, fatally weakened by the folly of the Fourth Crusaders who had destroyed the one State powerful enough to prevent Muslim incursion into Europe. Although the Byzantines were restored by the end of the thirteenth century, the unity of their Empire had been broken beyond repair.

The Ottoman Empire and religious tolerance

The Ottoman Empire, being Muslim, was a complete break with the past. But, in another sense, it was a continuation, with its capital being the same as of the Byzantines.

In some ways, the Ottoman Turks showed a greater degree of tolerance to religious dissent than many of the Christian countries in Europe. Christians, however, still had legal disabilities, which lasted right up until the nineteenth century. For instance, Christians had to pay more tax and had a limited career path in public service, as the senior officials had to be Muslim.

Above all, the Ottomans defined their subjects by their *religion* through organising the *millet* system. A millet was a basic unit of society. Everyone belonged to a particular millet. Some millets were Christian, such as the Greek and Armenian ones. All Orthodox Christians in the Balkans were under the Greek Orthodox millet, whether actually Greek or Slav, such as Serbian or Bulgarian. Catholic Hungary was under Ottoman rule for a while, but not nearly as long as the Orthodox Balkan area.

In terms of self-identity, therefore, being Orthodox was tremendously important. It made all the difference to who you were and to what you could do. It was also a preservation of an historic memory, of Byzantium, of the good old days of the great Christian Orthodox Empire. So in relation to the concept of 'palingenetics', of ultra-nationalism stemming from powerful myths and symbols, Orthodoxy, both a *religious* and a *political* identity under the Ottoman Empire, is a classic case.

Moscow: the third Rome

There was one important exception to the notion of all Orthodox Christians being also under Byzantine rule before the Fourth Crusade. This was Russia, or, more strictly speaking, the myriad of Russian-speaking States, including the Grand Duchy of Muscovy, whose rulers provided the nucleus of what was to become the Russian Empire.

Muscovy, soon to rule over Russia itself, regarded Moscow as the 'third Rome', and the spiritual heir to the Byzantine heritage. For centuries afterwards, Russia saw a large part of her rôle, politically and spiritually, as the protector of the Orthodox. This was one of the causes of the Crimean War in the nineteenth century, and was behind warm support for nationalist movements in the Balkans, leading up to the First World War.

The Ottoman and Russian Empires had one important thing in common – autocracy. Both were ruled by single individuals, whether Sultan or Tsar. Democracy did not thrive in such hostile conditions. Indeed it was regarded as a positively dangerous concept.

Orthodoxy under the Tsar

The Tsar was very much in charge of the Orthodox Church in Russia, controlling the key appointments. Obedience to the Tsar was almost an act of religious obligation. The Orthodox Church was effectively a Department of State, propping up the Tsarist autocracy. State and religion went closely together and Russia was very aware of its role as the leading Orthodox power. Until the middle to end of the nineteenth century, it was *the* Orthodox power, the nation not under foreign domination.

This linkage between State and Orthodoxy was to carry on, rather controversially, into Communist times. Stalin, while suppressing any kind of independent thought, let alone free religious expression, did not hesitate to use the Orthodox Church as a means of patriotic identity to mobilise people against the Nazi invasion. World War II is known in Russia as the Great Patriotic War, and the Orthodox Church played its full part in guaranteeing patriotic ardour to repel the German invaders. The Communists infiltrated the Orthodox Church very effectively after the war was over, and even today there is dispute as to who collaborated with whom.

The Russians strongly supported Slavic independence movements in the nineteenth century in countries such as Serbia and Bulgaria. Russia was a kind of older brother figure, helping out fellow Orthodox Christians under Muslim rule. It is reckoned that around 40 per cent of the Sultan's subjects were Orthodox, and Russia never hesitated to use that fact to interfere in the crumbling of the Ottoman Empire, an issue that has become known to historians as the Eastern Question.

Orthodoxy and the State

When the nearly independent Balkan States began, they imitated the Russian/Byzantine 'Caesaro-Papist' tradition, one of close links between State and Church. The Governments swiftly took over control of much of what the Church could or could not do. In particular, the Churches of the new countries became what is called *autocephalos*.

In plain English, this meant that while they were still fully Orthodox, they put themselves under the rule of their own national Patriarch. This is why we have the Romanian Orthodox Church, the Bulgarian Orthodox Church, the Russian Orthodox Church and so on. It is not as if there are any *spiritual* differences between them. Rather, the distinction is essentially *political*. Each Orthodox Church is under the rule of its own national Patriarch.

This meant, as with the Russian Orthodox Church centuries before, each Orthodox Church did not look outward but inward, to their own Patriarch in their own country, as opposed to the Patriarch in Constantinople. The property of the Churches was often appropriated by the State, and the country's political rulers, who were also members of the Orthodox Church, had a strong voice in appointments to the Church hierarchy.

Orthodoxy and patriotic allegiance

As a result, there was a powerful national/religious identity. The Orthodox Church was the Romanian Orthodox Church, the National Church, the local expression of Christian faith.

150

We can thus see how this could in time translate into the *only* expression of Christianity in a particular country. Orthodoxy had been the remnant of Byzantium, the old Byzantine Empire, the inheritor, in turn of the old Roman Empire. To be Orthodox was to be part of that heritage, its heir and custodian. Orthodoxy had kept the flame alive during the centuries of Muslim rule and oppression. To be an Orthodox Christian was therefore to be a patriot, a survivor, and, in a sense, a crusader against the enemy outside. The Christians in the West, split spiritually from Orthodoxy since 1054 – and in practice for some centuries prior to that – had failed to come to Constantinople's aid effectively in 1453. They had betrayed Orthodoxy, so they too were part of the enemy.

The consequences for self-identity, and for primary self-identity in particular, are obvious. Orthodoxy and patriotism, mixed with a slight dash of siege mentality, go very much together. This includes Russia, too, since they also had had to liberate themselves from Muslim oppression back in the days of Tsars like Ivan the Terrible, who conquered the armies of the Golden Horde.

Other consequences for the nature of Orthodoxy

As many have pointed out, the Orthodox never had either a Reformation or a Counter-Reformation. Protestantism was new, and had the zeal and dynamism of something fresh, even though one of its major doctrinal claims was that it was not new, but a restoration of the original Church, a *reformation* of a Church which had gone astray.

Likewise, although the Catholic Church has the motto *semper idem* – always the same – it too had to make considerable adjustments to counter the Protestant threat.

So on neither side was there stagnation. Both wings of Christianity in the West, Catholic and Protestant, had to adapt or change. Ideas were important, debate essential, and change, or active reaction to change, at the heart of the Church.

The isolation of the Orthodox Church
None of this touched Orthodoxy. In some ways this was ironic, since much of the impetus for the Renaissance came from scholars who fled the falling Byzantine Empire and fled westwards. For centuries it was the civilised East that could look down on the barbaric West. The Byzantine Empire never experienced the Dark Ages, so all the learning that had accumulated over the centuries was never lost.

Unfortunately for the East, it was the hitherto barbaric West who benefited eventually. Apart from about one hundred and seventy years of Ottoman rule in Hungary, the West did not fall to Islam. It retained its independence, even if only by narrow margins. This meant that Western countries could continue to run their own destinies, unlike their Christian compatriots under Ottoman rule. Furthermore, although Russia was regaining her independence as the Balkan States were losing theirs, the Islamic legacy remained for centuries afterwards. Pluralism, tolerance, genuine democracy never took root. Despite all the heroic efforts of Tsar Peter the Great in the late seventeenth and early eighteenth centuries to modernise his backward country, Russia never fully became part of the West. The literary debate between Slavophiles and Westerners in the nineteenth century showed the strong resistance to Western culture, even among the intellectual élite. The great twentieth-century Nobel Prize winner, Alexander Solzhenitsyn, is an excellent example of a present-day Slavophile. Russia, to the Slavophiles, was, and still is, different, with Russian Orthodoxy being central to that difference.

The lack of local rivalry within Orthodox countries

One of the differences between Catholic and Protestant, on the one hand, and Orthodoxy, on the other, is the lack of rivalry to Orthodoxy within its own domain. In countries that were Orthodox, Orthodoxy was *the* form of Christianity. Only in the late eighteenth century, when Russia absorbed many Catholics in the dismemberment of Poland, was there a major grouping of non-Orthodox. Even there, and in the Lutheran minorities in Estonia and Finland and the Catholic minority in Latvia, the heartlands of Russia were unaffected and remained almost entirely Orthodox. In the Balkans, the territories under Muslim rule were again nearly all Orthodox if Christian, and Muslim if not.

In the West, by contrast, there was always a rival form of Christian faith. For much of the time, individual countries might be monolithic – Protestant Sweden or Catholic Bavaria, for example. But people could and often did emigrate. When King Louis XIV of France revoked the Edict of Nantes in 1685, the decree which had given freedom of worship to French Protestants (or Huguenots) since 1598, over four hundred thousand Huguenots emigrated, thus depriving France of some of its most dynamic industrialists and workers. Some went to England, some to Northern Ireland, others to Prussia (the up and coming Protestant kingdom), and still others all the way to the New World.

In time, too, legal penalties against those of a different faith were lifted, such as by Emperor Joseph II in relation to his Protestant subjects. The French Revolution was completely secularist, and therefore anti-clericalist, in opposition to the Church.

The contrasting growth of religious diversity in the West

We will see the detailed reasons for the expansion of toleration in the West later on. The important point here is that the existence of two rival Churches had ended the possibility in the West of a monolithic Church, imposing uniformity, impervious to any kind of change. The Catholic Church could not undo the Reformation, and, in effect, by the end of the Thirty Years War in 1648, had to give up that hope.

Protestants were certainly not going to change and the very nature of Protestantism, with its continuous division into different denominations, increased that diversity all the more. In addition, while State Churches in Protestant countries normally had the senior hierarchy chosen by the State, the 'Free' Churches were, by definition, entirely self-governing. No Baptist or Methodist leader was appointed to office by a politician. Furthermore, becoming Baptist or Czech Brethren was often a *choice*, involving the willing consent of an individual. Likewise, someone born in Catholic Cologne could always move a few miles to a nearby Protestant-ruled city.

The principle of consent in West and East

This vital principle of *consent* was completely absent in Orthodox countries. You were born Orthodox and would, as likely as not, die Orthodox. As well as having no *Christian* rivals, Orthodoxy prevailed in societies where choice was not really an option. The Balkans produced no great thinkers of independent framework, and much though Catherine the Great of Russia admired the Enlightenment philosophers, she actually increased serfdom rather than setting existing serfs free. Until the 1860s, only one hundred and thirty or so years ago, countless Russians were literally owned by their masters. They were as unfree as the slaves in the USA, who were freed the same decade that serfdom was abolished in Russia. Serfdom in the West, by contrast, had disappeared some while before, admittedly often for economic reasons rather than from any sense of obligation or justice. Subjects of the Ottoman Empire, while not slaves, were not exactly free, and the Ottomans used to kidnap Christian children, train them as élite soldiers, or *janisseries*, and indoctrinate them forcibly into becoming zealous Muslims.

As a result, consent was not a realistic option. Because of the close tie between political and spiritual loyalty, your allegiance was *local*, politically and spiritually.

This brings us to the key issue of the next chapter – the issue of ultimate loyalty, and the tie between loyalty to a *belief* and loyalty to a *place*. This is why you can easily be an American and also Jewish, Catholic or anything else, and still be regarded as a loyal patriot. But if you want to be a patriotic Russian, you will invariably have to be Orthodox.

Before we go into detail, we need to have one further look at history to see how Western/Orthodox differences became exaggerated.

9

The Ottoman Inheritance

We have now seen some clear distinctive features in the past between Catholic and Protestant Churches in the West, and the Orthodox in the East.

As we saw in Chapter 3, the way in which we look at the past can radically alter the way we interpret the present. Few nations can escape guilt. The West is very guilty here, from British imperialism and France's 'civilising mission' through to the extremes of Nazi anti-Semitism. Britons who yearn for the good old days of the Empire constitute a present day example of longing for a racist, imperialist past. When it comes to the issue of religious nationalism, Orthodoxy gives us the clearest manifestation of a mis-used past. Once again, the causes are historical, and we must examine them in order to understand the present, especially as it relates to a conflict such as the war in the former Yugoslavia.

Some historic causes of Orthodox intolerance

Historians have argued that Orthodox clergy were never as well educated as their counterparts in Protestant and Catholic countries. This was to result in many unfortunate consequences. But this had little or nothing to do with Orthodox spirituality. Byzantine clergy were easily as learned as those in the Catholic West, and the Orthodox Church, in its early years, produced many of the finest Christian theologians and Church Fathers, men whom the whole Church, Orthodox, Catholic and Protestant, look to today with reverence for their insights and wisdom. Rather, the reasons for this discrepancy of education are historical.

The promotion ladder in Catholic and Protestant Churches

First, in both Catholic and Protestant countries, preferment to the rank of Bishop was theoretically open to *any* priest. This is not so even today in the Orthodox Church. Like Protestant clergy, but unlike Catholic, ordinary grass roots parish clergy may marry. But, unlike the Protestant Churches, no married clergyman may ever become a Bishop. Only monks may do this, and monks are, by their calling, all celibate.

The consequence of this is that the Catholic and Protestant Churches, both of which allowed parish priests to be promoted, had very different social compositions from the Orthodox. In the whole of the West, Catholic and Protestant, it was a custom for the younger sons of royalty and aristocracy to enter the Church as a vocation. As the novels of Jane Austen show us, it was perfectly acceptable for someone of 'good family', whether titled or simply gentry, to enter the Church. Many Anglican parish priests were from high social class backgrounds. Many also went from parish life to becoming Bishops or Archbishops.

The same applied in the Catholic Church, except that priests could not marry. (Some had mistresses and illegitimate children, as visitors to some of Salzburg's lovelier palaces will know – but that is another story and not exclusive to Catholic priests.) Within the Holy Roman

Empire, some Archbishops and Bishops were also secular rulers, as Princes directly loyal to the Emperor. Three Archbishops, those of Cologne, Mainz and Trier, were also Electoral Princes, that very élite group who, theoretically at least, elected the Holy Roman Emperor. Since these holders of such prestigious dioceses were also rulers of sometimes quite extensive principalities, it was all the more important that they be of the highest birth. Consequently, many such Prince-Bishops, as they were known, came from the Empire's royal families, such as the Wittelsbachs of Bavaria, and, in some cases, from as high as the Imperial Arch-house, the Habsburgs, themselves.

By and large, this did not happen in Russia or any of the Orthodox countries, except, perhaps, for tiny Montenegro, where the Bishops secularised themselves and became the hereditary ruling dynasty.

The different career path of Orthodoxy and its consequences

This had consequences for independent thought and leadership. In the West, clergy were part of the social and economic élite, either by birth (and thus kin to many of the top families) or by virtue of a high-ranking Church position. Some have argued that only in Russia did the clergy take the kind of leading position in society assumed by their Western counterparts. One further consequence of élitism in the Western Church is seen in the example of a Wittelsbach Archbishop who had prestige not simply because he was an Archbishop, but also because he hailed from one of the Empire's oldest and most eminent families. He thus had a personal social position not dependent on an office given to him.

Within the Orthodox Church, there was no similar 'career path' to follow. If you married and became a parish priest, you stayed at that bottom level for the rest of your career. The idea that you could start in a parish and work up to being a Metropolitan or Patriarch was simply not possible. The lower ranks of the clergy did not, therefore, attract recruits from the higher ranks of society. This social phenomenon was to have important consequences.

First, many priests remained poor, depending on any scraps of extra money that they could get from funerals, weddings, and the like. Priests often ended up being stuck in their first parish for most, if not all, of their career. Since many of them had been raised in the area where they became a priest, this meant in effect that they never really left home.

As well as coming from the poorer parts of society, Orthodox clergy suffered from other limitations. Often, even the poorest Catholic clergy had to go a long way from home to attend seminary, sometimes completely outside of their home culture to Rome. By contrast, Orthodox clergy frequently never went further than the next village. This exacerbated the problem of the lack of clerical education and meant that the Orthodox priest was not exposed to outside influences or to different perspectives. Their understanding of difference was inevitably curtailed and they lacked the experience of the wider world that can in and of itself give greater understanding of the real complexities of life.

Some practical side-effects of Orthodox limitations
This narrow-cast view has an obvious effect on tolerance. The more limited and literally parochial your world-view is, the less likely you are to escape old and deep-seated prejudices. Your presuppositions are never challenged, your views never held up to outside scrutiny and to debate. You cling, even if entirely subconsciously, to the prejudices with which you were raised, and to the

world-view of a narrow geographical area. The narrower your outlook and experience, the less likely you are to be tolerant.

Furthermore, since education for the poor was not a priority, the priests suffered from this as well. Many priests were semi-literate, as ill-educated as the peasants over whom they exercised spiritual authority. In fact, many priests were from peasant families themselves.

So when, for example, anti-Semitism was rife in areas where the poor sought scapegoats for their own misfortune, the priests would join in rather than discouraging their parishioners. In Russia, over-educated clergy were not averse to stirring up anti-Semitic pogroms, which, as viewers of *Fiddler on the Roof* will recall, were encouraged at the highest levels.

Religion and intolerance in the Yugoslav context

As should now be obvious, the link between religion and nationalism that we have been examining applies in full measure to the former Yugoslavia.

Numerous books based on eyewitness reporting have been published on the Yugoslav conflict. One of the most acute, *Slaughterhouse: Bosnia and the Failure of the West*, is by the American journalist, David Rieff. He makes some telling observations about the rôle of religion. Rieff points out that during Tito's time, most people were comparatively secular in outlook. Religion may, in our terms, have been part of their self-identity but not the prime constituent.

However, now that Yugoslavia was falling apart, the focus of prime self-identity was changing. Rieff comments,

Religion mattered not so much in and of itself . . . but rather as the main vehicle of ethnic and national allegiance in new states that were bent on defining citizenship almost exclusively in terms of ethnic identity.[1]

So, in other words, if you belonged now to Serbia, you were a *Serb*: Serbia was the State of the Serbs. Similarly, Croatia was the national State of the Croats. This created a major problem for those inhabitants of the new States who were not part of the majority: ethnic Serbs in Croatia, ethnic Albanians, Romanians and Hungarians in Serbia. As for Bosnia, it was a complete mess, since *ethnically* speaking it was a mix of Muslim, Serb and Croat, all living side by side, and frequently in the same village.

Furthermore, we have noted that Serbs, Croats and Bosnians (of any description) were ethnically much the same in origin. So what made them different? I would argue that above all *religion* made the difference, a religious divide fossilised by history, and by the historical divisions caused by who ended up in any particular Empire.

For, as Rieff shows, the ethnic differences that now made up the rationale for separate countries are in reality 'cultural rather than ethnic'.[2] He goes on to elaborate this crucial point,

> What made someone a Croat was the fact that he or she was a Roman Catholic, just as what made someone a Serb was membership, however attenuated, in the Orthodox church. Not that actual religious devotion mattered all that much either in Croatia or Serbia. What counted, once the nationalist mythmaking had been successful, *was the way in which religion was put to use* [italics added].[3]

The misuses of religion
Religion 'put to use': we see here, in a well-known

example, the concept of 'national myth making' that we discussed earlier. This is the 'palingenetic' core of ultra-nationalism as described by sociologists and intellectual historians. People may not have been particularly regular in their purely *spiritual* obedience, such as saying prayers, going faithfully to church, affirming inwardly the doctrines of the Church and so on. It is likely that if you asked the average Orthodox Serb or Catholic Croat what precisely the *doctrinal* differences were between Orthodoxy and Catholicism, they might have tremendous difficulties in outlining them, or giving more than the haziest description even if they could. How many in today's Balkans have ever heard of the *filioque* clause, the great divergence in doctrine between Orthodox and Catholic, on whether the Holy Spirit proceeds from both the Father *and the Son* (*filioque* in Latin) as Catholics and Protestants believe, or simply from God the Father, as taught by the Orthodox Church?

The split took place as long ago as 1054, yet to some people it is as if it happened yesterday. Pope John Paul II has tried to achieve good relations with the Orthodox Churches, but in many areas the old bitterness is still present.

Rather, it seems that religious expression is more an issue of tribal, ethnic loyalty than it is of heartfelt spiritual sentiment. This is well-illustrated by a true story from another religious trouble spot, Northern Ireland.

A Catholic Minister in the British Government was lunching with one of his permanent officials who was an agnostic. Some Protestants were outside, shouting slogans against the Minister. In order to calm them down, the official bravely went outside to reason with them.

'I am not a Christian,' he declared. 'But surely, since as Catholics and Protestants, you are all Christians, cannot all of you get along with each other?' 'We're not Christians,' the protestors shouted, 'we're Protestants!'

Such an interjection reveals a great deal about the essentially nationalist basis of religious nationalism. In theory, Orthodox and Catholic should be in full agreement with the basic biblical definition of murder, namely 'you shall not kill,' stated unequivocally in the Ten Commandments and binding on all Christians to this day. Yet wholesale massacres of completely innocent women and children have been committed by supposedly practising Orthodox and Catholic Christians, all over the former Yugoslavia.

The new religious nationalism

The religious element of nationalism is something that has, all too frequently, been ignored by secularist scholars. Again, this is quite understandable, however regrettable it might be in terms of an accurate understanding of what is happening in so much of the world today. To comprehend Bosnia or Iran without giving full weight to the inherent importance of religion as a *prime* motivation is, to me, quite incomprehensible. Others, though, may attribute it solely to conditioning. They might say that because I am a practising Christian myself, it is natural to attribute religious motivation to others.

This is the issue of *a priori* and *a posteriori* thinking that we examined earlier. Do we really look at the issues first, and then decide? Or do we work out our framework first and fit evidence into the grid we have already constructed? The issue of the rôle of religion in creating nationalist fervour is an excellent example of how difficult it is to know whether we are being objective or not: 'I'm an objective scholar, carefully weighing up the evidence, but Professor X is a dangerous extremist, peddling rubbish under the false pretence of learning . . .'

163

Thankfully, for me at least, there are those who are not religious, outwardly or in their writing at any rate, who have stressed the importance of understanding the religious motivations behind much of today's current nationalistic ferment. Religion is, as we saw, at the centre of much of Professor Huntington's 'clash of civilisations' thesis.

The adaptability of nationalism

Another academic who would hold to the central rôle played by religion is Professor Anthony Smith, of the London School of Economics. He was in fact pointing out the rôle of religion as early as the 1970s when Communism was still prevalent. In his book, *Nationalism in the Twentieth Century*, he observed that we 'need to examine the more traditional religious sources of nationalism, as well as some of the non-religious ideas that collided with traditional beliefs.'[4] For, as Smith acutely points out, 'nationalism can only be understood as a fusion of strands from several sources, religious and non-religious, as they come into conflict at the dawn of the modern era.'[5]

As we saw, some historians and sociologists believe in a happy compromise between the 'primordial' school of thought and the 'modernist' school. This is a compromise between the view that nationalism has always been there, and the view which sees nationalism as a 'construct' or result of the modern era, the world of 1789–1989, between the French Revolution and the fall of the Berlin Wall.

The advantage of nationalism as a force is that it is very adaptable. It can, rather as Hinduism has done in religious terms, vacuum up current intellectual fashions while retaining its core belief. For example, in much of the nineteenth century, nationalism was perceived by many as politically liberal. Semi-revolutionary republican idealists like Mazzini, the Italian champion of freedom, were at the vanguard of nationalism. Now, by contrast, nationalism is seen as anything but liberal.

But, as Smith concludes, 'it is just this confluence of different sources that allows nationalism to combine, transform, yet always remain a recognisable ideology.'[6]

Nationalism then, can be like the chameleon, changing its colours to suit the environment. I would argue that today, in our post-1989 world, religion is a vital ingredient of much contemporary nationalism, and that we fail to grasp this at our peril.

Remembering Kossovo

If we look in detail at nationalistic myths, we can see the present-day results very clearly. We can also see why, for example, that while the Croats are far from blameless, there is a good historic reason why the nature of Serb religious nationalism is more virulent than its Catholic Croat counterpart.

The Croat President, Franjo Tudjman, may at times see himself as a modern-day Crusader, as a champion of Christianity from the hordes outside. But there is a crucial distinction between the Croat and Serb experiences.

Croat independence was extinguished centuries before that of Serbia or Bosnia. There was never a great Croat Empire, in the way that there was a huge Serb Empire under their leader Stephan Dushan, whose domain encompassed parts of the Balkans for longer than even the greatest pan-Serb dream of today. This is not to say that there was no such thing as Croat patriotic feeling, simply that the powerful sentiment of faded glories that dogs Serbia cannot, historically speaking, be present in Croatia.

Croatia: Catholics under Catholic rule

Equally, if not far more important, is the fact that the rulers of present-day Croatia, namely Hungary and Venice, were *Catholics*. However much they might be seen as an oppressor, the Hungarians and Venetians, and the Austrians in Dalmatian Croatia after 1815, were fellow Catholics, co-religionists. They may have been nationally and politically alien, but they were *spiritually* the same.

This invariably creates somewhat of a common culture, more so in Catholicism, because in the liturgy, the language used would have been identical in Venice, Budapest and Zagreb. All Catholics used Latin for the Mass, all Catholics swore allegiance to the same Pope in Rome. The experience of foreign rule, however unpleasant it may often have been, was not therefore so alien in religion, one of the most important parts of an individual's life.

Muslims under Muslim rule
For the Bosnian Muslims, the same applied. They may well have been ethnic Slavs, *racially* the same as the Serbs within the Empire and the Croats outside. But under Ottoman law, because they were Muslims, they did not suffer from any of the penalties under which Christians were placed. Ottoman oppression, in that sense, was never racial. If you were a Muslim, it mattered not what racial background you came from. You were treated as a fellow believer, as a member of the House of Islam. Throughout Ottoman history, many senior members of the Government, right up to some of the very highest positions in the Empire, were held by people who, ethnically speaking, were not Turkish. They were, however, Muslims, and that is what counted most.

The consequences for Croatia and Bosnia
Therefore neither the Croats nor the Bosnian Muslims experienced the traumas of alien rule by people whose

religion was different. By an irony of history, the Croats were not under Muslim rule at all, unlike many of their notional Hungarian overlords. Hungary was defeated by the Ottoman army at the battle of Mohacs in 1526, and was not liberated until 1699. However, the westernmost part of the pre-1526 Hungarian kingdom remained in Christian hands, under the Habsburgs, who now acceded to the (much reduced) Hungarian Crown. Croatia, and what is now Slovakia, were part of this rump kingdom, with the Hungarian capital being for a while at Pressburg, the town today called Bratislava and the capital of the newly independent Slovakia. Thus while Hungary proper had 170 years of alien Muslim rule under the Ottomans, Croatia remained in firmly Christian, Catholic, Habsburg hands.

Why Serbian memories are different

The Serb experience was traumatically different. They went down to defeat in 1389 at Kossovo, not to be free again for nearly five hundred years. The psychological trauma of defeat must have been colossal, especially since Serbia had been one of the mightiest of Balkan kingdoms not long before. The fall of Serbia even predated the collapse of the Byzantine Empire by sixty-four years, and the fall of Bosnia itself.

Ottoman rule was Muslim rule. Although the Ottomans were, in comparison, far more lenient to their Christian subjects than Christians were to conquered Muslims, such as in Spain after the conquest of Muslim Granada after 1492, their religion, Islam, had long been seen as the enemy of Christianity. Although there were reverses for the Ottoman forces,[7] they were to continue their expansion for nearly three hundred years, always managing to retain the initiative over the oft-divided Christian armies in the West. Not until the failure to capture

Vienna in 1683, can it be argued that their decline began. When Eugene of Savoy, the great Austrian general, swept into Hungary in the 1690s, the reversal finally started. But even then most of the Balkans remained in Ottoman hands, and a brief Austrian capture of Serbia itself remained short-lived. It took Greek independence in the 1820s and 1830s truly to reverse the Islamic tide so far as the Christian Orthodox peoples of the Balkan peninsula were concerned.

The sense of humiliation felt by the Serbs must therefore be colossal, something that is imprinted in the national psyche. One can easily comprehend how a very unhealthy national self-identity could build up over centuries of despair and resentment. It has not just political repression, but alien and spiritual repression, a treble burden for a nation to bear, especially one that had itself once been so proud and commanding.

The Russian experience

Much the same can be said of the Russians, although their time under the yoke of Mongol rule, that of the Golden Horde, lasted in effect for only two hundred years, from the thirteenth to the fifteenth centuries. Scholars disagree, as so often happens with history, the *direct* extent to which the Russian people suffered. Muscovy, the State which under Ivan the Terrible was to form the nucleus of the future Russian Tsarist State, will serve as an example. The area of Muscovy was a tributary of the Golden Horde rather than under their direct rule. There were no mosques in Moscow, nor did the Mongols try to impose Islam on their tributary subjects. But there is agreement among many writers that the *psychological* damage done was colossal, and some have argued with conviction that that scar remains very much in place today. Western Europe, which so nearly fell to the Mongol armies, was spared the most terrible fate.

In addition, Russia was also invaded from the West, by the forces of both Catholic Poland and Protestant Sweden. Much of the core original Russian heartland, including the original Rus itself, was for centuries under Polish rule, including the old capital, Kiev. Western Russia and the Ukraine (which literally means 'the borderlands' or 'frontier country') has what is called the Uniate Church. The Uniates, who were viciously persecuted under Communist rule, are liturgically Orthodox, but *ecclesiastically* Catholic, having ultimate spiritual allegiance not to an Orthodox Metropolitan, but to the Catholic Pope in Rome.

The Ukraine is still divided politically and theologically down the middle, between the Catholic/Uniate West and the Orthodox Russian-orientated East. Some writers, such as Samuel Huntington, wonder whether the Ukraine can remain a single country, or fall apart, with the Eastern half possibly rejoining Russia.

Russia has suffered from complete economic devastation in the two world wars of this century and lost millions murdered or killed in battle in both of them. It is probably not surprising therefore that Russia has been rather paranoid towards outsiders for much of its history. The Nazi occupation was peculiarly horrible, as their ideology led them to believe that Slavs were, like Jews, genetically inferior, *Untermenschen* or sub-human. Millions of Russians died as a result of this pernicious doctrine.

I was once at an international relations conference, at which a British Sovietologist spoke about the then USSR's edgy attitude to the rest of the world. Much of it, she argued, was not caused by Communism as such, but by Russian history. Some have stated that many Soviet expansion plans were old Russian imperialist designs in a new guise. But as she concluded, while the Russians had a historic right to be a little paranoid, with their history of being invaded by the Mongols, the Poles, Napoleon, Hitler and others, surely they did not have the present-day right to be quite *so* paranoid.

Fortunately for us today, Russia is not invading anyone, nor is she killing people on a massive scale, whatever historical scars she might possess. Events in Russia move so rapidly that it would be foolish to predict what might or might not happen, since things might well change between my writing this, the manuscript's proof stage, publication itself, and events in the months following publication.

How the past haunts the present

However, recent events in the former Yugoslavia tell us that that part of the world will seldom be out of the news. Here, historical events have a dreadful way of impinging on the present. People in the 1990s have been slaughtered because of events that happened to the ancestors of the murderers in the 1390s, six hundred years ago. Serbs still have a powerful sense of victimhood, believing that the world is against them.

To some extent, this is a vicious circle. If you slaughter thousands of innocent women and children, people are obviously going to be against you! The television pictures of Serb concentration camps, and the news of the genocidal murder of thousands of Muslims at Srebrenica shocked the civilised world. Serbs resented the fact that the Western community had singled them out for punishment. It is true that both Croats and Muslims have undoubtedly committed atrocities too, some of them very terrible. British troops arriving in the area swiftly came to the cynical, but probably fairly realistic, view that 'there are no good guys in Bosnia.' Yet the scale of murder, ethnic cleansing and rape committed by Serbs, while in no way excusing guilty Croats or Bosnians, is on an incontestably greater scale.

The psychology of ethnic cleansing

Why is this? It is clear that in some cases, criminality was caused by individual sick, deranged or depraved minds, the kind of serial killer mentality warped enough to kill whatever the nationality. War simply gave such psychopaths cover for committing crimes that would, in normal circumstances, have been condemned, with their resultant imprisonment or judicial execution.

But there has clearly been a *national* psychopathology at work. To slaughter the thousands of Muslims in Srebrenica would have taken more than a few psychotic individuals to carry out. Many of those taking part in such atrocities would be people who, in normal circumstances, would not have been expected to participate in such barbarity.

The Bosnian Muslims and the Ottoman Empire

The Bosnian Muslims, the principal victims, were a *political* unit under Tito. This was, in a way, a continuation for them of the old Ottoman millet system, under which people had also been classified *religiously* rather than *ethnically*. A Bosnian Muslim's allegiance to Islam was more important than being a Slav. So they were thus identified not with their fellow Slavs, the Slavic but spiritually Orthodox Serbs, but with their fellow Muslims, the racially separate but spiritually Islamic Turks.

Prime self-identity was consequently not ethnic (Bosnian and Serb are in that sense the same), but religious. It was religion that was the centre of focus, and their religions were quite distinct.

Bosnian Muslims, being co-religionists of the Ottomans, prospered in ways not open to those remaining Christian. As invariably happens, this led to resentment and jealousy by those less fortunate. In addition, the Bosnian Muslims collaborated in other ways as well with the Ottoman ruling class. Collaboration with the enemy is seen as bad news in all such situations, from the 'quislings' in wartime Norway, to the tax collectors in New Testament times. Resentment against those seen as collaborators is always present, and the swift justice meted out, such as in post-1945 France, more frequently resembles that of the lynch mob than that of a formal court of law.

Ottoman occupation of Serbia ended in the nineteenth century. While Bosnia remained notionally under Ottoman rule right up until 1908, *de facto* it ended in 1878 when Austria-Hungary was given the right to occupy and administer Bosnia-Herzegovina under the Congress of Berlin. The ethnic strife in the area made the Balkans, then as now, a volatile place. Not for nothing were the Balkans known in those days as the 'powder keg of Europe'.

Evidently, with Ottoman rule in the Balkans now over for more than a century, there is no one among the Bosnian Muslims alive today who could be accused of compliance with the Turks. Even if there are any centenarians among Muslims alive now, it would be their great-grandfathers at the very nearest generational remove who would be in the slightest way guilty of collaboration.

The Serb victim mentality

But as some commentators, such as the exceptionally astute Croat writer, Christopher Cviic, have pointed out, there is in the victim-orientated Serb mentality a sense in which today's genocide and ethnic cleansing is a revenge on five hundred years of Muslim rule. Present-day Serbs cannot get back at long dead Ottomans. But they can revenge themselves on the *spiritual* and very much alive co-religionists of the old Ottomans, the Bosnian Muslims.

Thus, what to us is extremely *irrational*, is, to a paranoid, victim-centred group of people, completely normal. When we say that the slaughter at Srebrenica was an irrational act of barbaric madness, we are acting according to our own Western 'rational' world-view. By the standards of the perpetrators, reflecting their own thought processes, their actions were completely rational and entirely justified.

The logic of murder

It is this remorseless, false but sincere inner logic that makes such people so immensely dangerous. They genuinely believe that what they are doing, however much outsiders condemn it, is entirely justified. It is the same mentality as that of the cult, where the dictates of the founder, however weird, are automatically followed, even if, as at Jonestown, it leads to everybody committing suicide.

As we observed in the first chapter, if people are made complicit in violence, they will then feel that they have to collaborate with the perpetrators in order to protect themselves against the revenge of the victims. No doubt many of the Serbs taking part did so reluctantly. But, for example, their new home might be that formerly lived in by a Bosnian Muslim family, some of whose members had been murdered and where all the survivors had been ethnically cleansed. In such circumstances, a 'request' from a Serb general or Serb irregular militia leader is not really one that can easily be turned down.

Why the Nations Rage

People in the West, men as well as women, were horrified by the mass rape of Bosnian Muslim women. All this can be seen as part of the same national psychosis.

It is probably true that the testosterone charge many male soldiers get from fighting – and from winning in battle against your enemy – may have been a factor in some of the brutal rapes which took place. But, as feminist writers and criminologists often agree, rape is as much about power, domination by men over women, as it is about sex. The rape by Serb men of Bosnian Muslim women falls all too tragically into precisely this category.

Rape and genocide as revenge

The warped motivation for such terror is twofold. First, it is an act of national revenge, part of the same process that led to whole towns and villages being 'ethnically cleansed' and expelled, and the menfolk of the female rape victims being slaughtered and buried in mass graves. As we saw both from this chapter and examples cited in earlier chapters, the Serbs see the Bosnian Muslims as 'Turks'. The ultimate degradation in the chauvinistic warrior-orientated world is to rape a man's woman, to despoil his 'property'. When the villain in *Rob Roy* wished to humiliate our hero, Rob Roy himself, one of the dastardly things he did was to rape his wife. In that sense, the rape is part of the revenge motive, a paying back for centuries of Muslim rule.

As those who have seen the film or who have read Scott's novel will know, Rob Roy's wife also became pregnant as a result of the rape, despite her efforts to lose the rapist's seed. Part of this is connected to the machismo revenge motive – not merely do you humiliate the man by desecrating 'his woman', but you make her bear your child and not his.

However, in racial/ethnic terms, it is far more than this. In the mass rape of the Bosnian Muslim women, all the fathers of any children born will be *Serbs*, not Bosnians. The ethnic identity of the child is seen as being that of the father, not the mother.

Now, as we saw at the start of the book, the Serbs and Bosnian Muslims are *ethnically* the same for all intents and purposes. Genetically, all such children, conceived in such horrific circumstances, would be pure Southern Slavs through both parents. But we have come to realise that, in the topsy-turvy world of nationalism, such medically correct facts are not the point. In the nationalistic mindset, Orthodox Serb and Bosnian Muslim are entirely different.

The second motive then for what one can only describe as 'ethnic rape' is in fact genocidal. The children born to these women will be Serbs, not Muslims. Thus the number of future Serbs born will be greater and that of Muslims proportionately diminished. The womb will be like so many of the towns and villages, 'cleansed' of Muslims and repopulated by Serbs. The Muslim 'race' will contract as the Serb grows larger. Thus will further 'Turks' be cleansed from Serbian soil.

Real and distorted perceptions of truth

I have mentioned the way in which Serbian President Slobodan Milosevic exploited the six-hundredth anniversary of the Serb defeat at the Field of Blackbirds, Kossovo Polje, in 1389. The idea of celebrating a defeat is a contradiction in terms to most people, but quite normal to someone with a paranoid/victim mentality. After all, it shows you that people are always after you! What makes it worse is that the overwhelming majority of the people of the Kossovo province are ethnically Albanian Muslims. It is as if the majority of inhabitants of Agincourt were

175

English, or to Americans, as if the British, having burned down the original Presidential home in 1812, turned it into the British Embassy. These are the mildest of parallels compared to how the Serbs feel about Kossovo.

The Albanians are neither Slavic nor, for the most part, Orthodox, the majority being Muslim. So their presence acts as a permanent reminder that Kossovo was a defeat.

Some have said that Milosevic is a very medieval character, acting not just as a political leader, but in the traditional manner as 'father of the nation'. Above all, he has exploited very fully, maybe because he believes it himself, the Serb sense of betrayal. Not merely do the Serbs feel victimised, they feel betrayed. The 'West' did not rescue them in 1389 nor did they rescue Byzantium in 1453. The Catholic West abandoned the Orthodox East to the oppression of the infidel Turk. Such an interpretation would be hotly disputed by present-day Hungarians and Austrians. The Ottomans ruled much of Catholic Hungary between 1526 and 1699 and did their best to conquer Austria too.

But as always with such seemingly irrational feelings, it is not so much the *actual* truth as the *perceived* truth which counts. The perception might, under cold analysis, be proved false or at least be shown to be severely exaggerated. We have seen though, with 'palingenetics', that it is a central *myth* that drives contemporary ultra-nationalism. Serb leaders like Milosevic may not actually believe that there is a Catholic or Catholic/Masonic/Jewish plot to get Serbia. Events such as Catholic German recognition of Croatia have, however, a strange effect on seemingly otherwise intelligent and outwardly normal people. Germany is *Catholic* (actually, it has many Protestants too, but that is ignored) and *Catholic* Croatia is helped by her. It must be a plot!

Mythology and other excuses for murder

Serbs are not unique in such odd behaviour. The mentality of the militias in the backwoods of the USA, or that of the more extreme form of English nationalist, which sees Vatican conspiracies everywhere, is proof of that. If the Oklahoma bomb was the result of a militia conspiracy, dreamed up by people who see a malign United Nations plotting to take over God-fearing America, it shows that the paranoid mentality is without question not limited to any one particular grouping. But when, as in Nazi Germany or among many present-day Serbs it takes over a powerful State-backed grouping who can and do murder on a genocidal scale, then it becomes a major threat to peace.

I gave the example of the Serbian soldier who told a visiting US Senator that he killed 'Turks' without a qualm. David Rieff has given a similar example, one that demonstrates the victim mentality clearly, and the extent to which history/myth is used to reinforce it. Based on his experiences as a war correspondent in the former Yugoslavia, he writes that when

> one went into a village where fighting had taken place, it was often easier to get a history lesson than a reliable account of what had occurred earlier the same day.[8]

Significantly, Rieff goes on to observe that it

> was not just in televised speeches and press releases that Serbs talked about their defeat at the hands of the Turks on the field of Kossovo in the late fourteenth century . . . Some of them talked in this way on the battlefield.[9]

My own experiences in the area have led me to the same conclusion. Time is compressed. Events of fifty years ago are as if they happened just this morning! Rieff continues:

> In a Bosnian Serb position near the northern town of Priejedor, I was once sent on my way with a handshake, a jerrican of homemade slivovitz, the local plum brandy, and the word '1389' – the date of the Serb defeat at Kossovo.[10]

To be fair to the Serbs, Rieff also details gruesome crimes committed by Croats and Muslims. The horrors perpetrated by the Serbs can never exonerate Croat or Muslim war crimes, just as Hitler's genocide cannot be used to excuse barbarities committed by the Allies, even if such heinous acts were on a far smaller scale than those orchestrated by the Serbs or Nazis.

However, one does wonder whether the sheer magnitude of Serb bloodlust is psychologically motivated by the experience of oppression that they had. Two wrongs never make a right. The Ottomans slaughtered thousands of Bulgarians in the 1870s and hundreds of thousands of Armenians in the First World War. Such genocidal fury does not permit the Serbs of the 1990s to commit the same kind of butchery in historic retaliation. It does, though, give part of an explanation, and also a reason that people can give themselves when they seek to justify their enormities to their own consciences and to those of their friends, neighbours and families.

Genocide in the cause of history

Rieff shows how history can be manipulated in the present by those seeking an excuse for their behaviour. As he observes, such warped thinking can be

> terrible, as when, throughout the war, the Bosnian Serb forces referred to Bosnian government troops as

the Turkish army [italics added], and quite explicitly mobilized soldiers in the name of avenging their defeat in 1389 at Kossovo.[11]

What makes this kind of thinking all the more ridiculous is that the Bosnian army is *not* exclusively Muslim, even though the Muslim contingent might be by far the largest. There are in it Orthodox Serbs and Catholic Croats who, very bravely, have decided that they are *Bosnians* first and foremost and who, by their action, demonstrate that they still hold to the dream of a genuinely multi-ethnic, multi-religious unitary Bosnian State. Theirs might now be a sadly faded dream, perhaps impossible to realise after years of genocide and bitter conflict. But idealistic though they might be, their very existence in the Bosnian army at all is a remnant of that dream. It is also additional proof, if such proof were ever needed, of the complete absurdity of calling the Bosnian Army 'Turkish'. That is the world of paranoia, and of religious nationalism.

Destroying a nation's memory

Before going on to look at Orthodoxy in Greece and Russia, there is one last example of the victim mentality in action.

Croat friends of mine were outraged when they got the impression that many in the West were more upset at the Serb shelling of the lovely old Adriatic town of Dubrovnik than they were at the shelling and killing of numerous Croat cities like Vukovar or Osijek. I agreed with them at the time, and do so now. A human life is always worth more than an oil painting or some other priceless art object. Naturally one does not want to see either an innocent human life or a world famous medieval fresco being destroyed.

179

But if one has to choose, a human life should always come first.

However, as with the rape of the Bosnian Muslim women, the instinct behind the destruction of such objects is the same. It is genocidal: what one might call 'architectural ethnic cleansing'. It is as if malign forces destroyed the Lincoln Memorial, the Library of Congress, Westminster Abbey or every Anglican parish church and every Southern Baptist church building. Indeed, that is very much the equivalent of what the Serbs and ironically, to a lesser but certain extent, the Croats did in Bosnia.

Destruction as psychological murder

The National Library of Bosnia was *the* repository of Bosnian history. Such an archive collection is a folk memory encapsulated, the written evidence for the cultural history of a people. Numerous objects in that collection were not just valuable, they were literally irreplaceable. The symbolic value to the Bosnian people was enormous. It had, of course, absolutely no military value whatsoever. Yet the Serb artillery attacks in Sarajevo destroyed it utterly, and with that destruction, most of the contents. Similarly, in the vicious fighting between the two halves of Mostar, one Croat, one Muslim, the world-famous medieval bridge across the city was destroyed in the conflict. It, too, dating from Ottoman times, was a powerful symbol.

That was the reason why, like the old National Library in Sarajevo, it had to be destroyed. The war, like those of any nationalist/religious variety, is heavy with symbolism. Conflict, being stirred up by myths, involves the destruction of other people's values, symbols and myths as well as the creation and continuation of your own. Not merely must you cleanse the land of your enemy, you must destroy their past as well. It must be as if they have never been. You have your past that inspires you today, revenging Kossovo, or whatever it may be. If you destroy their past, they have no core symbols to which they can look back and take strength. So, in time, they are destroyed as a people.

Religious destruction as ethnic cleansing

This is why there was also wholesale devastation of many religious buildings, especially mosques. If a prime part of your enemy, of the difference between you, is their religion, then it follows that if you destroy the centres of their religious worship, their churches or mosques, you destroy them too. Mosques, churches, monasteries, basilicas, all have very little military value. But they have enormous *symbolic* presence. They embody the religious traditions of a people.

For centuries, villagers have worshipped at the Church of St A, or at the mosque in B. In many towns and small communities, churches, Catholic and Orthodox, stood side by side, nearby the local mosque. The presence of such different places of worship so close together was symbolic not just of diversity, but also of mutual tolerance and acceptance. You may not be a Muslim, but you pass the mosque every day on the way to work.

It was precisely such tolerance that had to be eliminated once the fighting began. Such diversity was symbolic of the fact that at one stage people were more marked by what united them: all Yugoslavs, all simply Bosnians, without a qualifier (Bosnian Serb, Bosnian Muslim). With nationalism to the fore, people were now almost more marked by whom they hated than whom they tolerated or even loved. The mosque, the church: it had to go.

Final observations on tolerance in Greece and Russia

We have seen that Serbia is by no means unique in her brand of nationalistic Orthodoxy, though no other group is as murderous, if indeed they are murderous at all.

Likewise, we have noted that it is not spirituality that necessarily makes the difference. In the past, both Catholics and Protestants have acted in totalitarian ways to those of other forms of Christian persuasion, even to the extent of putting 'heretics' to death.

No one is executed in Orthodox countries for being a Catholic or a Protestant. However, in very recent times, people have actually been jailed for converting someone from Greek Orthodoxy to Protestantism. This was the Costas Macris case in Greece, where a Greek Protestant, along with some Protestant missionaries, were imprisoned for leading a boy born Greek Orthodox into becoming a Protestant.

Several leading Western Christians were able to intervene on behalf of the imprisoned Protestants who were eventually released. But the fact that something like this could happen in Europe in the 1980s is, in itself, quite extraordinary and very revealing. After all this was happening in Greece, a country to which many Britons and Americans have for centuries looked as the fountain of Western learning and classical civilisation.

The Orthodox legacy in Greece today

While we may think of Greece in terms of Plato, or as the birthplace of democracy, the reality has been rather different. Even ancient Greece was a slave-owning State, with most inhabitants having no vote. But more important has been the fact that for two thousand years, Greece was part of an Empire, and an absolutist one at that. She was first under the Roman/Byzantine Empire and then the Ottoman. For one thousand of those years, Orthodoxy was at the heart of the Empire, with the Patriarch under effective imperial control. As with other Balkan states, Orthodoxy was a symbol of resistance, of being authentically Greek, of the 'good old days' when Greeks ruled the civilised Eastern world. Not until the 1920s, and defeat at the hands of Kemal Ataturk's Turkish armies did Greece give up her claims towards formerly Byzantine territory in Asia Minor.

On my own trips to Greece back in the 1970s, I was astonished at the fear felt by many Protestant Greeks of being discovered, of their unpatriotic, un-Greek Protestant form of Christianity becoming known. As the Macris case revealed, the antipathy towards non-Orthodox Christianity within Greece is still very marked. To be truly Greek is still to be Orthodox, even 500 years and more after the fall of Byzantium.

Russia: patriotism and Orthodoxy

In Russia, Orthodoxy and patriotism still fuse together. Anyone writing about a country so rapidly changing as Russia, does so at their peril. At the time of writing, Yeltsin has just recovered from major heart surgery and is resuming power. By the time you read this, matters could be radically different or exactly the same.

However, the remarks made in 1996 by General Lebed are very revealing of the Russian psyche, whether or not Lebed ends up in a position of power or as one of the might-have-beens of history. In a speech, he referred to Russia having three religions: Orthodoxy, Islam and Buddhism. Commentators at the time pointed out two flaws in his remarks. To begin with he was critical – as are many Orthodox – of Western 'sects', such as the Mormons. Second, he omitted any references to Jews.

There have been Jews in Russia for centuries, and to many, Lebed's omission was worrying.

But I would add to these remarks that he also omitted references to other mainstream forms of Christianity. No mention was made of Catholics, or of long-standing Protestant denominations in Russia such as the Lutherans or Baptists. A Baptist Russian is surely a Russian? Well, maybe not, according to the Lebed/Orthodox criteria. There are major differences between Mormons and Lutherans, yet the Orthodox world-view (and not just in Russia) has a tendency to lump them together and regard most Protestants as 'sects'.

Many object to the rather culturally insensitive methods of evangelism coming from the West, and it is hard at times not to feel some degree of sympathy. But many sincere and sensitive Protestants and Catholics have been tarred with the same brush as the extremists. Not all the strange sects are insincere, however much one might disagree with their views.

Tolerance, human rights and proselytism

In expressing such sentiments, I am revealing my own Western pluralistic background, one of tolerance for the market-place of ideas. In so doing, I am also revealing a very major cultural difference between the two kinds of Europe that have grown up historically. This is not to claim any superiority on the part of the West – Hitler was a West European, after all, and racist colonialism is also a product of Western Europe, as many an African, Asian, Australian or native North or South American will attest.

Tolerance has its problems as well. Racism and pornography are often defended by civil libertarians in the name of 'free speech'. People then wonder about the violence prevalent in society and about the decline in family

184

values. Tolerance is therefore a two-sided phenomenon, with an all too forgotten dark side to place alongside its many benefits. Tolerance, and what you allow in the name of tolerance, can sometimes be the lesser of two evils rather than an unalloyed benefit to the entire human race.

This is all to put in context the great debate in human rights and religious circles about the issue of proselytism. As a puzzled Orthodox Bishop put it, 'We don't send Russian Orthodox Bishops to Rome, so why should the Pope be encouraging Catholic missionaries in Russia?'

Territoriality and Christian faith
The 1996 conference of the Helsinki Commission on Human Rights in Warsaw addressed this very issue. At the heart of it were strong Orthodox objections to Western missionaries coming to Orthodox countries to preach their version of Christianity. Orthodox countries are *Orthodox*. That is their version of Christianity. Other countries have theirs – Catholic or Protestant – that is for them.

Western Christians come, by contrast, from a tradition of pluralism and mutual tolerance. In Britain and the USA, some Christians are converting to Orthodoxy, in some cases as they want a fully liturgical tradition, one that does not ordain women to the priesthood, but which is also not Catholic. They are free to do so, or not, as the case might be. While America is still a very Christian country, it does not matter, in public terms, which variety one chooses. While an atheist might find it hard to become President, by and large atheism is no bar to a career in nearly all fields. Furthermore, in the USA, there is no State Church: you can, under the Constitution, be freely anything you like. Your patriotism is not tied up with your religious view.

Here we see the nub of the issue. It is the question of

tolerance, pluralism and *territoriality*. In the West, the bond between a particular form of Christianity and the State has by and large been dissolved. In the East, the two have remained entwined. It is to this vital question that we must now turn.

Section Four

The Rise of Tolerance

*'I disagree with you,' the French
eighteenth-century philosopher, Voltaire,
is claimed to have stated, 'but I will fight
to the death for your right to say it.'*

Such a dictum is in many ways the embodiment of the
Western concept of tolerance. The right of toleration is
enshrined in the United Nations Declaration of Human
Rights. It is almost a hallmark of Western civilisation
that tolerance is to be encouraged in all places and at all
times. It is a value that we hold dear, and a distinction
of which we are proud.

But where does tolerance come from? Why is it a
Western virtue? Is it something innate in the Westernness
of the West? Such thinking, while subconsciously common among many of us in the West, is surely dangerous. For, like the infamous 'White Man's Burden', such
thoughts go on to imply natural superiority over those
nations for whom the concept is alien. Racism is not the

187

sole prerogative of the political right. If, as I trust we should believe, all races are fully equal, then toleration should be a universal value, prevalent everywhere.

The fact that tolerance is not a worldwide concept means that we ought to examine how it arose. The history of our own century, one in which the land of Goethe and Schiller, of great painters and musicians, saw the scale of intolerance grow so massive that six million Jews were slaughtered, shows that the West is no more virtuous than any other part of the globe.

Tolerance must, therefore, have arisen from a set of particular historic circumstances unique to the West, but not implying any superiority on our part. Historically, the predominance and global political/economic preponderance of the West is very recent. For centuries, the lands of Islam were culturally far ahead of Europe. The civilisations of Islam and of China were technically far superior to the comparatively backward West. Yet the world's most widely-spoken language is English, not Arabic or Chinese. While many Asian countries are doing their best to catch up, ours has been the 'American century'.

There was a time when the West was no more tolerant than any other part of the world. What caused the change? That is the theme of Section Four.

Chapter 10 examines in detail 'The End of Christendom and the Rise of Tolerance'. What were the historical factors which resulted in the freedoms which we now take for granted? In the discussion, I use the arguments, which I find convincing, of West African Professor Lamin Sanneh, a convert to Christianity from a Muslim background, but now living in the USA, at Yale. He demonstrates clearly how the clash between two rival kinds of Christianity, Catholicism and Protestantism, created a healthy competition which prevented the stifling religious uniformity of other parts of the world from prevailing in the West.

Chapter 11, 'The Consequences of Tolerance', looks at the results of the rise of tolerance, and the inevitable clash which that creates between the West and those cultures where such a concept is absent. It gives a warning, too. If we forget the religious nature of toleration, as our own culture becomes increasingly secular, we become in danger of being unable to defend tolerance against its many foes outside the West.

10

The End of Christendom
and the Rise of Tolerance

Having examined the Orthodox Eastern part of Europe,
we now turn attention to the Western half. We do so in
order better to understand why the history of religion and
tolerance has taken a very different turn the other side of
the religious divide.

The consequences of the fall of Christendom

Until the sixteenth century, Western Europe was also
known as *Christendom*. It was the land where one form
of Christianity held sway and to which everyone bore
allegiance. It was a very Christian world altogether,
with the institution of the Church holding sway over
the whole of life at both a national and a local level.
Peasants in the fields might not know much doctrine,
but the festivals of the Church were intimately memo-
rised and practised in every village. Every Christian
owed spiritual allegiance to the Pope, whether serf or
king.

The Reformation was to blow this apart, and nothing
that Emperor Charles V could do, let alone any Pope, was
able to bring it back together again. The old certainties
and the old unity were gone.

The End of Christendom and the Rise of Tolerance

The nature of Christendom
Christendom was more than just a set of beliefs. It was a political concept as well as something spiritual. We have seen already that Christendom was not, unlike Byzantium in its heyday, all under the same political ruler. No king of France, England or Castile would ever concede *political* allegiance to the Holy Roman Emperor in the way that he gave *spiritual* obeisance to the Pope. In fact, Emperor Charles V's own grandfather, the wily King Ferdinand of Aragon, made sure that appointments to major Church offices were made locally so far as possible, rather than by a distant Pope whose political sympathies might not be guaranteed.

Nevertheless, in cultural terms, there was a strong sense of unity within Christendom, especially since the world outside looked either mysterious or threatening. Christendom was thus *territorial* – you were born into it, baptised according to the rites of the Christian Church and you were to live your entire life under its auspices.

Christendom and Orthodoxy
The parallel with Orthodoxy is therefore strong: in neither area was there *choice*. Woe betide anyone whose teachings ran contrary to that of the Church, as many would-be Reformers discovered. Not only that, but the lack of choice was officially bolstered by the power of the State. Heretics were not just against the Church, but ran contrary to the world order of which the Church was only a part. Men such as the Czech reformer Jan Hus were deemed as threatening by the Emperor as by the Pope. A spiritually independent view was in effect an act of political rebellion.

In time, all this was to be changed by Protestantism. This is not to say that Protestantism was an ideal alternative. It took Reformation leaders themselves many generations to understand the change. Individual Protestant leaders also suffered from prejudices, bigotry and social blindness. However much one might dislike Luther's anti-Semitism or his political support of the German Princes against the peasants, his *theological* doctrine was revolutionary. When confronted by the might, not just of the Church, but also of the Emperor, Luther defied them. 'Here I stand, I can do no other' was not merely spiritual; it had far-reaching results politically and socially as well. Those words marked the end of united Christendom, with effects in Western Europe and now elsewhere that are with us today. This is because Protestantism, properly understood, is a matter of choice.

Protestantism and the birth of choice

Christendom was a matter of *birth*. You were born into a Christian country. Evangelism had brought Christianity to Europe in the first century, with the Apostle Paul's visit to Macedonia. Yet apart from bold attempts to spread the gospel to pagan Lithuanians, and from efforts like that of William of Rubruck to take Christianity to China, the great age of missionary endeavour had long since diminished. Spreading the gospel via the sword, such as in the reconquest in Spain, was as close as the Middle Ages came. The missionary age of Francis Xavier, the great Jesuit missionary to India and Japan, was still to happen.

Initially Protestantism was no improvement. The somewhat introverted approach of Christendom remained. Territorially speaking, the ties between what you believed and where you lived remained unaltered. This was embodied in *cuius regio, eius religio*: whose kingdom, his religion. Such a formula was a political compromise, a fix to prevent worse conflict breaking out between

Catholic subjects of the Emperor and those Princes who had decided to follow the new Protestant doctrines. The phrase makes a telling point: it is the *Prince* who decides the faith of the region. His decision decides for everybody. If he is Protestant, then that is what the State will be.

Consequently, Protestants soon behaved toward Catholics as the pre-Reformation Catholic authorities had behaved toward Reformed martyrs, such as Hus and Tyndale. My college at Oxford is situated in the same street as the place where those prominent Protestant martyrs, Cranmer, Latimer and Ridley, were burned at the stake for their beliefs under Catholic Queen Mary. Under her Protestant sister Elizabeth, England became consolidated as a strongly Protestant, Anglican country. The martyrs became established as folk heroes. However, by contrast, in Cambridge, when I journey daily to my college, St Edmund's, I pass the Church of Our Lady and English Martyrs. These martyrs, canonised recently, are *Catholics*, executed for their Catholic beliefs under Queen Elizabeth. To be Catholic was to be suspect, even a traitor. The territorial link continued.

Christianity in a 'post-Christian' age

By the twentieth century, however, such displays of territoriality have become not merely unknown but unthinkable. It is hard to imagine a leading Anglican Bishop in England or an eminent Southern Baptist leader in the USA writing the kind of letter that we saw in Chapter 7 from a Romanian Archbishop. The idea that the Church could use the State's power to enforce something spiritual via political means is now beyond the pale.

In the USA, moreover, it is often the Christians who complain that the State has gone too far the other way. Christians who want to display a manger scene at Christmastime now have to use private property to do so because to use public property is now regarded as a breach of the separation of Church and State. Likewise, it is difficult for Christian high school students to have private prayer meetings at State-run high schools for the same reason. So, if anything, the process of secularisation in the USA is taking matters a long way in the opposite direction. This is probably not at all what the Founding Fathers intended. Their aim was to prevent a coercive State Church rather than to banish Christianity altogether from the public square.

All this is happening in one of the most religious countries in the world: church attendance in the USA has remained high and is probably still the highest of any nation in the industrialised world. While Christianity may no longer enjoy the *public* place that it once did, the *private* place of Christianity in the USA is as high as ever and flourishing.

Much of the zeal for worldwide mission and the global spread of Christianity has also come from the USA. Billy Graham is surely the best-known and most internationally revered Protestant Christian in the world today. This vibrancy extends to Catholicism in the USA, with American Catholic missionaries renowned for their work among the poor. Protestant Christian relief agencies based in America show love of neighbour on a mammoth scale. Whatever quirks American Christianity might show – and much of the European criticism of it is often more snobbish than based upon reality – few can doubt that it is very much alive and well.

The American Christian phenomenon
An enormous amount has been written on the phenomenon of American Christianity. As Baptist historians in the USA will tell you, the tolerance experienced today did not exist at the beginning. Many American Christians

descend from those who fled intolerance back in Europe, the Puritans being the most well-known, with Catholics in Maryland being another group. Although tolerance might have taken a while to become universal, the fact that there was no official Church of America to which citizens had to conform made a huge difference.

Consequently, American Christianity is today almost bewilderingly broad, with groups of all sizes and views, some huge, such as the Southern Baptists, Methodists and Catholics, some tiny, with often just a few loyal followers focusing on a particular person. Individualism is as much a characteristic of Christianity in the USA as it is of the nation itself.

Much of America is *very* secular, though, with pockets strongly hostile to any form of religious belief. Yet in a State so very religious in its private make-up, this too is tolerated. In fact, for good or ill, you can invent your own religion and find adherents somewhere in the sprawling country.

Some sociologists have gone as far as to argue that the pluralistic secularism of the USA is the illegitimate descendant of Protestantism. The fact that we have a free and secular society stems, they argue, from the circumstances of the Protestant Reformation itself. As a Christian sociology professor put it, he might dislike Marxism, but at least in today's woolly, hang-loose, post-modern world, they believed *something*! Similarly, many Protestant Christians might not like the avowedly secular nature of today's society, and my private sympathies would be with them in many ways. But paradoxically, it could be the effect of the Protestantism to which we devoutly adhere that created such a climate. How did this happen?

Protestantism and the rise of tolerance
This is one of the most important issues raised in the

book. It is at the heart of the differences between East and West, within Christianity, and also between Western Christianity and Islam.

We need first of all to look at the central issue of territoriality and religion. It is, I will argue, the split between the two in the West which has allowed the rise of tolerance to take place.

This issue is highly pertinent not just to 'Christian' countries where the split did not happen, but also to those in which Islam predominates, in particular, what we described earlier as the 'anti-modern' variety of Islamic faith. So this is an argument relevant to many countries, where pluralism and tolerance are suppressed or discouraged. For one of the main objections to the West that exists in the Muslim world is precisely that Church and State *are* separated.

In the now well-worn phrase 'born again' lies the nub of the Protestant revolution and the rise of modern tolerance. As Luther discovered, the 'just shall live by faith'. That discovery transformed him and in turn led to the Reformation and to the end of Christendom.

It is important to say here that present-day Catholicism is radically different from its sixteenth-century predecessor. As we saw, the fact that, unlike Orthodoxy, Catholicism faced domestic rivalry, in the shape of an alternative form of Christianity, can be said to have done the Church tremendous good. The Church had to think through all she believed with greater clarity. She also had to make her teachings attractive.

Once the French Revolution came, the demise of territoriality in Catholic countries became stronger still. By the twentieth century, Vatican II in the 1960s changed Catholicism yet further. In the United States, many still within the Church go further and call themselves Catholic Evangelicals. 'Evangelical' or *evangelisch* was originally a term for Lutherans, which it still is in many German-speaking countries. Anything therefore said about historic Catholicism needs to be seen in this context.

Protestantism and early nationalism

As we saw in Chapter 3, 'Imaginary Kingdoms', there is a good argument for saying that the Reformation led, indirectly, to much subsequent nationalism. Once the homogeneity of Christendom was broken up, people naturally sought alternative allegiances. To many, this was the nascent nation-state. Politically speaking, much of the Reformation can be understood in proto-nationalist terms, a growing German consciousness rebelling against the imposition of an Italian Papacy and an Emperor who claimed universal jurisdiction. The Reformation in England also had strongly nationalist consequences: the Church of *England* seeking independence from Rome.

However, it was not that simple. The Protestant Reformation was not monolithic. There was no *one* Protestant Church, like the one Catholic Church. Protestantism was no sooner begun than it started to fragment: into Lutheranism, Calvinism, Zwinglianism, Anglicanism, and then a stage further: into groups like the Anabaptists, who rejected the authority of the nation-state altogether. Since no monolithic form of Protestantism emerged, rigid, coercive uniformity became more difficult to impose.

Protestantism, individualism and choice

Protestantism argued that it was going back to the New Testament model of early Christianity. Here the key text is what Jesus says to Nicodemus in John 3:16: unless you are 'born again' you cannot enter the kingdom of God.

Christian conversion, therefore, is a matter of individual choice or decision. You *choose* to be a Christian, or, if you take the Reformed view of Calvin, the influential seventeenth-century Protestant theologian and writer, God chooses you. Physical birth does not enter into it. You can be born a lawful citizen of a predominantly Protestant country, but, according to this doctrine, you are not thereby a Christian. You still need to be 'born again'.

This theological doctrine was, in time, to have massive political consequences and far-reaching implications for tolerance too. Many a contemporary humanist may despise Christianity, but the fact that he is free to do so without any adverse effects, such as imprisonment or even death for blasphemy, is because of the Protestant doctrine of the centrality of the second and spiritual new birth.

The demise of territorial Christianity

Initially, Protestant States did not immediately understand the need for tolerance. In Christendom, allegiance to the State and allegiance to the Church went together. There was no such thing as the 'secular State' as we understand it today. The State was Christian, and that meant that loyal subjects had to give allegiance to the form of Christianity which was recognised by the State.

Soon some Christians began to look in detail at the biblical teaching on Church and State. Luther himself had the 'two swords doctrine' – one sword was the State's and one belonged to the Church. Others began to understand Christ's own teaching on God and Caesar in a somewhat broader light.

Christ, in his teaching on God and Caesar (Caesar = the State) taught that we render to God the things we owe to God and to Caesar the things we owe to Caesar. For example, we give the State our secular obedience, keeping its laws, paying our taxes – tax being the particular issue that Christ was talking about in this teaching.

If one considers the issue further, certain other questions naturally arise. What is my *ultimate* allegiance? As both the Apostles Paul and Peter in their epistles teach believers, Christians are enjoined to obey the State. But the State is created by God. The State itself is not God, nor can it ever be. The *ultimate* loyalty of the Christian is not to the State but to God himself.

God and Caesar: Christianity and divided loyalties

For the early Christians this was the key political issue. The State was not some kindly Christian institution but the pagan Roman Empire. There, Caesar was not just your secular ruler, he was your God as well to whom you had to give both spiritual and political loyalty. For the polytheistic majority of the Roman Empire this did not create a problem. To pay homage to just one more God did not diminish your allegiance to the deities which you worshipped already. But the Christians did not have that option. Christianity is all or nothing. Christianity alone is true. So they refused to sacrifice to Caesar as God, and thousands of them were martyred for their faith as a result.

In the sixteenth century, the issue was more problematic. There was, in Western Europe, no pagan Empire demanding worship or death. Your secular ruler might, while being a professing Christian, be of a different Christian persuasion from your own. Under the compromise which Charles V made with his Princes, they had, as we saw, the right to choose the mode of Christian expression for that State. Soon there were not just Lutheran Princes in Germany, but Calvinistic ones as well, expressing the growing diversity of opinion within the Reformation itself.

So not only had the old homogeneity of Christendom been broken up, but a mosaic of very different options was arising, with States holding very different views living alongside one another. As the diversity grew, many Christians eventually found themselves espousing beliefs which had no State endorsement at all. Anabaptists in Germany and the early Baptists in England had no State where the ruler held their particular theological position.

Where did the ultimate loyalty of such people lie? The answer is that it had to be the *Church*. Furthermore, this was a Church constituted not of people who lived in a particular place, but who were united by what they believed. *Faith*, not *geography*, determined the constitution of the new Churches. What you believed was no longer linked to where you lived. You could be a Baptist anywhere.

In the 'anywhereness' of Christian belief we see the origins of the USA, the 'land of the free'. If the State would not allow you to practise your Christianity in the way of your choosing, then you could go somewhere where you could. To many Christians persecuted at home, the shores of America were a welcome haven, freedom to worship God as you felt he wanted you to rather than as some Prince or Bishop dictated. Loyalty was to God and not to the State.

The French experience
Some States began to realise that in fact the State should *not* coerce its citizens into any particular mode of worship or style of Church allegiance. France had been racked by civil war in the sixteenth century, much of it religious, between the Catholics and the Huguenots, the latter being the name given to the fast-growing Protestant minority.

The political leader of the Protestants was Henri of Navarre. He eventually succeeded as King of France, but still needed to conquer Paris. He therefore made a political conversion to Catholicism. But he did not forget his Protestant compatriots. Various attempts had been made in France during the turbulent 'Wars of Religion' period to come to an agreement on toleration. None had lasted long. But once the fighting was over, Henri, now King Henry IV, made an Edict at the town of Nantes in 1598. The Edict of Nantes was not ideal, in that it restored Catholicism to areas from which it had been expelled, making it difficult for Protestants to expand there. But Protestants themselves were given full freedom of worship, and equal civil liberties. You could now be a loyal Frenchman and a Protestant. The King might be Catholic, but you could be his devoted and obedient servant and reject his faith. A vital link between Christianity and territoriality had been broken.

Henri's grandson, King Louis XIV, revoked the Edict and many Protestants had to flee as a result. This was greatly to benefit the economies of Britain, the Netherlands and northern Germany (especially Prussia) since the French Huguenots had many trading skills. But within a century of Louis' death came the French Revolution, and the end of State Catholicism. Since then, France has been an increasingly secular country on the one hand, and has offered complete tolerance for Protestants on the other.

Freedom and the triumph of personal faith

John Locke was one of the greatest seventeenth-century English philosophers. The USA today descends, philosophically, in many ways from his thought. He was also to have a profound influence on the issue of religious freedom and tolerance.

For, as he argued, true religion is incompatible with State coercion. Making someone go to church against their will does not make them a Christian. This is because it does not make any outward conversion they make valid.

As the old saying goes, 'a man persuaded against his will is of the same persuasion still.'

True faith is as the result of '*inward* change'. Christianity, by this token, is the consequence of an essentially voluntary act. It is, in the words of Lamin Sanneh, the 'triumph of personal faith'. Inward change, personal faith – these are not things, if they are to be genuine, that can be brought about by external force.

The results of Locke's teaching on tolerance

Politically speaking, the results of Locke's philosophy are plain. He believed that any society held together by coercion was a tyranny, as did the Founding Fathers of the USA a century later. Locke, who lived from 1632 until 1704, had seen civil war in his own homeland. Religion and tolerance were of great importance in that struggle, between those who wanted an enforced Church and those favouring freedom of worship.

When Locke wrote his famous work, *Epistola de Tolerantia* (or *A Letter Concerning Tolerance*) in 1689, he was in exile in the Netherlands, a country that had itself had a major struggle for freedom against tyranny in the sixteenth century. (His other well-known work, *An Essay Concerning Human Understanding*, was published around the same time, though he had been working on it for many years previously. This work is justly fêted for its groundbreaking methodology.) It is with his views on tolerance, though, that we are concerned here.

His views on political tyranny applied equally to religion, as he pointed out. True faith is something that cannot be tyrannically coerced upon an individual. This means that in one of the most important of all areas of life, someone's religion, the State has no say.

Locke had spent time in Montpellier, in France, and had been greatly influenced by the idealism of the Edict of Nantes. Now King Louis XIV had repealed it, and had become the enemy of freedom. With the accession in 1689 of the Dutch leader, William of Orange (William III), to the British throne, Locke was able to return to his home country. Both Britain and the Netherlands were to be central to the struggle against the expansionist tyranny of Louis of France in the wars that were now to follow.

Locke and religious freedom

The dramatic impact of Locke's thought on religious freedom can easily be imagined. He finally snapped the bonds between *faith* and *territoriality*. For if faith was 'inward change' then no State could legitimately command outward coercive obedience. Every free citizen could choose their own form of faith. Being British no longer meant anything spiritually, although formally speaking the British took until the nineteenth century legally to remove restrictions on non-Anglicans altogether. In the new USA, religious coercion was banished by the founding constitution itself. The Virginia Baptists, whose early persecution has been so ably documented by John S. Moore, were persecuted no more. Baptists, Presbyterians, Methodists, Catholics, Episcopalians (= Anglicans) were all equal before the law.

The very nature of State power was thus drastically reduced. Power over the soul as well as the body had been an integral part of political control over the subject. Your core beliefs were open to integration by the agents of the State. Not any more – now the belief of every citizen was free and sacred.

Locke also, some have argued, believed that atheism cannot defend true religious toleration. This is because toleration itself is based on a religious idea, that of *personal* faith.

Individualism versus intolerance

The notion of personal faith has much relevance today in the debate on the scope of religious toleration and individual freedom. Opponents of the forces of 'Jihad' often find it difficult to argue with the forces of *intolerant* religion. Anti-modern, or fundamentalist, views are frequently against the propagation of tolerance. In some cases, this is because they see liberty being replaced by licence, a misuse of freedom to do literally anything. Muslims in strict countries are, as we have observed, often horrified at the moral flabbiness if not outright decadence of the West. Sometimes, too, this can be caused by the woolliness of Christians, so anxious not to appear offensive that, for example, they let all kinds of undesirable things enter into our schools. It can take local Muslim parents to galvanise Christian and non-Christian parents alike into a campaign to ensure drug-free, pornography-free schools.

This is not to say that non-believers lack a clear rationale for their view; far from it. But in the increasingly *Jihad versus McWorld* environment, appeals to the brotherhood of humanity, while working well within a secularised mindset, do not hold much water with someone whose entire world-view is religious. 'Modernity' or 'McWorld' has, as we saw earlier, sometimes increased the Jihad mentality rather than placating it.

Even in societies that are technologically very advanced, such as the 'Tiger' economies in East Asia, there are those arguing that the 'Asian way', which downplays individual freedom at the expense of the wider community, is preferable to the West.

The consequences of Jihad and civilisational clash

If Huntington's controversial theory of civilisational clash has any truth in it, discussions of this nature become more than just theoretical. They will, for example, make a huge difference both to trade and to international relations. As Professor Bernard Lewis and others have shown, mutual understanding between Islam and the West is important, and may become increasingly vital as time progresses.[1]

Is Western interference in the human rights of other countries a new form of imperialism? Should we defend political dissidents in China or Myanamar, and try to prevent the execution of those who convert from Islam to Christianity? In the West, we certainly believe these rights to be inalienable and self-evident, as the US Constitution reminds us. For much of today's humanity, these arguments are more than relevant, they are life and liberty or death and imprisonment itself.

Christianity and the concept of freedom

Free will is a doctrine that pervades the Christian Bible. Not all Christians agree with each other on the tension between free will and God's choice. If equally sincere theologians have wrestled with it for nearly two thousand years, this is not the place to pronounce one way or the other, whatever my own views. But choice, the need to be born again, personal faith, all point to a biblical support for tolerance.

This is something that we will examine in more detail later. In the context, though, of discussions with intolerant world-views, Christians can argue *both* for tolerance *and* for a fully integrated Christian world-view. You can have faith without coercion, an all-encompassing belief system and pluralistic tolerance. Christians therefore have a way of influencing and reaching out to Muslims that the modern secular rationalists do not and cannot have. It is not either Jihad or McWorld, an intolerant society or a homogenised and anonymous consumerist morass.

When rendering to God means *not* rendering to Caesar

Locke wrote his books in revolutionary times. Much has been said or written about the French Revolution and the origins of 'modernity'.

Modernity, here, means not just modern, but a whole framework of associated views. One of the most important of these is that there are such things as absolutes. At a conference on modernity and 'post-modernism', a leading theologian told the audience that most scientists were 'modernists'. They believe, for example, that $2 + 2 = 4$, and that this holds absolutely true absolutely everywhere. One of the great appeals of Marxism was that it was supposed to be 'scientific' – absolutely true – and was therefore much more modern or advanced than earlier modes of thought. Nazism made similar claims.

In the 'Age of Modernity', religion was often deemed to be 'unscientific' or pre-modern. One can see this early on in the modern period, with the French Revolution's 'Cult of the Supreme Being', a kind of classically inspired atheism, showing the fundamentally anti-religious root of much of the Revolution's thinking. One of the most influential thinkers behind the eventual French Revolution was the eighteenth-century philosopher, Jean Jacques Rousseau. His view that human beings are born free but are everywhere in chains gave birth to a romantic notion of human nature. This notion was swiftly exposed in the gore of the Terror that followed the initial stages of the Revolution, and has been shown to be tragically wrong in the horrors of the twentieth century.

Yet in the revolutions of Locke's own time, those of the seventeenth century, religious men such as Oliver Cromwell were among the ideologists and leaders of events. The same faithful group of Christians, the Puritans, that played such a key rôle in the establishment of

New England were also instrumental in the overthrow of royal tyranny back home in the reign of King Charles I. Recent historiography has shown that the motives of some Puritan leaders were not as black and white as earlier historians have supposed, nor were all the Royalists quite as dreadful. Few are likely to dispute, though, that religion was central to the thinking of both sides.

The end of the divine right of kings

Charles genuinely believed that he had a mandate from God to rule: the 'divine right of kings'. The Puritans, fighting on the Parliamentary side, equally believed from their own understanding of the Bible, that the kind of rule which he practised was tyrannical and therefore mistaken.

This was a revolutionary view: that there was an authority over and above that of the King, and that the King could *legitimately* be overthrown by his subjects. It was not entirely new. The Dutch, in their revolt against Philip of Spain and foreign rule, had had similar debates some decades earlier. Like the Dutch, the Parliamentarians formed a Republic.

In the former instance, it did not last long. Charles II was invited back from exile in 1660. In 1688 his brother, James II, was regarded by many as attempting to reintroduce the royal tyranny they had thought long vanquished. In the end, James fled, and his Protestant daughter Mary was invited to share the throne with her Dutch (and Protestant) husband William of Orange. Twice in one generation, in 1649 and 1688, a British king had been overthrown. Then, when the Protestant branch of the Stuarts looked as if it was coming to an end, Parliament passed an Act of Succession limiting the throne to Protestants. In 1714, a German prince, the Elector of Hanover, became King as George I, in preference to many of Stuart lineage whose genealogical claims were far better than his.

The Age of Absolutism
The eighteenth century has often been seen as the Age of Absolutism, from King Louis XIV of France at the outset to Catherine the Great of Russia at the other end, and Frederick the Great of Prussia in between. I choose these sovereigns as they are Catholic, Orthodox and Protestant respectively. All three variants of Christianity were affected by the increase in royal power.

Few historians now believe in what is called 'the Whig interpretation of history', in which view Britain's Protestant parliamentary system grew inexorably to ever greater freedom and happiness, leading to Britain's rise to become the greatest world power in Victorian times. As we saw in earlier chapters, inevitability in history is hard to predict.

Nevertheless, while most would now say that there was nothing inevitable or foreordained in Britain's rise, her history has had a major impact on the cause of tolerance, and, through Britain, so in turn with the USA.

Britain and the rise of religious toleration
As far back as the seventeenth century, devout Christians such as the Puritan poet, John Milton, believed that a monarch, if a tyrant, *could* be lawfully overthrown. The King was as accountable to God as his subjects, and, if he disobeyed God, he could be deposed.

We see through this that there are limits on the obedience which rulers may require from their subjects. They cannot be coerced to believe what they reject, to worship in a way that they find abhorrent. Even though a ruler might find their theology objectionable, it *must* be tolerated.

Christian thinkers of the time took this further. Some groups, like the Levellers and Fifth Monarchy Men took it a *lot* further, thinking the kind of politically revolutionary thoughts that were not, in some cases, to reappear until the twentieth century, influencing many of the Christian Socialists of our own time. (If American readers find the juxtaposition of the words Christian and Socialist somewhat startling, it is worth pointing out that in Britain the Labour Party has been, slightly jokingly but also seriously, described as 'more Methodism than Marx'.)

Most, though, were not so extreme. By no means did all the Puritans favour the beheading of Charles I even though they had not hesitated to fight on the Parliamentary side in the Civil War. With his grandson, James II, exile was the result rather than execution. It is worth remembering with James, that, while *politically* inept, in *spiritual* terms, he would have given both Free Churchmen and his fellow Catholics religious freedom many years earlier than turned out to be the case. His deposition did result in greater tolerance for dissenting Protestants, though not for Catholics.

Tolerance and the limits of power
But whether the option was death or exile, the central point is that leading politicians had established the principle that there was a limit to royal power and that *political* tolerance would not countenance absolute rule. Historians might disagree on exactly how much power was still exercised by the Sovereign – some have likened William III's power, for example, to that of an American President today. Be that as it may, the principle of collaborative government, the 'Crown in Parliament', had been established. If that looks similar to the more formal checks and balances in the US Constitution, that is, perhaps, no coincidence.

Levels of tolerance are bound to increase in such a society. The eighteenth-century Methodist Revival of the Wesleys and Whitefield was not outlawed, and the distinguished Christian lady, Selina Countess of Huntingdon, was able to introduce it even into aristocratic circles. The Wesleyan preachers did not suffer the same fate as the Lollard followers of Wycliffe had some centuries earlier. The influence of their American counterparts, such as Jonathan Edwards, on the whole of society, was enormous. While not everyone may agree today that the Wesleys helped indirectly to stop the equivalent of the French Revolution from taking place in England, their own impact on the country was considerable. When Revolution came to the American Colonies, it was a swifter and considerably less bloodthirsty affair than that in France a few years later. America had no equivalent of the Terror, the guillotine or of Napoleon.

Civil freedom, therefore, as Sanneh has shown, can be said to have Christian roots. Not everyone enjoyed that freedom immediately. For all Jefferson's fine statements about liberty, he continued to own slaves. In Britain, active Christians such as William Wilberforce were able to see the end both of the slave trade and then in 1833, a month after his death, the end of slavery itself. In the USA it took a civil war. One can legitimately argue, though, that while the early Americans took time to realise exactly how far the principle of freedom and tolerance should be applied to those of African and native American descent as well as European, they had at least understood that such principles existed and were at the centre of human life and happiness.

11

The Consequences of Tolerance

Tolerance and the rise of secularism
Eventually, as the memories of the beginning faded, people in countries such as Britain and the USA forgot the Christian roots of their freedom. This is, in a way, not surprising. God, as the saying goes, has no grandchildren. Christianity is a matter of personal faith. Having Christian parents does not guarantee Christian children or grandchildren. Every generation must begin again.

This is a continual Old Testament theme – remembering what God did in times past, that he must be followed and obeyed today. As Christ himself said to the Pharisees, people who emphasised the outward while often forgetting the inward, that being descendants of Abraham did not save them. While as Christians we may sorrow at the increasing secularisation around us, and weep for those who have no personal faith, the *fact* of secularisation should not surprise us. The people at the time of Amos were no different in their slothful materialistic ease than the America or Britain of the twentieth century. Technology may have changed, but people remain the same.

Consequently, once the State no longer had the right to enforce a *particular* religion, it ceased to have the right

211

to impose *any* religion. Atheism, agnosticism or any other kind of belief therefore became possible in a pluralistic society.

Likewise, because Christianity was seen as *personal*, rather than something imposed by the State, Christianity itself became privatised. In Western Europe and the USA, this has led to the marginalisation of Christianity from public life. Western society has created what one African Christian has described as a 'bland consensus', one that is powerless either to understand or to engage effectively with the forces of Jihad. Only in recent years have Christians sought actively to re-enter the 'public square' of national life, often doing so through the political right, in the USA, and the political left, as in Britain.

It is still too early to say whether such activity will be successful, and this book is not the place for a discussion, especially since for me to come down politically on one side or another would have the regrettable result of losing readers on the opposing side of the political spectrum. Without in any way revealing my own political prejudices, I can say that politics is an issue in which my fellow Christians are as unfortunately intolerant to each other's opponents as their secular counterparts.

The modern, often bland, secularism of 'McWorld' is thus an *indirect* consequence of the Reformation, one that the Reformers in a fully religious age could never have foreseen.

Catholics and competition

Protestantism did not just create tolerance by dividing into separate forms itself. It also did so, as hinted in earlier chapters, by providing Catholicism with active competition. Recent historians have argued convincingly that the pre-Reformation Catholic Church was not quite as moribund as Protestant historians have maintained –

certainly not at grass roots parish level, whatever the corruption and political interference at the upper reaches of the hierarchy.

Competition proved the key: the Catholic Church had to adapt to survive. We now know that the Counter Reformation was successful in many countries, and with permanent results. Countries where the tide was turned remain Catholic today, over four hundred years later.

The Catholic leadership, both in Rome and in Vienna, where successive Holy Roman Emperors wrestled with the problem politically as well as spiritually, did not know this at the time. Poland, Austria and Bohemia (now the Czech Republic) had huge Protestant minorities in the sixteenth century, and, with statistics being uncertain, it is even possible, as some historians speculate, may have had *majority* Protestant populations.

Catholic responses to Protestant competition

Some of the turning around was violent, as was so often the case, on both sides, in that unsettled area. I have had the privilege of staying many times in a lovely old castle in Austria. It is now owned by an actively international but American-based Christian charitable foundation. The purchaser was a courageous German-American who had the wisdom to see the evils of Hitler in his native land long before others did. Back in the sixteenth and seventeenth centuries it was a strategic castle owned by the Prince-Archbishop of Salzburg, who owed direct political allegiance to the Emperor. Many early Protestants were held in the dungeons – now inhabited by bats – and maybe martyred there for their faith. The castle having passed into Protestant hands in the 1960s, their prayers must have been answered, albeit not in ways that they could have imagined three hundred years ago!

The other powerful armoury in the Counter Reformation was doctrinal and spiritual. The shock troops were the Society of Jesus, the Jesuits. The Society did not restrict itself to Europe and to combating Protestants. It did what the Church had not done for centuries, and began the major task of evangelism overseas – beyond Europe, outside the old Christendom.

The Age of Discovery and the consequences for tolerance

Protestants had begun the same task, with missions to the Native Americans. Mission itself, long neglected, began again in earnest. Soon Christ's words to spread the good news to *all* the world were, finally, being taken seriously. Here again competition helped, as Calvinists (sometimes thought of as the shock troop equivalent within Protestantism) and Jesuits spread Christianity globally, always aware that the others might get there first.

Oxford and Princeton historian, Professor J. H. Elliott, has made an important point about the 'Age of Discovery' which is also relevant to our discussion on tolerance. He points out that European explorers came across civilisations in the age of exploration after Columbus who were entirely alien to anything that West Europeans had seen before. There was considerable theological debate, for example, about the human nature of recently discovered South American tribes. Were they human? If so, how did they fall into God's plan? In China there was often heated debate among missionaries about which Chinese word should be used when translating the word 'God' into that language.

Western Christianity and the challenge of diversity

All these debates showed that Western Europe was having

to come to terms with *diversity*. This was a major intellectual challenge, and meant that Westerners had to look at many of their own most basic suppositions in the light of it. As other historians have shown, Christians encountering old civilisations, such as China and India, had to work out what in the Christian gospel was essential – an irreduceable core – and what was in fact European cultural accretion that was not an integral part of the message of Jesus Christ.

These challenges were new. The fact that while the Catholic Church, especially after the Council of Trent, gave itself a rather monolithic face in Europe, but found it very hard to agree on cultural issues in Asia, is, in itself, encouraging.

Back to Byzantium

The division of Western Christendom, while a cause of sorrow to many within it, turned out to have been a major benefit. Western Christianity grew worldwide, making converts in lands where any kind of Christianity had been unknown. In time, the harshness of the immediate Reformation/Counter Reformation era gave way to tolerance, to an attitude that said in effect, 'I still don't agree with you, but I tolerate your right to be wrong.' Tolerance did not imply some mushy denial of your own claim to truth, but affirmed the right of people to proclaim freely what they believed truth to be. One could – if mathematicians allow this to be possible – call this 'highest common factor truth' as opposed to 'lowest common denominator truth'.

(Post-modernists, for whom the only truth is that there is no truth, may not like this. The fact that they are allowed to proclaim freely and openly their world-view, though, is a result of people in the past who believed passionately that absolute truth exists, defending, sometimes to the death, their right to propagate their opinions.)

In Eastern Europe, the historic situation was very different, in particular in those countries dominated by Orthodoxy. This latter point is important as the division is *religious*, not racial. Czechs, Slovaks, Slovenes, Croats and Poles are all indisputably part of the Slavic world. Their history, though, has been *Catholic*, and those areas of, say, Poland, under Russian rule were not under Orthodox hegemony for very long. Russians (by far the biggest Slav group), Bulgarians, Macedonians and Serbs are *Orthodox*. Croats, Czechs and Poles, for example, too, have always used the Latin alphabet, whereas Russians and Serbs use the Cyrillic, which is similar to the Greek.

The legacy of Genghis Khan

Historically, as we have seen, the Orthodox countries had the grave misfortune to be conquered by non-Christian forces for prolonged periods: the Russians by the Mongol Horde and the Balkan states by the Turkish Ottoman Empire. While Central Europe (and to a lesser extent some Mediterranean countries) were threatened by Muslim invasion, only part of Hungary was actually conquered and most of the old area of Christendom left unscathed. Protestant Europe, being further away, never suffered in this way at all.

The scars that this left were terrible, leaving traces that remain today even in Russia. Some have described Stalin as an essentially Asiatic figure, more Mongol Khan than European ruler. While this is not exactly complimentary to Asia, no Asian leader, Ghengis Khan included, ever competed with Western Europe's Adolf Hitler for barbarity. There is a cultural point in the statement. Russia was always a dictatorship. Indeed, the period of parliamentary democracy and government she has had since 1991 is the longest she has ever had, unless one

The Consequences of Tolerance

counts the half-hearted concession to democracy between 1905 and 1917, which buckled under the pressure of both war and revolution.

Russia was at the frontier of Europe and Asia, often invaded from both sides, Poles on the one hand and assorted nomadic groupings from the East. The ability to form a democracy often includes the presupposition of internal stability and external security.

Some have said that the monolithic uniformity of China prevented her from having a renaissance or industrial revolution that would have opened her up earlier, and to much greater advantage and mutual benefit, to the outside world. The same, I would argue, could be applied to Russia. History, rather than anything innate in the Russian personality, forced her into an introverted and unproductive mould.

Cultural isolation and the consequences for tolerance

As for the Balkan States, four centuries of alien Ottoman rule is enough to sap any society. A renaissance or industrial revolution under foreign oppression is a rather unrealistic prospect! Croats and Czechs may have been under *foreign* domination, but it was the rule of fellow Catholics, of people raised in the same common West European culture. The Serbs did not have that chance.

All this had an equally oppressive result on the Orthodox Church, with consequences that exist today for her attitude towards toleration and diversity. This is not to excuse current intolerance in any way, but to put it in historical perspective.

Orthodoxy was isolated, politically and geographically, from the Reformation. The Orthodox Church never had a Luther or a Calvin, neither did it have a Loyola

217

or a Xavier. There was no equivalent of Protestant-ism's ninety-five theses or of Catholicism's Council of Trent. While the Catholic Church proclaims that it never changes, in reality it was the monolith of Orthodoxy to which the phrase *semper idem* (always the same) could really be applied.

The effect of absolutism on Orthodox faith

Consequently, Orthodoxy was never challenged, from outside or inside. To the majority of its adherents, it was *the* form of Christian faith, the faith which had survived against both Mongol invasion and Ottoman rule. Its theological opponent, Islam, was not a rival, but an enemy, a very different notion from the Protestant and Catholic conflict of Western Europe. The link between Church and State was never broken, between faith and territoriality. Pluralistic democracy was unknown, as Orthodox people lived either under the autocracy of the Tsars, rulers with all the power of the old Byzantine Emperors, or under the Ottoman Sultan, who, while not Christian, had inherited the physical remains of the old Byzantine Empire.

In a sense, the Orthodox never really had a chance. No Reformation, no Counter-Reformation, no Renaissance. Instead of a freely initiated home-grown Industrial Revolution, they had serfdom, an agriculturally-based slavery that in a country like Britain had died out by the fifteenth century at the latest.

Orthodoxy and tolerance today

Now we have a Russia that is democratic at long last but with all the instability natural in a country where genuine pluralist democracy has never been allowed to take root. In Serbia we have old-style patronage politics and the vicious ethnic cleansing of all who are not Serb. This is not a racial issue, as anyone who visits prospering, peaceful, democratic countries such as the Czech Republic or Slovenia can readily attest.

No, it is Orthodoxy and history that have made the difference, bestowing a double whammy on countries that have lived under their burdens. Communism, itself by origin a Western philosophy, for long provided a protective veneer, a better, because more excusable, rationale for Russian expansionism than Pan-slavism or simple aggression. How much better to say that you have troops in Hungary or Poland because you are defending 'socialism' against the capitalist West than to say that you are acting in the tradition of Russian defensiveness against outside attack.

Orthodoxy and the fear of foreigners

Now that Communism has imploded, the lands of Orthodoxy are far more vulnerable than they have been for many years, if not for decades. Outside forces seem more threatening than ever before. Old, atavistic Russian fears are being aroused. The Serbs, deprived of the cocoon of Yugoslavia, are feeling exposed.

Not surprisingly, the faith of these countries, Orthodoxy, is also feeling very threatened. Orthodoxy is their national religion, the comforter and source of identity in troubled times.

In the nineteenth century, some Western missionaries, such as Lord Radstock, attempted to bring other kinds of Christianity to Russia. They did not get very far and then the Revolutions of 1917 put an effective end to those efforts. Many Protestants did live in Russia, or in Russian provinces beyond the Urals, but these were mainly of ethnic German ancestry. Orthodoxy within the boundaries of Russia proper did not have any real competition, except for the Uniate Christians, in areas conquered from Poland and now in the Ukraine. Even the Uniates, while owing spiritual allegiance to Rome, were Orthodox in liturgy.

Satellite invaders

Ironically, the problem facing Orthodoxy is very similar to that of their old enemy, Islam. Islamic countries feel deeply unhappy about the invasion of McWorld. Washing machines and cars are all very well. But along with such useful gadgets come the insidious *cultural* effects of the modern world, not just Western goods, which are neutral, but Western *values*, which are not.

As even non-Christian commentators have pointed out, one of the extraordinary things about a soap opera such as *Dallas* is that, although the background of the story is set in a town in the middle of America's 'Bible Belt', there are no practising Christians portrayed in the stories. This is also despite the fact that the family upon whom the imaginary Ewing family is based have many active Christians in their midst. Protestant mainstream Christianity, so central a part of the real city of Dallas, is marked by its absence.

Although conspiracy theorists will no doubt disagree, much of this bias is completely unconscious. The script writers and producers of such shows simply do not meet active Christian people in the course of their everyday real lives. Nor, for that matter are there that many active Christians aiming for Hollywood. Culturally, though, the result is a very incomplete picture of life in the West.

A wall of misunderstanding: the myth of the 'Christian' West

Yet, like the Muslim friends in the Middle East on whose screens I watched *Dallas* some years ago, most Muslims, including many leaders in their own societies, do not comprehend that. To them, the West is 'Christian', as they are Muslim. They see the greed and immorality of the fictitious Ewing clan, and take that to be an accurate portrayal of Western Christian values. They see their own young people listening to Western rock music, with its frequently anarchic lifestyle statements, and they become gravely concerned. The fact that many Westerners are too, from Robert Dole on the right to Tipper Gore on the left, does not percolate through as strongly as one would like.

As Lamin Sanneh said, the West is too dominated by its 'bland consensus' to be seen to be doing anything in a way in which the Muslim or Orthodox worlds would understand. For repression, which might certainly deal with many social problems of our time, is an instrument incompatible with the pluralistic society in which we live. It is, as one might describe it, the flip side of tolerance. Franco's Spain crushed Protestants, it also crushed a lot of crime as well. Post-Communist Prague has complete political, economic and religious freedom. It also has a greatly increased crime rate, prostitution and the new-style Eastern European Mafia.

This is the problem in Russia, and accounts for the desire of many Russians to have 'strong leadership'. With democracy has come unprecedented inflation and street violence, causing economic hardship and physical fear to many who, under the old Soviet system, were left alone. Most peasants did not fear the KGB – they simply got on with life in the village much as their ancestors had done under the Tsars.

Keeping out the decadent West

For such people (not the Westernised intellectual élite we see on television interviews), Mother Russia is Orthodox Russia. The West has brought, to such minds, crime, inflation and chaos. The West is greedy and decadent

– look at what they put on television, with soap operas and a lifestyle that demands a thoroughly un-Russian materialistic view of life. Who except for the new Mafia can afford the kind of designer clothes one now sees in the smart shops of Moscow or St Petersburg?

The West is Protestant or Catholic, with the Pope, a member of the old Polish enemy, sending in Catholics to take people away from Orthodoxy. Wealthy American evangelistic organisations are holding crusades and spreading their often bewildering Protestant doctrines. Orthodoxy itself is being invaded, and in its own heartland.

Christians such as Pope John Paul II and Billy Graham, both of whom share a real and longstanding spiritual concern for Russia, would be the first to protest that the two things are not linked. Their desire to see a spiritually renewed Russia is of an utterly different order from the big Western corporations who see post-Communist Russia as a means of enlarging their profit base. The Pope has often criticised the thoughtless materialism of 'Western values'.

The 'social teaching' of the Catholic Church is as critical of the defects of capitalism as it is against the tyranny of atheistic Marxism. Catholic and Protestant leaders alike are implacable in their opposition to the greed, selfishness and mindless hedonism that marks so much Western society. In this, in the West, they are often in full accord with Muslim leaders' own strictures. Regrettably for Christianity, though, all Westerners are frequently tarred with the same brush, whether Christian or secular.

The right to be wrong

The right to be wrong can have mixed consequences. Freedom of religious and political thought can also create societies in which crime flourishes, families break up and many other antisocial or immoral activities take place.

In the West, we see this as the price of freedom. I have an atheistic Jewish lawyer friend in the USA. Politically, he is strongly liberal. But when it comes to freedom of speech, he would even extend such freedom to anti-Semites, pornographers and racists. He is zealously opposed to all three of those categories of people as many people would be who do not share his liberal politics. Yet there is a logical consistency to his view, however much I might dislike it and wish to censor such moral filth. (In Britain, the propagation of racism is theoretically illegal.) Freedom of speech is . . . freedom.

Such liberal views are anathema to Muslim societies, and increasingly to many in Orthodox countries, such as Russia. The West, they argue, pays too high a price for freedom.

Liberty or licence?

Liberty but not licence? Can one have true liberty without the concomitant problem of rampageous licence along with it? We saw earlier that post-Fascist Spain and post-Communist Central and Eastern Europe were not exactly encouraging in this regard.

For those of a totalitarian mindset, the very fact that such a question could be posed is proof enough of the West's decadence. In a theocratic State, there is no question of liberty to commit licence. Adulterers are stoned, or at least discouraged, rather than having their promiscuous lifestyles glamorised on television.

Where, though, do you draw the line? Who decides where to draw it? Who chooses those who make the decision? Above all, on what grounds is the choice made? While some Christians on the radical right might agree fully with Muslims who uphold family values, I have yet to hear of a Christian leader proposing the death penalty for adultery. Furthermore, many Muslim intellectuals are now arguing that capitalism is inherently wrong, if not actually immoral. On this issue, they surely part company with the Christian religious right, for whom capitalism is the best economic system.

Christianity and the defence of freedom

Can a secular West solve such a dilemma? Or is Christianity a better defender of Western values? We have seen that Christianity is a faith of choice, entered into voluntarily, not at the point of a gun. Freedom is a Christian value. Yet Christians also believe in absolutes, morals and values. Can Christianity be the defender of freedom against Jihad?

Such a question is bound to provide a very contentious answer. Yet we live in potentially tense times. Perhaps it is time for me to come off my fence, and give some views of my own. We in the West have become very complacent, feeling superior in our reactions to those different from ourselves. It is easy to be snobbish to the great unwashed outside the gate of our cosy city. But, in my view, they are our fellow humans, our equals. We are all kith and kin, sharing a common humanity. We must take very seriously views which are radically unlike those of the 'bland consensus' of the secular West. Section Five of this book is devoted to discovering how this might be done.

Section Five

Religion and Tolerance: A Possible Perspective

I trust that by now we have come to some understanding of why the nations rage, and of the rôle played by religious nationalism in creating that wrath.

At first glance, the future might seem gloomy. No sooner do we finish one Cold War than various pundits start to predict a new one. War and brutal mass murder erupt on a scale not seen in Europe since the Holocaust. Americans, immunised by history and by safe distance from the kind of terrorism well known in Europe, begin to feel the rage of militant Islam at home as well as abroad.

International relations theorists, like Sir Harry Hinsley, came up with a theory in the 1970s which states that the consequences of nuclear war would be so dreadful, if not terminal, that conflict between the Superpowers would be unlikely. The Hinsley thesis was not merely an adjunct of deterrence theory – nuclear bombs deter war. Rather it was part of a longer-scale historic theory. This was that the more complex war becomes, the higher the stakes become, the less likely that war is to happen. In this scenario, nuclear weapons are simply the most complex of all weapons in their potential for damaging both victim and aggressor.

To the considerable relief of millions in both East and West, the end of the Cold War removed the threat of a Superpower conflict leading not to victory for one side or another, but to the aptly-named MAD or mutually assured destruction. World War III, had it taken place, could have been the assured destruction of the human race, if the 'nuclear winter' some scientists feared destroyed those who somehow managed to survive the nuclear exchanges themselves. As someone who lives in the eastern part of England, near many US Air Force bases, this was good news since I would almost certainly have died in any first strike of Soviet nuclear missiles against American bombers in Britain.

The bad news is that, since war no longer means nuclear devastation, the consequences of going to war have ceased to be so absolute. Wars are no longer proxies, with the pawn of one Superpower attacking another. Escalation of war will no longer lead to global Superpower Armageddon and the end of humanity.

War is therefore feasible in a way that it has not been since the invention of the atomic bomb. Serbia can invade Bosnia and slaughter its inhabitants without fear of a nuclear strike on Belgrade. In that sense, the world is not a safer place, but more dangerous.

The one remaining Superpower, the USA, might come to your aid if you are attacked. But, as Croats and Bosnians found to their cost, it might choose not to as well.

The British-born Yale historian, Paul Kennedy, has come up with the interesting theory of imperial over-stretch. In his bestseller, *The Rise and Fall of the Great*

Powers, he points out that many Great Powers – sixteenth-century Spain, twentieth-century Britain, for example – begin to stretch their resources too far. In the end, their imperial obligations become too much and they have to abandon them. The USA, he argues, might be in exactly that position as the twenty-first century dawns. The burdens of being the world's policeman will be too much.

The tremendous length of time that it took the United Nations to act in Bosnia shows that the UN will find it hard to assume the global policeman rôle. In any case, the UN is only the sum of its members, and if they disagree among themselves, then the UN will be powerless.

If religion is to be a key component of future conflict, as some argue, then religion can surely be part of the solution as well as the cause of the problem. If the UN is toothless, and America is severely overstretched, then maybe those of us who believe in some of the world's major faiths can try to ensure that religion creates a climate of peace, not one of nationalistic war.

Chapter 12, 'The Parable of the Good Bosnian Muslim', aims to work out a possible optimistic scenario in which this happens. It would be based not on what has been called the 'bland consensus' of McWorld, but on a recognition of the key rôle of religion in world affairs and international relations. We can give honest acknowledgment of profound religious differences with no woolly pretence that such distinctions do not exist. It would seek to heal the political and cultural splits within Christianity, without asking for the abandonment of deeply-held theological distinctive characteristics. It would build bridges with Islam because it would not be based on the kind of flabby secularism which Islam so despises.

Why the Nations Rage

It may not work. Wars may continue to be fought, and nations to rage against one another. But unless we try, we may not have a chance to do so for very long.

12

The Parable of
the Good Bosnian Muslim

The nature of Christianity, with three mainstreams of
Orthodoxy, Catholicism and Protestantism, and many
subdivisions within the last of these, shows how exceptionally difficult it is to get any consensus on many of the
key issues.

In trying to come to any kind of Christian perspective
on nationalism, anyone who attempts a conclusion is
bound to be under attack from many sides, probably
all at once. In addition, these will not be related to the
attacker's theology on other issues. When it comes to my
own views on nationalism, Christians with whom I am
in fullest agreement on other significant doctrinal issues
disagree with me profoundly and I with them.

A Christian perspective?
At the beginning of this book, we saw how historians aim
to be objective, while recognising that this goal might
not, in reality, be obtainable. When it comes to some
Christian-based reflections on nationalism – Christianity
being the faith community from which I come – I am
very aware that I am entering a minefield.

The dictum 'I am objective, but you are prejudiced' is

highly applicable here. Nationalism goes to the core of our self-identity. To attack beliefs in this area, however gently or 'objectively' one tries to do it, can arouse the deepest passions and hostilities. All Christians have a tendency to baptise their own views on particular subjects and elevate those particular feelings into absolute Christian truth. I am not immune, as people who read this chapter might well discover. What I can say in my defence is that people reading this chapter are not immune either! The parable Christ told of the mote and the beam, in which we tend to condemn someone for the tiny mote in their eye while cheerfully ignoring the huge beam in our own, applies as much to the debate on nationalism as it does to other contentious subjects.

With those important caveats in mind, let us look at some possible Christian perspectives on nationalism. I take them from the Bible rather than from any writer or theologian. I do so because the Bible is something that all Christians, of whatever description, are supposed to have in common.

Back to the Garden
'Racism is wrong.' I would trust that all well-meaning people would be in happy accord with such a statement. The converse, that unity among all kinds of humanity is right, should equally be a point of assent for people of goodwill.

Yet generalised statements such as these can, in an age of violence and hatred, seem rather mushy: true but woolly, if you like. While, like Le Carré's fictional character, George Smiley, it might be better to be a sentimental woolly liberal than a murderous fanatic, in today's harsh world sentiment is not enough.

Salvation religions believe what they teach to be true. At the core of both Christianity and Judaism is a belief in the central unity of the entire human race. We are *one* race, created in the image of God. This is the message of the Genesis story, one now given an unusual backing by the 'Out of Africa' DNA geneticists.

This controversial theory, invented by geneticists at University of California, Berkeley, and confirmed by experts at London's Natural History Museum, is far from religious. Indeed, one gets the impression that when *Time* and *Newsweek* called it the 'Eve theory' (that we all descend, apparently, from one 'mitochondrial' [= maternally inherited] DNA ancestress in Africa), the scientists putting it forward were embarrassed. The last thing they wanted was to be thought of as helpful to Christian creationists. As with all scientific theories as well as supporters, it has its zealous opponents, especially among paleontologists. Since I am no geneticist, I cannot say whether such a theory has scientific credibility. Pleasant though it would be to support something which demonstrated objectively and scientifically that we are indisputably *one* race, I have to leave such conclusions to others.

The oneness of humanity

It is encouraging, though, that some scientists are supporting the concept which many religions, not just Jewish or Christian, propound on the oneness of the human species. This is a theological proposition which does not depend on 'emigrationist' or 'diffusionist' scientific theories. It is at the heart of Christ's message and of the Ten Commandments, to love our neighbour as ourselves. Hatred is wrong for a reason – we are *all* in God's image, we are *all* one family.

The Church itself is to be a microcosm of the oneness of humanity. In the Church universal, all its members are God's people on earth. Christ, in giving the 'Great Commission' instructed his disciples to spread the news to *every* nation. No one was to be exempt, no one was undeserving. The message of Christianity was *universal*. As the Apostle Paul put it, in Christ all are made one. There are no Jews, Greeks, slave or free, male or female – *all* are one. Within Christianity there are no racial divisions, no class distinctions, no gender divisions. A black female slave and a wealthy male Roman were equal before God if they were both Christians, they were fully brother and sister in Christ, one not more special than the other.

It is not surprising, given the revolutionary nature of this teaching, that people regarded the early Christians as folk who were turning the world upside down. In a society which had plenty of racism, sexism and privilege, for these things to be of no importance was genuinely radical.

Christian concepts of self-identity
Christianity, as any personal faith, is the ultimate self-identity and a very complete form of belonging. This was something which some early Christians themselves, like St Peter, found hard to cope with at first. He was used to Jewish national distinctive features. For him to understand that the Jew/Gentile barrier had been demolished by the new Christian Church took a while, as the Bible is honest enough to tell us. Paul, too, had been very nationalistic, a proud member of the Pharisees, a Jewish religious grouping who had done much to keep Jewish cultural and separatist traditions alive. Now he was consorting with former pagans, people who ate meat which was not Kosher, the kind of individuals with whom no Pharisee would ever have wished to associate.

The Christian Church, therefore, is a model, or paradigm, or God's ideal. As Paul discovered when asked to take the message to Europe, the gospel is international.

The noted Christian author, John Stott, has called the church a 'supranational community' something that was apparent from the day of Pentecost, when St Luke carefully describes the broad ethnic and racial diversity of those who became Christians on that day.

Christianity as a deterritorialised religion

In the context of our theme of territoriality, one can say that Christianity is a *deterritorialised* faith. This too was apparent at Pentecost – Luke emphasises that everyone heard the gospel *in their own language*. Unlike Islam, another international faith, Christianity has no official language. From St Jerome to the Good News Bible, Christians have translated the Bible into the languages of the people to whom they were preaching. Peter's concept of the 'priesthood of all believers' has, in practical terms, meant that Christians have a keen desire to study biblical teaching for themselves. This has necessitated careful translation, from internationally-used languages such as English or Spanish, to obscure tribal dialects spoken by as few as several hundred people. Not everybody has enjoyed this process: many Christians prefer the majestic words of a liturgy written when language was more image-filled than the rather basic popular language of today.

The consequence has been that Christianity has become truly worldwide. While those groups who want *every* people group to have heard the Christian message by AD 2000 might be being slightly optimistic, the fact that the goal of Christ's Great Commission is even in sight shows that no one nation is potentially excluded. Christianity embraces Silicon Valley to Stone Age civilisations, with all shades of humanity in between. Everyone is equal, from a Calcutta roadsweeper to a Fortune 500 Chief Executive Officer. God sees the faith, not the passport;

spiritual wealth, not economic. There is no nationalism in a Church where all the inhabitants are as one people under God. Peter, who used to be so particularist in his world-view discovered this and passed it on to us in his epistles.

A global faith

This marks a distinction from Old Testament times, when God's people and a particular race overlapped. Even there, though, the prophecies of men like Isaiah, Amos, Hosea and Jeremiah make clear that being born Jewish did not save you. It was righteousness that exalted a nation, not your genetic accident of birth. Those not born Jews could become Jewish, as the existence of proselytes shows us. (Naaman the Syrian would be the best known Old Testament example.) At the very beginning of the Jewish race itself, God told Abraham that through his descendants *all* the nations of the earth would be blessed.

In the story of the Tower of Babel, we see how nationalism was the result of sin. Humanity had been one. Now, because of its arrogance and rebelliousness against God, it was split. Nations were born, the realisation of the common bond of all humanity broken. With the coming of the Church, the curse of Babel is overcome. A Christian garbage collector in Los Angeles and a Christian investment banker in London have more in common with each other than they do with people from their own ethnic, racial, economic, social or gender backgrounds. A Swahili speaker, a Chinese speaker, a Quechua speaker and an English speaker who are all Christians may not understand each other's human languages. But they do share the language of Christian love and reconciliation. When I have seen a Christian Arab and Messianic Jew embrace, and in public, it was impossible to feel anything other than deeply moved.

The Parable of the Good Bosnian Muslim

Good Samaritans

Christ's parable of the Good Samaritan is the ultimate biblical teaching on the issue of religious nationalism. We interpret it as loving our neighbour as ourselves, or being good to despised people. To interpret it at the purely personal level is quite right.

But who is our neighbour? Is it just *my* neighbour? Is it simply showing Christian love to a family from an unpopular ethnic minority who come to live next door?

Christianity is, at the core, a faith of *individual* salvation. You cannot be born again for somebody else. We have a personal relationship with God as our individual heavenly father. But the New Testament continually emphasises the *corporate* nature of Christian faith as well.

The corporate nature of Christian practice

While the entry point is individual, we are together members of God's people on earth. We are not an atomised mass of individual molecules floating around. We are, as the foundational documents of Christianity teach us, the Body of Christ. What we do as Christians we do corporately as well as individually. We are members of the Church, and much New Testament teaching is about our collective responsibility, together, as Christians.

Nowadays, Christ's parable might be the Parable of the Good Bosnian Muslim (or the Good Serb or Good Croat). The Pharisee walking by is the religious nationalist. The Pharisees were the territorial religious nationalists of their day. The Samaritans were a national, despised enemy who had gone over to the other side centuries before, and were thereby deemed to be racially and spiritually contaminated: just like today's Bosnian Muslims. So when the Catholic Croat priest and the Serbian Orthodox

Archimandrite pass by the injured man, it is the Good Bosnian Muslim who helps him.

Loving our neighbour corporately means loving those of a different race or religious persuasion, affirming our common God-given humanity. This does not threaten our core spiritual values. We are not asking Orthodox, Muslim, Catholic or Protestant to give up any spiritual or doctrinal distinctive characteristics. The Samaritan did not make conversion to Samaritan religion a precondition of help, nor did the injured man make conversion to Judaism a precondition of accepting it.

Loving our enemies

Christ was a realist not a woolly idealist. When the Bible says that you should love your enemies or love those who treat you badly, people often miss the point of what he is saying. If you love your *enemy*, that means you *have* enemies. Having enemies is part of the human condition. So much mushy thinking today tries to forget or deny the existence of such a thing as an enemy. Christianity does not. But you must *love* your enemies, not massacre them, rape them, ethnically cleanse them. You must love neighbours – Muslims, Croats, Tutsis, bosses, business rivals – as *yourself*.

Christianity is about reconciliation, yet all too often it is against fellow 'Christians' that 'Christians' fight – rather like the Protestant ladies in Northern Ireland who were Protestants, not Christians, and who hated Catholics.

Citizens of heaven

Our citizenship, the New Testament emphasises, is in heaven. As Christ himself put it, Christians are in this world, but not of it. We may live in England, Rwanda, Serbia, but ultimately we are not English, Tutsi or Hutu, Croat or Serb. We are Christians, citizens of heaven,

God's believing people here on earth. Earth is a place of temporary sojourn, not the place of our ultimate destiny or belonging.

The nation-state, our ethnic group, cannot therefore command the Christian's complete obedience. There are some things which I can render to God alone, and this final allegiance is one such thing.

It is thus difficult, if not impossible, to see how a genuine Christian can be a nationalist. I can be proud of my country's good achievements, of much of its culture and of its healthy characteristics. Such features can, for a Christian, be seen as part of God's loving grace, things that thankfully and mercifully alleviate the full effects of humanity's fallenness. But that, scripturally speaking, is where it should stop.

There is a sense in which Christ was put to death for not being a nationalist. He refused to territorialise his kingdom. He refused to lead a nationalist rebellion against the Romans. This is not to condone Roman rule, simply a statement that this is not what Christ had come to earth to do. Barabbas the criminal was released, Jesus the innocent condemned, both at the request of the local nationalists. He was a king, but not in the sense that the religious nationalists of the day implied.

As we saw from Pentecost, the post-resurrection kingdom that Christ established was a multi-racial supra-national community. It is this that Christianity urgently needs to recover. Too much of this century has seen people killing each other in the name of God. What kind of image of Christianity has ethnic cleansing given to Muslims? Rwanda and Burundi are theoretically two of the most Christianised countries in Africa. They are among the most hate-filled on earth: as the *Independent* newspaper put it on 15 November 1996, an area now filled with 'satanic violence'. Northern Ireland has some of Europe's highest church attendance rates and equally some of its worst communal hatreds.

Prince of Peace

One of Christ's main appellations is 'Prince of Peace'. Peace is inherently incompatible with war and hatred. It is the recovery for all Christians, Protestant, Catholic and Orthodox alike, of love of neighbour and of love of peace, that must be central to a return to a genuinely, actively Christian self-identity and world-view.

Should this happen, the chances of religion being manipulated for mythic, nationalistic, territorial ends should be greatly diminished. Christians will be reaching out not just to each other, Orthodox Serb to Catholic Croat, Christian Tutsi to Christian Hutu, but to those of other races and beliefs. What I have called 'highest common factor unity' will not require us to give up any of our own beliefs. Orthodox Christians would not be required to submit to the Pope, nor would Catholics be compelled to abandon their interpretation of the Mass or Protestants their understanding of the priesthood of all believers. Tolerance does not mean abandonment of distinctions and differences. Rather it is permission to be different, to have distinct views without life-threatening consequences, to live together in peace despite racial, cultural or ethnic differences.

Orthodoxy and the spiritual nature of Christianity

Tolerance should help Orthodox Christians who feel under siege from the West. Christianity, properly understood, is not *territorial* but *spiritual*. Orthodox Christians who take their faith seriously, rather than wearing it as a tribal badge like the Protestant ladies in the story, can be helped to understand that they have more in common with their fellow Christians than they do with anyone else.

The Parable of the Good Bosnian Muslim

Rather than being terrified of Catholics or Protestants, they can work together towards common goals. Some Orthodox themselves have realised that they need to do more about the poor and underprivileged in their own societies, if only to prevent incoming Catholic and Protestant missionaries from assuming a monopoly on social concern. They could revive the missionary zeal of St Cyril and St Methodius, the great Orthodox preachers, and spread the gospel to the spiritually needy.

This might seem a pipe dream. Back in 1988, the fall of the Iron Curtain, the disappearance of Communism and the implosion of the Soviet Union might all have seemed pipe dreams too. The future is by definition unpredictable. However, if we are aware of the nature and causes of the problems we face, we can hope to effect positive changes. Catholics and Protestants were once as territorial as Orthodoxy is now. Germany, after being the cause for two world wars and the home of the Holocaust, has for decades now been a peaceful member of the family of nations. England and France are NATO and European Union partners despite nearly nine hundred years of armed conflict. Things have changed, and can do so again.

The dreams of an optimist?

An optimist, they say, is someone who believes that they live in the best of all possible worlds. The pessimist is someone who fears that the optimist may be right.

Both optimists and pessimists have had ample cause to assert the truth of their claims since 1989. Communism, with all its repression, has been overthrown in Europe. The genocide of Bosnia has shown that large-scale barbarities can exist in Europe in a way we thought had expired over fifty years ago.

The nations continue to rage, just as Christ said they

would, until the end of time. Things could get far worse. They may improve. Totalitarian States of any hue can fall. While I was writing this chapter, the last Romanian Communist leader was peacefully elected out of office, to be replaced by a candidate whose politics would have been inconceivable under Ceaucescu seven years earlier.

Currently, the Islamic dictatorships, whether pro-Western and Sunni, such as Saudi Arabia, or hostile and Shia, like Iran, look impregnable. Once, many areas of the world which are now monolithically Muslim were either Christian or had large Christian and Jewish minorities. Human rights activists regularly receive reports of people being executed secretly or imprisoned for conversion to Christianity. Only a few years ago I had a handbook of Christian prisoners behind the Iron Curtain. A year or two later, with the fall of the Iron Curtain, they were all free. Tolerant Muslims might gain control, granting similar freedoms in their countries. Maybe even Islam itself could give way to pluralism, tolerance and democracy.

Is this a pipe dream? Perhaps, then possibly as much a pipe dream as someone who would have predicted the fall of Communism and the end to the threat of nuclear holocaust in 1989.

Giving peace a chance

Nationalism has been with us a long time. It will surely be with us for a while longer in some guise or another. But to be informed is to be forearmed. We have ignored religion as a force in contemporary nationalism to the detriment of thousands of innocent people who have lost their lives in vicious conflict.

To understand is to be able to act. If we engage with the protagonists in language that they can understand, they may be willing to talk, rather than dismiss us as bland Western materialists. Not every Orthodox Archbishop

The Parable of the Good Bosnian Muslim

or Muslim Imam is totalitarian. Some might be open to understanding a different point of view. Countries like Russia and Romania still have many traces of their past, and these scars might take years to heal. At least we are on the way.

The nations rage. If we know the reason why, peace will always have a chance.

Appendix A

Nationalism: A Glossary of Specialist Terms

Civic nationalism: The civic variety of nationalism includes within it everyone living in a particular country. The United States is a good example of a civic nationalist country. You can be a loyal American citizen, whatever your ethnic background, religion or race. Everyone is *included*.

Clash of civilisations: This phrase was popularised by Harvard Professor Samuel Huntington in articles and a book of this name. His thesis, which is controversial, states that all of humanity is divided into certain core groupings or 'civilisations'. The prime basis of a civilisation is religious: Western, Orthodox, Islamic, Hindu, etc. I have devoted Chapter 5 to Huntington's views. They have relevance to the notion of religious nationalism and war. Huntington believes that future conflict will be based on clashes, and maybe even wars, between religion-based civilisations.

Ethnic cleansing: The exclusion of an ethnic grouping from a country or area by forced exile or murder.

Ethnic nationalism: This states that your prime loyalty

is to your ethnic grouping and to your nation-state. A nation-state is the political expression of the dominant ethnic group within it. For example, in Serbia, only those of Serbian ancestry are truly Serbs. Serbia is the nation-state of the Serb people. People in Serbia who are not of Serb ancestry are therefore *excluded* from the Serb nation-state. This has led to *ethnic cleansing*, the exclusion or 'cleansing' of a country by forced exile or murder of all who do not belong to the Serb race. This concept is explained in some detail in Sections One and Two.

Nationalism: This is usually held to mean an ideology which states that an individual's primary secular loyalty is to the nation-state. The *Encyclopaedia Britannica* gives such a definition.

Palingenetic: The word used by Roger Griffin of Oxford Brookes University to mean a form of ultra-nationalism which uses myths to bolster its case. Nazi Germany and the myth of the German, or Aryan, Master Race is the example which Griffin himself uses. I argue in this book that Serbian religious nationalism can also be described by this term.

Religious nationalism: This ideology says that your religion and your ethnic identity go hand in hand. If you are a loyal subject of country X, then you *must* believe in religion Y to be a proper national of that State. The converse can also apply in some cases: loyal followers of religion Y are members or supporters of country X. Thus, nationalism is not simply an ideology which demands that an individual's prime *secular* loyalty is to the nation, but their *religious* loyalty as well. The nature and consequences of religious nationalism form the main theme of the book.

Appendix B

Ethnic Groups in
the Former Yugoslavia

One of the best and most tragic examples of religious nationalism today is the war in the former Yugoslavia. It might be helpful to have a short description of the main players. I have used the word ethnic, rather than nations, since not all ethnic groups had nations of their own.

Yugoslavia as such only existed from 1918 to 1941 and again from 1945 to 1991. Not even in Roman times was it ever under the same political administration. Up until 1918, when it came into being, the northern part was in the Catholic Austro-Hungarian Empire. Much of the coastal part (Dalmatia) was under the rule of Venice, the city-state which existed until 1797, when it was defeated by Napoleon. The coastal regions were under Austrian rule again until 1918. All these regions are Catholic in faith.

The southern part was independent until the fourteenth century, when it was conquered by the Muslim Ottoman Empire. The region, whose inhabitants are Orthodox in faith, gained effective independence in the mid-nineteenth century.

The central part was also conquered by the Ottomans and remained under their rule until 1878 (legally until

1908). This area, Bosnia-Herzegovina, saw many conversions to Islam. The area has in it Catholic and Orthodox Christians, and Muslims. A much fuller story is given in Section Three.

The former Yugoslavia had several republics within it, each of which has now become independent. Some republics had more than one ethnic grouping, and this has been a major cause of war. Two have been involved in very little fighting, and are predominantly at peace. For that reason, I have not described them in detail elsewhere. These are Macedonia and Slovenia.

Following is an alphabetical listing of the former Yugoslavia's republics and a somewhat brief description of each.

Bosnia: Unlike Croatia or Serbia, Bosnia has no predominant ethnic or religious majorities. Even if it is mainly 'Bosnian', that in itself is a contentious statement, since many Croats and Serbs deny the separate existence of Bosnians in their own right, claiming instead that they are really Croatian or Serbian. As well as Catholics and Orthodox, Bosnia has a large Muslim minority, which makes up the biggest simple minority in Bosnia itself. The lack of an ethnic or religious majority led to much vicious fighting and mass murder in the attempt to create one.

Much of Section Three is devoted to the intricacies of Bosnia, and the reason for the carnage which has taken place there. It is perhaps unique in being a country where Islam, Catholic Christianity and Orthodox Christianity all clash with one another. This makes it the best, but also the most tragic, part of the world in which to examine religious nationalism. In Tito's Yugoslavia, Bosnians of all descriptions managed to live together without bloodshed. The Bosnian capital, Sarajevo, was a showpiece city of inter-ethnic togetherness, and was the site for one of the Winter Olympics. Now Sarajevo, and Bosnia as a country, are synonymous with some of the most barbaric examples of conflict since the Nazi atrocities of World War II.

Bosnia, and what happened there, is the reason why a study of religious nationalism is so important. If we do not learn the lessons of Bosnia, and how to prevent such conflict from taking place again, then there may be many more Bosnias ahead of us.

Croatia: One of the republics in which much of the recent fighting has taken place. It is mainly *Croat* ethnically and *Catholic* in its religious expression. Present-day Croatia is a mix of the old Croatian kingdom along with the coastal province of Dalmatia, which is also ethnically Croat, but with strong Venetian (Italian) cultural links. Unfortunately for the Croats, Croatia had an historically *Serb* population along its southern border. These Serbs were brought into the country in Habsburg times, to form the (Austrian) 'Military Frontier' against further Ottoman invasion. In the recent fighting, Serbia seized much of this region, known as the Krajina, because the 'Krajina Serbs' ostensibly needed protection against the Croats. Subsequently, with not a little help from the Americans, Croatia reconquered this region. They expelled the Serbs, many of whose families had lived there for centuries. This was in revenge for Croats from the eastern part of Croatia (called Slavonia) who had been expelled, or 'ethnically cleansed' when Serbia tried to prevent Croatia from becoming independent.

Dalmatia: see **Croatia**.

Kossovo: One of two self-governing regions within Serbia during the rule of Tito (see **Serbia**). This area was predominantly ethnically *Albanian*, and therefore had a mainly *Muslim* population. Unfortunately for the Albanian majority, Serbia's most sacred site, *Kossovo Polje*, the place where Serb armies were defeated in 1389, is at the heart of the province. Serb nationalists never accepted Kossovo's semi-independence, and when Yugoslavia broke up, the Serbs abolished provincial independence and re-absorbed it into Serbia proper.

Krajina: see **Croatia**.

Macedonia: This is a country whose ethnic mix should have led to terrible fighting, but for wise leadership and the presence of American troops from early on. Many say that *Macedonians* are a genuine Slavic race of their own. Others dispute this. Bulgaria say that Macedonians are really Bulgarians. Serbia calls Macedonia 'Southern Serbia'. Greece regards its use of the name Macedonia as an insult, since Greeks regard Macedonia as being the proper name for northern Greece. Macedonians at least have the Orthodox form of Christianity in common with Serbs, Bulgarians and Greeks. Macedonia has a large *Albanian* minority, the Albanians being a completely unrelated ethnic group, many of whom are Muslim by religion.

Montenegro: Along with Serbia, this country forms the rump of the old Yugoslavia. *Montenegrins* are Orthodox and very closely related to the *Serbs*, so further explanation will come under the heading, **Serbia.**

Serbia: Along with Montenegro, this country forms the rump of the old Yugoslavia. Nearly all of Serbia proper is ethnically Serb. Serbs are Orthodox. Tito, the Communist ruler of Yugoslavia for thirty years after the Second World War, was not a Serb and wanted to restrict their power. He created two self-governing regions within Serbia, both of which had majority non-Serb populations, but which still had big Serb minorities. These were **Kossovo** and **Voivodina** (see separate entries).

Slavonia: see **Croatia.**

Slovenia: overwhelmingly *Slovene* ethnically and *Catholic* in religion.

Voivodina: One of two autonomous regions within Serbia during the rule of Tito (see **Serbia**). Ethnically speaking, this province was a mosaic, with ethnic *Romanians* and ethnic *Hungarians* living there as well as *Serbs*. Like Kossovo, this province was also reabsorbed when Yugoslavia split.

Appendix C

A Rapid-glance Chart of the Former Yugoslavia and Related Peoples

The following summary gives country, ethnic group(s) and religion(s).

Albania: Albania is a separate country and was never part of Yugoslavia. The reason that Albanians are in this chart is that there are huge *Albanian* minorities in both Serbia and Macedonia. Albanians are ethnically unrelated to the Slavs, and may possibly be descended from the ancient *Illyrians*, the name given to the inhabitants of the Balkans in Roman times, long before the Slavs entered the peninsula. Most Albanians, maybe over 70 per cent, are Muslim.

Bogomils: The Bogomils were a religious group, whose views were regarded as heretical by all parts of the Christian Church in the Middle Ages. Many Bogomils lived in present-day Bosnia. Nationalist Serbs and Croats claim that the fifteenth-century Bogomils converted *en masse* to Islam after the Ottoman invasions, and that today's Bosnian Muslims are their descendants. As with the separate identity of the Bosnians as a Slavic group in their own right, this is a hotly disputed claim.

Bosnia: The biggest minority is Bosnian Muslim. The

next biggest is Serbian/Orthodox (the 'Bosnian Serbs') and the smallest is Croat/Catholic (the 'Bosnian Croats'). Some people in Bosnia simply see themselves as Bosnian regardless of ethnic origin or religion. Serb and Croat nationalists deny that a separate Bosnian identity exists.

Croatia: Mainly Croat and Catholic, but formerly with a large Serb minority.

Macedonia: Predominantly Macedonian/Orthodox, but with an Albanian/Muslim minority. Some claim that the Macedonians are Serb or Bulgarian in racial origin.

Serbia/Montenegro: Mainly Serb and Orthodox, but with a large Albanian/Muslim minority in Kossovo and many nationalities in Voivodina. Together Serbia and Montenegro combine to form the rump Republic of Yugoslavia, with the much larger Serbia as the predominant partner.

Slovenia: Slovene and Catholic.

Appendix D

Some Past Rulers of
Parts of the Former Yugoslavia

Austria: Most of present-day *Slovenia* used to be called the *Duchy of Carniola* and was under Austrian rule for centuries until 1918.

The Austro-Hungarian Empire: Strictly speaking, this did not exist until 1867. But in practice, it existed from 1526, when the Archduke Ferdinand of Austria became King of Hungary. *Bosnia* was under Austro-Hungarian rule from 1878 to 1918, and was legally annexed to that Empire in 1908.

The Byzantine Empire: Strictly speaking, this was no more than a continuation of the eastern half of the old Roman Empire itself. The western part of the Empire, based on Rome, fell to invading barbarians in 476. The eastern part, by contrast, survived nearly another thousand years, until 1453. Its capital was the city of *Byzantium*, which the Roman Emperor, Constantine the Great, refounded as *Constantinople* in AD 324. (This city still exists, and is called *Istanbul*). While theoretically the Roman Empire continued, the Byzantine Empire was effectively Greek, rather than Roman in character, culture and language.

Nearly all the Balkan peninsula was under Byzantine rule for hundreds of years, including what is now Serbia, Montenegro and Macedonia. The Serbs managed to gain independence and for a while had an Empire of their own, under Stephan Dushan.

Hungary: Hungary conquered *Croatia* in the early Middle Ages (excluding Dalmatia, which became Venetian). Croatia remained under Hungarian rule until 1918. Some say that the medieval kingdom of *Bosnia* was also under Hungarian rule, while others emphasise the considerable autonomy and practical independence of the native Bosnian kings. Either way, Bosnia was conquered by the Ottoman Turks in the fifteenth century.

The Ottoman Empire: The Ottoman Turks were a tribe from Central Asia that conquered what is now called Turkey, after the ethnic group who successfully seized it from the Byzantine Empire.

The Ottomans were *Muslims*, following the teachings of the founder of the Islamic faith, the prophet Muhammad. The Ottoman dynasty founded a vast Empire, which at its peak stretched from the Atlantic coast of Africa to today's Iran/Pakistan border. (Not all these territories were under Ottoman rule all the time, but it gives you an idea of its size. The Ottoman Empire was also long-lasting, surviving right up until 1918, when it lost to the Allies in the First World War.)

The Ottoman Sultan was also *Caliph*, the spiritual head of the Islamic religion, as well as the political ruler of the Empire. Thus, under their rule, religious and political elements were completely intertwined.

All of present-day Serbia, Montenegro, Macedonia and Bosnia fell to the Turks in the fourteenth and fifteenth centuries, and remained under Ottoman rule until the nineteenth century. The Ottomans divided their subjects not ethnically, but *religiously*. This was the *millet* system. Conversion to Islam held political and economic advantages. Many of the Slavic subjects of the Ottomans converted consequently to Islam, with the repercussions for today's Bosnian Muslims that have been sadly all too clear in relation to their ethnic cousins, the Serbs.

The Roman Empire: Much of the former Yugoslavia was part of the Roman province of *Illyria*, but some of today's Slovenia, especially *Istria*, was part of Italy itself.

The Venetian Empire: Venice is now a famous and historic Italian city. But until the end of the eighteenth century, it was an independent republic, under a ruler called the Doge. (Shakespeare's two plays, *The Merchant of Venice* and *Othello*, feature the republic.) Venice at one stage had a large Mediterranean Empire, which included Cyprus and Crete. It ruled the Adriatic coast of what became Yugoslavia, the province being called *Dalmatia*. Some parts of the old Roman Istria and Venetian Dalmatia remained part of Italy right up until 1945. Most of Dalmatia, however, became Austrian in 1815 and part of Yugoslavia in 1918.

Appendix E

Byzantium, Rome and the Split of Christianity

The East/West Roman split is important religiously as well as politically. Constantine the Great was the Emperor who made Christianity the official religion of the Roman Empire. In theory, Christianity remained a united religion until 1054. In practice, however, Western Christians followed the lead of the head of the Church in the old Western Roman capital, Rome. Today the Pope has the office of Bishop of Rome as one of his most important titles. Followers of the Bishop of Rome became known as *Roman Catholics* or simply *Catholics*, for short. Catholic means *universal* and the Catholic Church still claims to be the true and universal form of Christianity to this day. In the surviving Eastern half, Christianity remained the official religion. However, whereas the West dissolved into numerous barbarian kingdoms, the East remained united. Consequently, the link between Church and State remained far stronger, with the head of the Church being under the Emperor's control.

Doctrinal differences increased between the two halves of Christianity, with the formal split occurring in 1054. The Eastern half became known as the *Orthodox Church*, since it, too, claimed to be the true, or Orthodox, form of Christian faith.

So the split in versions of Christianity, Catholic and Orthodox, which marks the former Yugoslavia, can be seen to be the political result of a religious division over nine hundred years ago.

Notes

Section One: Nationalism and Self-Identity

1. Many variants of religious nationalism have been propounded. Huntington's is simply one of these, but possibly one of the best known and most influential.

Chapter 1 A Question of Identity

1. Tito was the ruler of the country from liberation in 1945 until his death over thirty years later.
2. This was James Baker, the United States Secretary of State. We will look at the fall of Yugoslavia in much more detail later, as it is a study *par excellence* of the rise of religious nationalism.
3. Although atrocities against the Jews were tragically evident in 1938, the true depth of the mass killing that we call the Holocaust did not begin *en masse* until after the war had begun.
4. As we will see, neither the Nazi regime nor the Serbs have been by any means unique in their modern-day application of ethnic cleansing.
5. In America, Ulster Scots are called Scotch-Irish, which should mean the same, although I doubt if many a Protestant Ulsterman would like to be called Irish of any description.
6. See his excellent book, *Blood and Belonging*, based upon the television series of the same name.

Notes

7. For example, Neal Ascherson's illuminating article in the May 1996 edition of *Prospect*.

8. See most recently Linda Colley's book, *Britons: Forging the Nation: 1707–1837* (London: Yale University Press, 1992). Arguably much of the 'Whig interpretation of history' was built on the notion of British Protestantism, and Liah Greenfeld has discussed this also in *Nationalism: Five Roads to Modernity* (Cambridge, Mass.: Harvard University Press, 1992).

9. Significantly, in some countries IFES includes Catholic students as well. For instance, in the USA, there is now the phenomenon known as 'Evangelical Catholics'. Many Catholic friends of mine in the USA would certainly fall into this category. However, in some countries, it was the students themselves who strongly opposed Catholic students from being admitted into the campus group. This was often because of very recent history of active persecution by Catholics of Protestant minorities, whether social, as in Austria, or political/legal, as in Spain, a country in which some forms of Protestant belief were actually illegal until as recently as the 1970s. As we shall see later, religious nationalism was all too often the cause of this intolerance, and of making Catholicism in Spain very different from that in the UK or USA.

10. The Montenegrins, closely akin ethnically to the Serbs, were the one group that liberated themselves early on from foreign domination, only to lose their independence in 1918.

11. We spoke together in French: Romanian is a romance language, derived ultimately from the Roman soldiers settled in the old Roman frontier province of Dacia. So just to add to the mosaic, Romanians are therefore not Slavic at all.

12. When I stayed in the region once, everyone watched the Wimbledon tennis championships on Italian television instead of Yugoslav.

13. The best analogy here is probably British English and American English: two languages that are inherently the same but which have increasing numbers of words unique

to their own variant, as unwary American travellers to the UK sometimes discover.

14. Slovenia is blessed with the fact that it is overwhelmingly Slovene both ethnically and politically.

Chapter 2 The New World *Dis*order

1. Many commentators also think that 'the modern age' or the 'Enlightenment era' is over as well; the 'two-hundred-year modernity project' is over. People who hold this view range from post-modernists, for whom any kind of irrationality is now acceptable, to Christian thinkers and theologians who advocate that secularism is now on the wane and that we are returning to a pre-Enlightenment Age of Faith. (Professor Thomas Oden of Drew University in New Jersey has made some fascinating and very insightful comments on this issue, including remarks made at the Oxford Centre for Mission Studies conference on modernity in Oxford in 1996.) But, while it is pleasant to think that an Age of Faith is on the way back, much depends on the *kind* of faith to which people are returning after the evident failure of secularist Marxism.

2. See the famous book by Norman Cohn, *The Pursuit of the Millennium*, in which he makes a convincing case that Marxism was a kind of millenarian or messianic belief system, albeit entirely secular rather than overtly religious (Paladin edition, 1970, pp. 108–9).

3. A view completely demolished as 'historicist' by the great Austrian (later British) political philosopher, Sir Karl Popper. As Benjamin Franklin accurately pointed out, the only things that are truly inevitable are death and taxes.

4. For example, Eric Hobsbawm, whose book *National-ism*, written at the time of the fall of the Berlin Wall, seemed to predict that nationalism would fade away. My description of Hobsbawm's rather rose-coloured spectacle view is British understatement compared to the wonderfully trenchant denunciation that Senator Daniel Patrick Moynihan gave in a lecture series in Oxford, now published by OUP as *Pandaemonium*.

5. Some people, of course, regard American liberal capitalism as thoroughly malign. However, they are often people
   who live in prosperous Western countries, or who have
   access to plenty of material comforts through being part
   of the national élite.
6. See also the many books by Christopher Hill, of Oxford
   University, on the Levellers, Diggers, Fifth Monarchy
   Men and other idealistic groups in England in the seventeenth century. Their millenarian views were both political
   and strongly influenced by their understanding of biblical
   Christian teaching.
7. In a very influential article, 'The Bent Twig: A Note on
   Nationalism', *Foreign Affairs*, vol. 51, 1972, pp. 11–30;
   reprinted as 'Nationalism: Past Neglect and Present
   Power' in the anthology of his work entitled *Against
   the Current* in 1979, pp. 333–355.
8. 'Nationalism', *Against the Current*, p. 337.
9. Ibid., p. 337.
10. Ibid., p. 337.
11. Ibid., p. 345.
12. Moynihan, *Pandaemonium: Ethnicity in International
    Politics* (OUP, 1993), p. 80. A thoughtful and helpful
    analysis.
13. *Pandaemonium*, p. 83.
14. See, for example, Norman Cigar, *Genocide in Bosnia:
    The Policy of Ethnic Cleansing* (Texas A & M University
    Press, 1996). The author is part of the US Marine Corps
    School of Advanced War-fighting. He shows clearly that
    the Serbs were by no means as innocent in the war as they
    now make out. The Serb Royalist forces, the Cetniks, were
    as keen to prevent Tito's Partisan (= mainly Communist)
    forces from gaining power after the war as they were to see
    the German and Italian Axis Powers from being defeated.
    Consequently many Serbs collaborated in varying degrees
    with the Axis to this end. Tito was not a Serb – he was
    part Croat, part Slovene, and many Croats fought with the
    Partisans against both the Axis and the nationalist forces,
    the Serb Cetniks and the Croat Ustase. So some Croats
    were on the 'good' side and some Serbs on the 'bad'. A

more popular version of much of the fighting can be seen in the Alistair Maclean story filmed as *Force 10 from Navarrone* with Harrison Ford and Edward Fox, which shows clearly that many Serbs fought on the Axis side.
15. Michael Ignatieff, *Blood and Belonging* (London: Chatto & Windus, 1993), p. 16.
16. Ibid., p. 2.
17. Ibid., p. 3.
18. Ibid., p. 3.
19. Ibid., p. 16.

Chapter 3 Imaginary Kingdoms

1. Anderson is also admired by post-modernists who react against the Marxist notion that objectivity and certainty are possible. The post-modernist interpretation, or 'discourse', is even more complex – those wishing to follow it up can consult the bibliography.
2. Anthony D. Smith, *The Ethnic Origins of Nations* (Basil Blackwell, 1986), pp. 6–18. This quotation comes at the end of Chapter 1, which is a very helpful summary of much of the debate.
3. Charles A. Kupchan (ed.), *Nationalism and Nationalities in the New Europe* (Ithaca, NY: Cornell University Press, 1995).

Section Two: Religion and Nationalism: The Origins of Conflict

1. Unfortunately, I was unable to include an analysis as this book came out just before I handed my own manuscript in to the publisher.

Chapter 4 The Field of Blackbirds

1. Scottish nationalists have sometimes said that if Scotland had remained politically separate, Scottish English dialect distinctions might have caused a separate form of English to appear. While we cannot ever know what might have been, the illustration reinforces the point.
2. Serbia and Montenegro are technically mixed, still calling

themselves Yugoslavia, but Serbia is the part that matters.

3. As Moorish Spain shows, Muslims could be more benign to minorities than were Christians of the same period. In fact, when newly reconquered Christian Spain expelled the former Moorish rulers, the Christians soon instituted the violent persecution of the remaining Jews and Muslims. When the Spanish Jews, the Ladinos, were expelled from Spain, it was in the Turkish-ruled Balkans that they found safety and tolerance. The Bulgarian-born Nobel Prize winner, Elias Canetti, is descended from such people. It was the supposedly Christian Germans who set out to destroy the Ladino Jews in the Holocaust, after centuries of peace and tranquillity under the Muslim Ottoman Empire.

4. David Rieff's important book, *Slaughterhouse: Bosnia and the Failure of the West* (New York: Simon & Schuster 1995), gives very helpful documentation on this issue as well.

Chapter 5 The Clash of Civilisations

1. 'The Clash of Civilizations?', *Foreign Affairs*, vol. 72, no. 3, Summer 1993, pp. 22–49. Huntington is Eaton Professor of the Science of Government at Harvard University, and Director of their Olin Institute for Strategic Studies. Now published in book form as *The Clash of Civilizations and the Remaking of World Order* (New York: Simon & Schuster, 1996).

2. Anthony D. Smith, *The Ethnic Origin of Nations* (Oxford: Blackwell, 1986), especially pp. 119–125.

3. Ibid. The whole of Chapter 5 is important reading (pp. 92–125).

4. Ibid., on the issue of Islam as a 'salvation religion'.

5. Bernard Lewis, 'The Roots of Muslim Rage', *Atlantic Monthly*, no. 266, September 1990. The article was the journal's lead story.

6. Ibid., p. 60.

7. Benjamin R. Barber, *Jihad versus McWorld* (New York: Times Books, 1995).

8. Samuel Huntington, 'The West and the Rest', *Prospect*, Issue 16, February 1997, p. 35.

9. Mark Jürgensmeyer, *The New Cold War? Religious Nationalism Confronts the Secular State* (University of Oklahoma Press, 1993).
10. Ibid., pp. 1–2.
11. Ibid., p. 2.
12. Ibid., p. 3.
13. Ibid., p. 3.
14. Ibid., p. 4; see also p. 7.
15. Ibid., p. 15.
16. Huntington, 'The Clash of Civilizations?', *Foreign Affairs*, p. 22. See pp. 22–25 for the core of the argument.
17. Ibid., p. 24.
18. Ibid., p. 25.
19. Ibid., p. 27.
20. Harold Isaacs, *Idols of the Tribe*, p. 1; quoted in Daniel Patrick Moynihan *Pandaemonium*, p. 65.
21. *Pandaemonium*, p. 64.
22. Ibid., p. 64.
23. Ibid., p. 64.
24. Ibid., pp. 41–42, quoting his own earlier article in *Newsweek*.
25. Anthony D. Smith, *Nationalism in the Twentieth Century* (Martin Robertson 1979).
26. 'Tribalism Revisited', *The Economist*, December 21, 1991, p. 45 (US edition).
27. George Kennan, *Around the Cragged Hill* (New York: W.W. Norton, 1992), p. 73.
28. Isaiah Berlin, 'Two Concepts of Nationalism', *New York Review of Books*, Nov. 21, 1991, p. 22.
29. Donald L. Horowitz, *Ethnic Groups in Conflict* (University of California Press, 1985), p. 13.
30. This is taken from a superb series by Robert Fisk in *The Independent* in October 1996.
31. Quoted in *Pandaemonium*, p. 145.
32. *Pandaemonium*, pp. 53–54.

Chapter 6 The Paradise of Belonging

1. *Richard II*, Act II, Scene 1, lines 40–68.
2. Review by Gerasimos Augustinos of Michael Ignatieff,

Blood and Belonging in *Mediterranean Quarterly*, vol. 6, no. 3, Summer 1995, p. 123.

3. Roger Griffin, *The Nature of Fascism* (Routledge: London, 1993) and (ed.) *Fascism* (Oxford Readers Series, OUP, Oxford, 1995), pp. 32–36.
4. Daniel Goldhagen, *Hitler's Willing Executioners* (London: Little Brown, 1996).
5. See his book, *Landscape and Memory* (London: Harper-Collins, 1995), which was also a television series.
6. Goering's enthusiasm for hunting was legendary.
7. Quoted in Baigent and Leigh, *Secret Germany* (Jonathan Cape, 1994), p. 226.
8. Jung, reference.; quoted in Baigent and Leigh, *Secret Germany*, p. 226.
9. Baigent and Leigh, *Secret Germany*, p. 226.
10. Ibid., p. 225.
11. For example, *Plotting Hitler's Death* on the resistance to Hitler. A review in the 22 November 1996 issue of the *Times Literary Supplement* (TLS) argues that only mentioned some of the resistance movements, and that the actual amount of resistance was therefore greater. A BBC television Everyman drama documentary in 1996 gave considerable detail about the Kreisau circle, the Christian-based resistance circle.
12. For example, *Secret Germany*. America has many books published about Nazism and the occult, some rather weird in themselves.
13. Quoted in *Secret Germany*, p. 226.
14. Quoted in *Secret Germany*, p. 227.
15. Quoted in *Secret Germany*, pp. 227–228.

Chapter 7 Blasphemers of Our Country's Faith

1. I am very grateful to Sam Ericsson of Advocates International in Virginia for providing me with this reference.
2. The Keston News Service, with a full-time journalist in Moscow, is an invaluable source of such material. It is part of the Keston Institute in Oxford, and can send the material by post or via the Internet to people who are interested.

Why the Nations Rage

3. *Pandaemonium: Ethnicity in International Politics* (Oxford and New York: OUP, 1993), p. 147.
4. Quoted in Roger Griffin (ed.) *Fascism* (Oxford: OUP, 1995), p. 222.
5. *Fascism*, p. 220.
6. See Roger Griffin's arguments in his book, *The Nature of Fascism*, particularly the opening chapters. While I can see much in his point of view, I tend more to seeing Fascism as very religious when it chooses to be. Like nationalism itself, one of the dangers of Fascism and one of the ways it finds people so easy to deceive, is its chameleon-like qualities.
7. Roger Griffin argued this at a fascinating seminar in Oxford in 1995. It is part of what he would describe as Fascism's 'mythic core'.
8. For example, in the works of Anthony Smith, who uses the term 'salvation religions'. See Chapter 4.
9. *Fascism*, p. 221.
10. Quoted by Moynihan in *Pandaemonium*, pp. 132–133. Bloom's writing was in *Commentary*, April 1947, in an article entitled 'The Peoples of My Hometown: Before Nationalism Crushed Rumania's Design for Living', p. 329.

Chapter 8 The Byzantine Inheritance
1. This is from the human point of view. Reformed theology within Protestantism makes God the chooser and not the individual. Either way, though, there is a *choice* involved.

Chapter 9 The Ottoman Inheritance
1. David Rieff, *Slaughterhouse* (New York: Simon & Schuster 1995), pp. 68–69.
2. Ibid., p. 69.
3. Ibid., p. 69.
4. Anthony D. Smith, *Nationalism in the Twentieth Century* (Martin Robertson, 1979), p. 17.
5. Ibid., p. 17.
6. Ibid., p. 17.

264

7. One such reverse was Don John of Austria's famous naval victory over the Turks at Lepanto in 1571.
8. Rieff, *Slaughterhouse*, p. 69.
9. Ibid., p. 69.
10. Ibid., p. 69.
11. Ibid., p. 69.

Chapter 10 The End of Christendom and the Rise of Tolerance

1. See Bernard Lewis, *The Middle East* (London: Weidenfeld & Nicolson, 1995), and the article in *Atlantic Monthly*: 'The Roots of Muslim Rage', no. 266, Sept. 1990, p. 60. Professor Lamin Sanneh's seminal Henry Martyn Lectures in Cambridge in 1995 have also been most helpful in giving inspiration for my own thoughts on tolerance, as will be seen in the next chapter of this book on tolerance and its consequences.

Bibliography

Almond, Mark, *Europe's Backyard War: The War in the Balkans* (London: Heinemann, 1994).

Anderson, Benedict, *Imagined Communities: Reflections on the Origin and Spread of Nationalism* (London: Verso, 1983; rev. ed., 1991).

Ascherson, Neal, 'When Was Britain?', *Prospect*, May 1996, pp. 25–29.

Augustinos, Gerasimos, 'A Review of Michael Ignatieff, *Blood and Belonging*', *Mediterranean Quarterly*, vol. 6, no. 3, Summer 1995, p. 123.

Baigent, Michael and Richard Leigh, *Secret Germany*, (London: Jonathan Cape, 1994).

Barber, Benjamin R., *Jihad versus McWorld* (New York: Times Books, 1995).

Baron, Salo Wittmayer, *Modern Nationalism and Religion* (Freeport, NY: Books for Libraries Press, 1947; rpt., Harper and Row, 1971).

Bell, Martin, *In Harm's Way: Reflections of a War Zone Thug* (London: Hamish Hamilton, 1995).

Berlin, Isaiah, *Against the Current: Essays in the History of Ideas* (London, The Hogarth Press, 1979).

——'The Bent Twig: A Note on Nationalism', *Foreign Affairs*, vol. 51, 1972, pp. 11–30.

Bibliography

——'Two Concepts of Nationalism', *New York Review of Books*, Nov. 21, 1991, p. 22.

Bloom, Solomon, 'The Peoples of My Hometown: Before Nationalism Crushed Rumania's Design for Living', *Commentary*, April 1947, pp. 329–335.

Brubaker, Rogers, *Nationalism Reframed: Nationhood and the National Question in the New Europe* (Cambridge: CUP, 1996).

Cigar, Norman, *Genocide in Bosnia: The Policy of 'Ethnic Cleansing'* (College Station, Texas: Texas A & M University Press, 1995).

Cohn, Norman, *The Pursuit of the Millennium* (London: Paladin, 1970).

Colley, Linda, *Britons: Forging the Nation: 1707–1837* (London: Yale University Press, 1992).

Cviic, Christopher, *Remaking the Balkans* (Chatham House Papers, London: Pinter, 1991; rev. ed. 1995).

Donia, Robert J. and John V. A. Fine, Jr, *Bosnia & Hercegovina: A Tradition Betrayed* (New York: Columbia University Press, 1994).

Eatwell, Roger, *Fascism: A History* (London: Vintage, 1996).

Esposito, John L., *The Islamic Threat: Myth or Reality?* (Oxford: OUP, 1992; 2nd ed., 1995).

Fernández-Armesto, Felipe, *Millennium: A History of Our Last Thousand Years* (London: Bantam Press, 1995).

Fisk, Robert, Series of articles featured in the International section, *The Independent*, October 7–12, 14, 18, 1996.

Fox, Frank, *The Balkan Peninsula* (London: A. & C. Black, 1915).

Fraser, John Foster, *Pictures from the Balkans* (London: Cassell, 1912).

Fukuyama, Francis, *The End of History and the Last Man* (New York: Free Press, 1992).

Garton Ash, Timothy, *We the People: The Revolution of 89* (Cambridge: Granta Books, 1990).

Glenny, Misha, *The Fall of Yugoslavia: The Third Balkan War* (London: Penguin, 1992).

Goldhagen, Daniel, *Hitler's Willing Executioners* (London: Little Brown, 1996).

Greenfeld, Liah, *Nationalism: Five Roads to Modernity* (Cambridge, Mass.: Harvard University Press, 1992).

Griffin, Roger (ed.), *Fascism* (Oxford: OUP, 1995).

——*The Nature of Fascism* (London: Routledge, 1991).

Hechter, Michael, 'Explaining Nationalist Violence', *Nations and Nationalism*, vol. i, no. 1, 1995, pp. 53–68.

Hobsbawm, Eric, *Nations and Nationalism since 1780* (Cambridge: CUP, 1990).

Horowitz, Donald L., *Ethnic Groups in Conflict* (Berkeley, California: University of California Press, 1985).

Horsman, Matthew and Andrew Marshall, *After the Nation-State: Citizens, Tribalism and the New World Disorder* (London: HarperCollins, 1994).

Huntington, Samuel, 'The Clash of Civilizations?', *Foreign Affairs*, vol. 72, no. 3, Summer 1993, pp. 22–49.

——'The West and the Rest', *Prospect*, Issue 16, February 1997, pp. 34–39.

——*The Clash of Civilizations and the Remaking of World Order* (New York: Simon & Schuster, 1996).

Ignatieff, Michael, *Blood and Belonging* (London: Chatto & Windus, 1993; Vintage, 1994).

Isaacs, Harold, *Idols of the Tribe: Group Identity and Political Change* (New York: Harper and Row, 1975).

Jelavich, Barbara, *History of the Balkans: Eighteenth and Nineteenth Centuries*, vol. 1 (Cambridge: CUP, 1983).

Jones, Steve, *The Language of the Genes* (London: Flamingo, 1993).

Jürgensmeyer, Mark, *The New Cold War? Religious Nationalism Confronts the Secular State* (Berkeley,

Bibliography

California: The University of California Press 1993).

Kaplan, Robert D., *Balkan Ghosts: A Journey through History* (New York: St Martin's Press, 1993).

Kennan, George, *Around the Cragged Hill* (New York W. W. Norton, 1992).

Király, Béla K. (ed.), *Tolerance and Movements of Religious Dissent in Eastern Europe* (New York: East European Quarterly, Columbia University Press, 1975).

Kupchan, Charles A. (ed.), *Nationalism and Nationalities in the New Europe* (Ithaca, N. Y.: Cornell University Press, 1995).

Lampe, John R., *Yugoslavia as History: Twice There Was a Country* (Cambridge: CUP, 1996).

Lewis, Bernard, 'The Roots of Muslim Rage', *Atlantic Monthly*, no. 266, Sept. 1990.

Lewis, Bernard, *The Middle East* (London: Weidenfeld & Nicolson, 1995).

Lockhart, R. H. Bruce, *Guns or Butter* (London: Putnam, 1938).

Lukacs, John, *The End of the Twentieth Century and the End of the Modern Age* (New York: Ticknor and Fields, 1993).

Malcolm, Noel, *Bosnia: A Short History* (London, Macmillan London Ltd., 1994).

Morgan, David, *The Mongols* (Cambridge, Mass.: Blackwell, 1986).

Moynihan, Daniel Patrick, *Pandaemonium: Ethnicity in International Politics* (Oxford: OUP, 1993).

Norwich, John Julius, *Byzantium: The Decline and Fall* (London: Viking, 1995).

O'Brien, Connor Cruise, *God Land: Reflections on Religion and Nationalism* (Cambridge, Mass.: Harvard University Press, 1988).

Palmer, Alan, *The Decline and Fall of the Ottoman Empire* (New York: Barnes and Noble, 1992).

Pfaff, William, *The Wrath of Nations: Civilization and the Furies of Nationalism* (New York: Simon & Schuster, 1993).

Pinker, Steven, *The Language Instinct: The New Science of Language and Mind* (London: Penguin Books, 1994).

Pinson, Mark, *The Muslims of Bosnia-Herzegovina: Their Historic Development from the Middle Ages to the Dissolution of Yugoslavia* (Harvard Middle Eastern Monographs 28, Cambridge, Mass.: Harvard University Press, 1993; 2nd edn., 1996).

Ramet, Pedro (ed.), *Religion and Nationalism in Soviet and East European Politics* (Duke Press Policy Studies, Durham, N. C.: Duke University Press, 1984).

Ramet, Sabrina Petra, *Balkan Babel: The Disintegration of Yugoslavia from the Death of Tito to Ethnic War* (Oxford: Westview Press; 2nd edn., 1996).

Rieff, David, *Slaughterhouse: Bosnia and the Failure of the West* (New York: Simon & Schuster, 1995).

Schama, Simon, *Landscape and Memory* (London: Harper-Collins, 1995).

Schulze, Hagen, *States, Nations and Nationalism: From the Middle Ages to the Present* (Oxford: Blackwell, 1996).

Silber, Laura and Allan Little, *The Death of Yugoslavia* (London: Penguin Books/BBC Books, 1995).

Smith, Anthony D., *The Ethnic Origins of Nations* (Oxford: Blackwell, 1986).

——'Gastronomy or Geology? The Role of Nationalism in the Reconstruction of Nations', *Nations and Nationalism*, vol. i, no. 1, 1995, pp. 3–23.

——*Nationalism in the Twentieth Century* (Oxford: Martin Robertson, 1979).

——*Nations and Nationalism in a Global Era* (Cambridge: Polity Press, 1995).

Thompson, Mark, *A Paper House: The Ending of Yugoslavia*

Bibliography

(London: Vintage, 1992).

'Tribalism Revisited', *The Economist*, December 21, 1991, p. 45, (US edition).

Ullman, Richard H. (ed.), *The World and Yugoslavia's Wars* (New York: The Council on Foreign Relations, Inc., 1996).

Voegelin, Erich, *Political Religions*, trans., T. H. DiNapoli and E. S. Easterly III, Toronto Studies in Theology, Vol. 23 (Lewiston, N. Y.: The Edwin Mellen Press, 1986).

West, Rebecca, *Black Lamb & Grey Falcon* (London: Macmillan, 1940, 1941; rev., 1955).

Westerlund, David (ed.), *Questioning the Secular State: The Worldwide Resurgence of Religion in Politics* (London: Hurst & Co., 1996).

Wilson, Duncan, *Tito's Yugoslavia* (Cambridge: CUP, 1979).